POST-CARBON INCLUSION

Transitions Built on Justice

Edited by
Ralph Horne, Aimee Ambrose,
Gordon Walker and Anitra Nelson

First published in Great Britain in 2024 by

Bristol University Press
University of Bristol
1–9 Old Park Hill
Bristol
BS2 8BB
UK
t: +44 (0)117 374 6645
e: bup-info@bristol.ac.uk

Details of international sales and distribution partners are available at bristoluniversitypress.co.uk

© Bristol University Press 2024

British Library Cataloguing in Publication Data
A catalogue record for this book is available from the British Library

ISBN 978-1-5292-2942-4 hardcover
ISBN 978-1-5292-2943-1 paperback
ISBN 978-1-5292-2944-8 ePub
ISBN 978-1-5292-2947-9 ePdf

The right of Ralph Horne, Aimee Ambrose, Gordon Walker and Anitra Nelson to be identified as editors of this work has been asserted by them in accordance with the Copyright, Designs and Patents Act 1988.

All rights reserved: no part of this publication may be reproduced, stored in a retrieval system, or transmitted in any form or by any means, electronic, mechanical, photocopying, recording, or otherwise without the prior permission of Bristol University Press.

Every reasonable effort has been made to obtain permission to reproduce copyrighted material. If, however, anyone knows of an oversight, please contact the publisher.

The statements and opinions contained within this publication are solely those of the editors and contributors and not of the University of Bristol or Bristol University Press. The University of Bristol and Bristol University Press disclaim responsibility for any injury to persons or property resulting from any material published in this publication.

Bristol University Press works to counter discrimination on grounds of gender, race, disability, age and sexuality.

Cover design: Andrew Corbett
Front cover image: Zhen Xiong, RMIT University

Contents

List of Figures and Tables		v
List of Abbreviations		vi
Notes on Contributors		vii
Acknowledgements		xi
1	Post-Carbon Inclusion: Transitions Built on Justice *Ralph Horne, Anitra Nelson, Aimee Ambrose and Gordon Walker*	1
2	Inclusion in Post-Carbon Urban Experiments *Ralph Horne and Louise Dorignon*	17
3	Histories of Heating: Looking Back, Moving Forwards *Aimee Ambrose, Jenny Palm, Stephen Parkes and Beth Speake*	36
4	Inclusive Rhythms: Chrono-Urbanism and De-Energization *Gordon Walker*	53
5	Alternatives to Justice for a Thriving Transition *Aimee Ambrose, Alvaro Castano-Garcia and Yael Arbell*	70
6	Housing Narratives for Post-Carbon Inclusive Societies *Ralph Horne, Anitra Nelson and Louise Dorignon*	84
7	Still Breathing Unequally? Air Pollution and Post-Carbon Transition *Gordon Walker, Douglas Booker and Paul J. Young*	104
8	Beyond Circular Economies: Rethinking Relations of Waste *Ralph Horne and Bhavna Middha*	120
9	Cool Inclusion: Thermal Inequality in an Overheating Climate *Elspeth Oppermann, Gordon Walker and Jamie Cross*	138
10	Pre-Figurative Hybrids for Post-Carbon Inclusion *Anitra Nelson*	156
11	Uneven Consumption and the Work of Being a High Consumer *Aimee Ambrose, Alvaro Castano-Garcia, Anna Hawkins, Stephen Parkes, Beth Speake and Yael Arbell*	174
12	Housing Retrofit for Post-Carbon Inclusion *Ralph Horne and Lisa de Kleyn*	189

13	From an 'Imperial Mode of Living' to a 'Caring Commons'	207
	Anitra Nelson	
14	Future Directions for Post-Carbon Inclusion	225
	Ralph Horne, Anitra Nelson, Gordon Walker and Aimee Ambrose	

Index   234

List of Figures and Tables

Figures

2.1	Framework for understanding post-carbon urban inclusion experiments	23
4.1	Diagrammatic representation of the '15-minute Paris' (*Le Paris du ¼ Heure*)	61
7.1	Cedar trees planted along a school fence to monitor their impact on reducing air pollutants in the school playground	110
9.1	The pyramid of thermal management processes and their relationship to energy	143
9.2	Keeping cool conceptualized within the capability approach	148
12.1	Changing life stages and emotional connection to 'home'	197
12.2	Dwellings and their surrounds present as opportunities and constraints	199
12.3	Sign boards for plants made from recycled wood	201

Tables

2.1	Paradigms of post-carbon urban inclusion experiments	24
4.1	Rhythmic de-energization principles within the 15-minute city concept	63
6.1	Underlying narratives of low carbon housing and inclusion	89

List of Abbreviations

BTR	build-to-rent
CA	capability approach
CE	circular economy
COP	Conference of Parties
DIO	do-it-ourselves
DIY	do-it-yourself
EC	European Commission
EU	European Union
EV	electric vehicle
FaDA	Feminisms and Degrowth Alliance
GHG	greenhouse gases
IE	institutional ethnography
ILO	International Labour Organization
IPCC	Intergovernmental Panel on Climate Change
LTNs	low-traffic neighbourhoods
NGO	non-government organization
PV	photovoltaic
SDGs	Sustainable Development Goals
UK	United Kingdom
ULL	urban living lab(oratory)
UNFCCC	United Nations Framework Convention on Climate Change
US	United States

Notes on Contributors

Aimee Ambrose is Professor of Energy Policy at the Centre for Regional Economic and Social Research at Sheffield Hallam University (UK). Her background is in sociology, town planning and energy studies. Her research interests coalesce around understanding how energy policies play out in the everyday lives of groups who are often overlooked in society, such as vulnerable households but also high consuming households. She has explored these issues in the context of low energy housing, energy poverty and changes to domestic heating fuels and methods. She uses research methods such as oral histories and walking interviews.

Yael Arbell is Research Associate at the Centre for Regional Economic and Social Research at Sheffield Hallam University (UK). She specializes in sustainable communities and inclusion and diversity in collaborative housing, including issues of racial justice and social inequality in community-led housing.

Douglas Booker is a PhD researcher in the Lancaster Environment Centre, Lancaster University (UK). Interested in opening the black box of air quality science to understand how it produces and represents knowledge of the air, he is co-founder and chief executive officer of National Air Quality Testing Services, a business set up to raise awareness of indoor air quality by developing air quality monitoring technologies and testing services.

Alvaro Castano-Garcia is a doctoral researcher in the Centre for Regional Economic and Social Research at Sheffield Hallam University (UK) with a background in environmental science. Current research interests centre on social justice in low carbon energy transitions, particularly just transition and high consumers. He is funded by the White Rose Social Sciences Doctoral Training Partnership.

Jamie Cross is Professor of Social and Economic Anthropology at the University of Edinburgh (UK) and Director of the Edinburgh Earth Initiative. He has a long-standing commitment to the ethnographic study of energy, technologies and markets against the backdrop of climate change. His books include *Dream Zones: Anticipating Capitalism and Development in India* (2014).

Lisa de Kleyn is Research Fellow in the Climate Change Adaptation Lab, La Trobe University, Bundoora (Australia). Her research considers environmental justice, governance and representations across a range of subject areas, including housing energy efficiency, climate change adaptation and natural resource management.

Louise Dorignon is Vice-Chancellor's Postdoctoral Research Fellow at the Centre for Urban Research, RMIT University, Melbourne (Australia). A geographer, she specializes in the production, lived experience and urban outcomes of apartment housing in Australia and Europe. Current research focuses on modular apartment prefabrication to enable more sustainable and affordable homes and support everyday experiences of post-carbon housing.

Anna Hawkins is Senior Lecturer in Environmental Social Science at Sheffield Hallam University (UK) with teaching and research interests related to just sustainabilities and equitable resource consumption. In recent years, her work has explored socio-spatial health inequalities, food insecurity, hard to reach energy users, and high consumers of resources.

Ralph Horne is Professor of Geography and Associate Deputy Vice Chancellor, Research and Innovation for the College of Design and Social Context, at RMIT University, Melbourne (Australia). He is interested in social and policy change to support sustainable urban development, housing and households. He combines research leadership and participation in research projects concerning the environmental, social and policy context of production and consumption in the urban environment. The spatial, material and contingent social and policy structures at play are the main focus of his work on both the making and shaping of future urban environments.

Bhavna Middha is Research Fellow in the Australian Research Council Research Industrial Transformation Research Hub for Transformation of Reclaimed Waste Resources to Engineered Materials and Solutions for a Circular Economy at RMIT University, Melbourne (Australia). An environmental sociologist, she researches various aspects of sustainable consumption such as food, energy and waste issues, as well as spatialities and just transitions.

Anitra Nelson is Honorary Principal Fellow at the Informal Urbanism Research Hub (InfUr-), Melbourne School of Design, University of Melbourne (Australia). An activist-scholar, her research explores ecologically sustainable non-monetary futures, eco-socialism, and degrowth. She is author of *Beyond Money, A Postcapitalist Strategy* (2022); co-author (with Vincent Liegey) of *Exploring Degrowth: A Critical Guide* (2020); and co-editor of both *Food for Degrowth: Perspectives and Practices* (2021) and *Housing for Degrowth: Principles, Models, Challenges and Opportunities* (2018).

Elspeth Oppermann is Senior Research Fellow at the Rachel Carson Centre, LMU Munich (Germany) and Yong Loo Lin School of Medicine at the National University of Singapore. A critical geographer specializing in adaptation to extreme heat, she focuses on how the social is co-produced through material-energetic relations, and on developing an inter-disciplinary, more-than-human thermo-ethnographic analysis of physiological heat management.

Jenny Palm is Professor and Director of the International Institute for Industrial Environmental Economics at Lund University (Sweden). She researches energy systems from social science perspectives – socio-technical systems, planning processes, governance, energy democracy, energy citizenship, energy justice, and technology diffusion and adoption. Objects of study are urban infrastructures and urban planning, energy communities and prosumers.

Stephen Parkes is Research Fellow at the Centre for Regional Economic and Social Research at Sheffield Hallam University (UK). Specializing in decarbonization of transport, with policy and academic studies for a range of funders – research councils, local authorities, charities and central government – current foci include active travel (walking, cycling and wheeling), autonomous vehicles and high consumers of energy and transport.

Beth Speake is Research Associate at the Centre for Regional Economic and Social Research at Sheffield Hallam University (UK). Her research interests and expertise focus on the impact of social security policy design and implementation on marginalized groups; gendered violence, abuse and trauma; and inclusive conceptualizations of violence.

Gordon Walker is Professor at the Lancaster Environment Centre, Lancaster University. He has a wide-ranging profile of research on the social and spatial dimensions of environment, energy and climate issues. This includes work on environmental and energy justice; applications of rhythmanalysis and social practice theory; community engagement and renewable energy technologies; and adaptation and resilience in relation to heatwave and flood risks. Books include *Environmental Justice: Concepts, Evidence and Politics* (2012) and *Energy and Rhythm: Rhythmanalysis for a Low Carbon Future* (2021).

Paul J. Young is Senior Climate Specialist at JBA Risk Management and Visiting Researcher in the Lancaster Environment Centre, Lancaster University (UK). He is a climate scientist and atmospheric chemist, with research interests in bringing natural, social and data science together to understand and address issues related to environmental change.

Acknowledgements

Aimee Ambrose and co-authors of Chapter 3 gratefully acknowledge funding provided by the Swedish Energy Agency (Energimyndigheten) and the Arts and Humanities Research Council (UK) under the CHANSE ERA-NET Co-Fund programme, which received funding from the European Union's Horizon 2020 Research and Innovation Programme, under Grant Agreement no. 101004509. Both sources enabled the research on which this chapter is based.

Gordon Walker, author of Chapter 4, gratefully acknowledges permission to reproduce gained from Micaël Dessi (https://micaeldessin.com/), illustrator of Figure 4.1, a diagrammatic representation of the 15-minute city. He also notes that Chapter 4 draws closely on arguments developed in his own book *Energy and Rhythm: Rhythmanalysis for a Low Carbon Future* published by Rowman & Littlefield in 2021.

Aimee Ambrose and co-authors of Chapter 5 gratefully acknowledge funding provided by the Sheffield Hallam University and the White Rose Doctoral Training Partnership for enabling the research on which this chapter is based.

Ralph Horne and Louise Dorignon, co-authors (with Anitra Nelson) of Chapter 6 gratefully acknowledge funding provided by the Australian Research Council Research Linkage Grant 'Housing Outcomes Metrics and Evaluation' (HOME: Grant no. LP150100089).

Gordon Walker and co-authors of Chapter 7 gratefully acknowledge permission granted by photographer Professor Barbara Maher to reproduce the photograph in Figure 7.1.

Ralph Horne and Bhavna Middha, co-authors of Chapter 8, gratefully acknowledge funding provided by the Australian Research Council Research Industrial Transformation Research Hub for Transformation of Reclaimed Waste Resources to Engineered Materials and Solutions for a Circular Economy (TREMS: Grant no. IH200100010).

Gordon Walker and co-authors gratefully acknowledge that Chapter 9 draws, in part, on research funded by UK Research and Innovation and the Global Challenges Research Fund through the Economic and Social Research Council (Award ES/T008091/1) as part of Cool Infrastructures, a multi-disciplinary project into life with heat in global cities.

Anitra Nelson gratefully acknowledges the following interviewees who informed Chapter 10 – Vincent Liegey and Logan Strenchock (Cargonomia); Andrea Vetter (Haus des Wandels, and Konzeptwerk Neue Ökonomie); and Nina Treu (Konzeptwerk Neue Ökonomie).

Aimee Ambrose and co-authors of Chapter 11 gratefully acknowledge funding provided by Sheffield Hallam University and the White Rose Doctoral Training Partnership which enabled the research on which this chapter is based.

Ralph Horne and Lisa de Kleyn, co-authors of Chapter 12, gratefully acknowledge funding provided by the Australian Research Council Research Linkage Grant 'Housing Energy Efficiency Transitions' (HEET: Grant no. LP170100420) and data collected by the HEET research team, including Dr Sarah Robertson, who conducted interviews and took the photographs included in this chapter.

Anitra Nelson gratefully acknowledges the following interviewees who informed Chapter 13 – Brenna Quinlan (Australian illustrator); Ashish Kothari and Shrishtee Bajpai (Kalpavriksh).

Co-editors Ralph Horne, Gordon Walker and Aimee Ambrose gratefully acknowledge and thank co-editor Anitra Nelson for taking on the important role of copy-editor and project manager for this work, without which this book would have not been possible.

1

Post-Carbon Inclusion: Transitions Built on Justice

Ralph Horne, Anitra Nelson, Aimee Ambrose and Gordon Walker

Introduction

As efforts to address the climate crisis (hopefully) continue to multiply across the urban world, two central questions are brought to the fore: first, how could these efforts be made effective and sufficient to address the climate emergency and heal the planet for future generations? Second, to what extent can effective actions also promote justice and inclusion? To address these questions, throughout the book we present case examples and empirical insights, together with consideration of both reformist and more radical ideas. Later in this chapter we introduce key terms, including but not limited to ecological modernization, circular economies, just transitions, socio-technical transitions and degrowth.

Decarbonization and inequality are entangled at multiple scales, whether planetary, national, regional, city, local community or house(hold). The implications and ramifications of such entanglement matter insofar as they might reinforce each other; they might present as a Faustian bargain. Beyond the unacceptable prospect of decarbonization and equality being regarded as mutually exclusive, the unfolding patterns and practices of adoption of so-called low carbon technologies also raise questions about the extent to which they are actually contributing to overall arrest of climate change, or merely shifting the problem around. For example, is the rush for minerals to feed low carbon technology unacceptably exacerbating global ecosystem decline? Is automation really freeing us from drudgery or fuelling modern slavery?

The starting point for this book is an optimistic view that decarbonization efforts will continue to grow and ultimately a post-carbon and more inclusive society could unfold – one where fossil fuels are no longer extracted nor required, and where people enjoy the capability, opportunity and dignity of effective participation in society, regardless of their identity, wealth, ability, background or culture. However, this possibility is heavily conditional and there are many different routes that could be followed in its pursuit. It is these routes and conditions that are the main topic of the book.

Post-carbon means 'after carbon' – it is about how things might be when fossil fuels are no longer coursing through the anthropogenic world's veins. It is about when the atmospheric balance of greenhouse gases is restored and when planetary repair – reversing deforestation, curbing methane, and so on – is well underway. Carbon, here, is simply a signifier for fossil fuels in direct combustion as energy and consumption (as in plastics) and as embodied in materials. Carbon (atmospheric CO_2) emissions generally refer to all greenhouse gases (GHG), that is, CO_2 and non-CO_2 GHG. CO_2 is a standard measure of all GHG emissions due to its propensity and long lifetime. Within total GHG, carbon, methane and nitrous oxide occur roughly in the following proportions: 15:4:1. An important distinction between post-carbon and decarbonization is made here. The latter does not address consumption *per se*, whereas 'post-carbon' allows for imaginaries where de-energization and fundamentally different ways of doing things are achieved in addition to decarbonization.

Framing the book in this way is not intended to enter the realm of optimistic imagining or visioning what futures without fossil-fuel-powered lives and economies may be like. We rather use it as a heuristic for bringing together critiques of current strategies for heading towards a post-carbon urban sphere, diagnosis of where exclusions rather than inclusions may materialize, and exploration of alternative practical ways of living that have been seeking to enact the degree of transformation that becoming post-carbon will need to entail.

The idea of urban decarbonization is deceptively simple. Reductions in residential and urban scale carbon emissions have long been identified as a priority and the Foreword to the Intergovernmental Panel on Climate Change Special Report on Global Warming of 1.5°C (IPCC, 2019) emphasises the importance of taking an integrated approach. In reality, a myriad of cost–benefit assessments showing uncertain and limited paybacks have tended to ignore the sheer complexity of the numerous and various urban and domestic arrangements that explain the failure of relying on economic rationales to progress the transition. Even where policies have been deemed successful, they have tended to have uneven, perverse or short-lived effects often due to and/or reinforcing socio-economic inequity. For example, the idea of gas as a 'transition' energy source in moving away from coal leaves much of the fossil fuel industrial complex intact – indeed, reinforced – and the inequalities of existing access to energy unquestioned.

Given the extent of the climate emergency and absolute imperative to limit warming to 1.5°C, much talk of decarbonization, net zero and low carbon transition is manifestly inadequate and reflects an unwillingness to part from an existing, damaging and exclusionary high carbon world order. At the same time, global society is highly unequal, with wealthier strata of Global North nations, global elites and transnational corporations generating the vast majority of the emissions, the consequences of which are already being felt hardest by disadvantaged communities in the Global South. Moreover, there is also widening inequality in terms of wealth, access to resources, environmental quality, health, housing, opportunity, and so on, both within and between countries, regions, neighbourhoods, social groups and even within households. High carbon fossil fuelled societies are inherently exclusionary – prioritizing the needs and wants of certain groups over the externalities – the grotesque damage to the planet that the most vulnerable others will bear. Through the transition away from fossil fuels, we have a unique opportunity to reformulate who should be prioritized and to make reparations for previous exclusion. The title of this book is therefore aspirational, reflecting the dual, overlapping and very pressing need to move rapidly to a post-carbon society that redresses the exclusion inherent within the current regime.

'Ultimately, a future low-carbon world may very well become more pluralistic, democratic, and just', writes Sovacool (2021: 14), in a review of 198 articles analysing 332 cases of energy justice in climate change mitigation. 'But', he concludes, 'the sobering results from this review also indicate without proactive governance it could be more antagonistic, exclusionary, violent, and destructive'. This book engages with the many ways in which efforts to decarbonize necessarily disrupt and reconfigure domestic and urban scale infrastructures and practices, but with a focus throughout on who is excluded, who is included and on how patterns of difference and marginality are implicated.

This book has four starting premises. First, that rapid decarbonization is necessary and that radically more sustainable and de-energized ways of urban living, transformations in housing and urban energy efficiency, and widespread deployment of renewables are all crucial aspects of this goal. Second, that housing and urban spatial economic, social and cultural inequalities are worsening and must be addressed. If not, there will be increasingly negative consequences for humanity, not just those in increasing poverty. Third, that efforts to rapidly decarbonize and address increasing, diverse and sometimes hidden inequalities are rarely matters that are addressed conjointly, for all sorts of reasons. As Lamb et al (2020) highlight in their literature review, decarbonizing actions can exacerbate inequality, and vice versa. Fourth, it is urgent, at this juncture, to examine a range of post-carbon inclusion agendas at urban and household scales, and critically evaluate ways forward, whether via 'degrowth', more conventional 'just transitions', or some middle course, like a 'generous transition'.

So, what does 'doing' post-carbon inclusion look like? In reality, we don't, and can't, yet know. At the highest and broadest levels of decision making it means changing mundane and economic activities such that emitting carbon is not needed. Moreover, to be inclusive, these changes necessarily involve attention to the need for, and to the processes of, transitioning to new mechanisms and arrangements for economic distribution, including between social groups and across gender, race, locale and abilities. To state a concern with 'post-carbon inclusion' means ensuring that approaches taken to transformation embody a commitment to a diversity of forms of inequalities and marginalization alongside the concern to mitigate climate change and regenerate planetary health.

The large and rapidly growing corpus of work engaging with mechanisms of change and purpose spans (at least) socio-technical transitions, justice and, indeed, just transitions. As introduced in Chapter 2, socio-technical transitions are envisaged as facilitated and managed decarbonization. For example, the multi-level perspective (Geels, 2010) defines mechanisms for regime change via protected niches, all unfolding against a backdrop of landscape factors. A managed socio-technical transition, if possible and successful, may 'deliver', for example, a renewable-energy-powered city. However, at what cost to inequality? Ideas of justice and distribution need to be introduced, which have not been a focus for socio-technical transition scholars. Instead, a substantial literature now exists on the meanings of justice that have been and can be enrolled in discourses of environmental, climate and energy justice (Walker, 2012; Bickerstaff et al, 2013; Schlosberg and Collins, 2014; Wood, 2023), and in just transition frameworks.

The term 'just transition' has gained increasing traction alongside decarbonization, given the risk that market-based restructuring will heavily impact communities dependent upon the economic activity of fossil fuel extraction (Newell and Mulvaney, 2013; Healy and Barry, 2017; Johnstone and Hielscher, 2017). As described in Chapter 5, a just transition is a central plank in the European Union (EU) Green Deal programme (European Commission, 2020). Elsewhere the United Nations Framework Convention on Climate Change (UNFCCC) has called for it, the International Labour Organization (ILO, 2015) has supported guidelines for it, the Canadian federal government created the Just Transition Task Force to support the coal phase-out (Government of Canada, 2019) and the Scottish government established the Just Transition Commission (Scottish Government, 2020). Ostensibly, these government-supported Keynesian-style interventions are designed to smooth the pathway and enlist support while also aiming to mitigate the worst excesses of market-based change. The term has broadened in scope, to encompass the consumption side of the equation, noting that those who lack the resources to invest in energy efficiency and low carbon technologies suffer disproportionately (While and Eadson, 2019). Nevertheless, a justice based approach to post-carbon inclusion requires us to look beyond just transitions (Chapter 5).

Aim, scope and approach

The aim of this book is to reflect upon efforts to shift towards post-carbon worlds, while also seeking to address inequality and exclusion at various scales – intra-community, regional, global, inter-generational and inter-species. It is presented predominantly from a 'western' perspective and concerns and draws empirically mainly on Western Europe and Australia, although there are several chapters that take an overtly global perspective on inclusion and thus draw out Global South–North issues. Later in this chapter we set out what work the post-carbon inclusion concept is expected to 'do'. We provide examples of the breadth of post-carbon inclusion as challenges at both domestic and urban scales, through both promising and problematic cases and patterns.

We also seek to bring notice to the traps, cautions and potential for capture of efforts towards post-carbon inclusion. Related to this, we take as an ontological starting point the failure of market-based solutions to the climate crisis to date, and the lack of time the planet and global community has remaining to wait for more attempts at ecological modernization and neo-classical environmental economic 'solutions' to be tried. Coupled to this is recognition of the failure of mechanistic, technocentric and behavioural solutions based upon ideas of free, individual choice, and of the triumph of technological ingenuity. The last 50 years has seen a predominance of these tools and this period has seen spiralling climate crisis and rapidly worsening biodiversity loss, rapidly degrading the global commons.

Even now, in the 2020s, the circular economy is being presented as the latest solution – a largely technological magic wand (Chapter 8) – and the solution to the housing crisis is seemingly new technology to be delivered via the same market and homeownership ideal that has created the problem in the first place (Chapter 6). In seeking to peel back the façade of these proposed 'solutions' to high carbon exclusionary society, this book calls for more attention to, first, the realities of everyday life as a starting point for change, rather than the assumed relations and their causes; second, the role of power, ethics and inequalities in governing the transition towards post-carbon inclusion; and, third, the importance of practising low carbon inclusion here and now, in ways that enhance knowledge sharing and test out how post-carbon inclusion can be.

Everyday life as a starting point for change

Studies of everyday life, utilizing relational approaches, are now increasingly recognized as essential in understanding and informing directions for the necessary changes to progress post-carbon inclusion. This means taking seriously studies of daily lives and how they are structured by unwritten rules, meanings, obligations and a myriad of material, moral and meaning-laden expectations. Thus, instead of assuming free choice is the key driver of what people do, we draw attention to social practices (Shove et al, 2012; Hui et al, 2018) as building blocks of what happens in daily life. We present rich empirical studies of such in Chapters 3, 10, 11 and 12. We highlight the roles of space, time and affect, and the entanglements of these in shaping diversity, dynamics and obduracies in everyday life (as in Chapters 3, 4 and 12). We seek to differentiate between people who are excluded through various means (both overtly and through more subtle mechanisms) by examining their capabilities to participate and function in society, including in particular activities and practices that might either further entrench a high carbon society, or lead towards post-carbon practices.

We see merit in utilizing the capability approach, as developed initially by Amartya Sen and Martha Nussbaum, as a normative framework or perspective on human welfare and wellbeing to engage with in considering the metrics, challenges and tensions of post-carbon inclusion (in Chapter 9, particularly, as well as in Chapters 2, 4, 8 and 12). Within this framework, justice is accomplishment-based, it 'cannot be indifferent to the lives that people can actually live' (Sen, 2009: 18), chiming with our focus on everyday life, its differentiations and inequalities.

Where capabilities and practices connect is when we pay 'closer attention to how successful performances of practice are distributed across populations ... understanding this as a reflection of differences in the capability to perform ... one way in which theories of practice and of justice as capability might be conjoined' (Walker, 2013: 187). Inequality is about recruitment to, and performance of, practices; analytically speaking, variations in the performance of practice should be understood as reflections of differences in capability (Halkier and Holm, 2021). Linking capabilities and social practice in this way distracts attention from individual focused capabilities towards societal change that supports these capabilities and embeds social justice as central to social practice analyses (Willand et al, 2021).

Inequalities, power, ethics and governing transitions

Coupled with the importance of the everyday is the centrality of power and ethics in transitioning away from planetary deterioration. Inequalities, and/or entrenched relations that hold together unsustainable practices that exacerbate climate change, are manifestations of power exercised either overtly or in a more subtle processes in shaping possible choices and silencing or side-lining others. Particular ethical stances are extended through power relations (Benatar et al, 2018) and, in turn, shape actual unfolding socio-technical transitions (Avelino, 2021). Normative arrangements shaped by powerful energy companies in turn entrench inequality of access to essential energy services (Sovacool and Dworkin, 2015).

In Chapter 2, we examine urban experiments and urban living labs (Bulkeley et al, 2019) as vehicles for inclusive socio-technical transitions, informing dialogues on power and possibilities through the proceeding chapters. This talks to a role for emphasizing and communicating such processes, and to amplify alternative narratives, actions and ideas. Stephens and Landsmark (2023) argue for diversification of leadership on decarbonization agendas in an effort to bring more inclusion. Pel et al (2020) explore routes to more inclusive social action on climate change that seek to account for neoliberal power.

Chapter 5 argues that just transitions should go beyond 'just' ensuring 'no-one is left behind' (as the European Commission [2020] Green Deal headline puts it) and address the core problem that created splintered industrial monocultures of mining communities in the first place. In so doing, it develops alternative ideas and complementary virtues to justice, and calls for complementary, multiple perspectives and philosophies based on generosity and care.

Practising low carbon inclusion here and now

The urgency for more radical action is now reaching mainstream society and this book seeks to add to scholarship in this direction. Given the aforementioned entrenchment of power relations and investment in the status quo, it is also important to surface the possibilities of systemic change, and to allude to what this might entail, from where it might emanate, and to what end. Such possibilities require a precursor of greater cooperation, reciprocity, solidarity, care and generosity to be prioritized above competition and the current dominant growth metrics of mutually assured destruction.

The IPCC (2022) report, *Climate Change 2022*, not only warns of an urgent need to change direction from a path to a 3°C average temperature rise, with severe impacts – including on people's food security and heightening risks of flooding, fires and storms. The report also criticizes gross domestic product as 'a poor metric of human well-being', pointing out that 'climate policy evaluation requires better grounding in relation to decent living standards' and that 'the degrowth movement, with its focus on sustainability over profitability, has the potential to speed up transformations' (IPCC, 2022: 5–105, 17–59). In fact, the report suggests that 'degrowth pathways may be crucial in combining technical feasibility of mitigation with social development goals' (IPCC, 2022: 5–32). Chapters 10 and 13 focus on degrowth, while Chapters 6 and 12 discuss the importance of establishing such legitimate narratives on alternative futures.

Degrowth self-evidently challenges ways of living in growth-driven societies. The degrowth movement seeks a normalizing (cooling) planet in the short to medium term, facilitated by living practices of solidarity – satisfying everyone's basic needs, no more, no less – with light ecological footprints. At the core of the degrowth analysis is a recognition that capitalist economies, polities and cultures are driven by economic growth at the expense of people and the planet. Essentially anti-capitalist and driven from the bottom up, degrowth advocates and activists focus on care for Earth, including reducing carbon emissions, and solidarity, which requires inclusion.

Even though the idea and initial theories of degrowth developed decades earlier, only in this century did degrowth emerge as an active movement in France and then spread through Europe. Often misrepresented and misunderstood, in a nutshell degrowth is to growth as *quality* is to quantity. Monetary quantities of costs and prices weigh down capitalists' calculations in their plans and budgets, their accounting practices, financial negotiations and arrangements, and trading targets. As with competing capitalists, the capitalist state measures its economic progress through a peculiarly quantitative, monetary, concept of growth. In contrast, degrowth advocates seek a world based on ecological and social values, applying principles of social justice, conviviality, solidarity, security and ecologically sustainable living for *everyone*. Degrowth transformation focuses on livelihoods of 'sufficiency', which the IPCC describes as 'a set of measures and daily practices that avoid demand for energy, materials, land and water while delivering human wellbeing for all within planetary boundaries' (IPCC, 2022: 1–41).

The authors of this book observe that it is a narrative-making accomplishment of entrenched interests in the status quo that view degrowth ideas as 'radical'. Types of stories foregrounded matter as we contemplate and enact post-carbon inclusion. Janda and Topouzi (2015: 529) talk about how energy efficiency 'hero stories' – showing how energy efficiency can be achieved in practice – are by far the most common narrative found in the literature. They argue that telling more 'learning stories' would help to balance and develop the inspiration provided by hero stories. 'In contrast with the hero story, which takes place largely in an imaginary world, learning stories in both their original form and their energy counterparts occur in all the detailed richness and idiosyncratic elements of the real world', write Janda and Topouzi (2015: 520). Following interpretivist traditions, learning stories help reveal unintended consequences and underlying ethical bases of policy.

Global circulations of ideas and actual practices of low carbon justice, generosity, altruism and inclusion, both between nations and generations, and species are, thus, powerful antidotes. While we argue for a social structures approach, this does not absolve us of personal responsibility. It is a question of which ethical rules we live by and these are built at the community level, legally but also socially. Hence, we have well-established taboos around assault and murder, but very unclear rules and lines of responsibility about violence towards and assault of the planet. As Chapter 11 argues, it makes no sense to ask people to limit high energy consumption while allowing advertising of such. Similarly, practices of thrift or moderation are not based in conscious, behavioural actions, but in deeper-rooted meanings, muscle memories, interpretations of social rules and semi-automated functions.

As we are shaped by our knowledge, social rules and material surroundings, all these must be aligned to lower consumption. This is where examples of how experiments and living arrangements demonstrating and testing post-carbon life become significant (Chapters 2 and 10 offer different, arguably complementary, perspectives on this). Similarly significant is Brand and Wissen's (2021) concept of an 'imperial mode of living' (Chapter 13), and needs to amplify, legitimize and celebrate multiple and diverse degrowth variants. What is critical in this work is to avoid judgement and, instead, heighten the validity and virtues of empathy, care, generosity, solidarity, cooperation, dialogue and sharing – as in Chapters 5, 7 and 13.

What work can post-carbon inclusion do?

As an organizing term, we make no novel claim for the idea of post-carbon inclusion. We use it as an heuristic concept, useful to the extent that it can be put to work. Such work lies in providing a substrate upon which urban phenomena can be examined, consistently raising the priority of striving for post-carbon worlds while attending to inclusion priorities. Thus, every chapter engages with post-carbon inclusion at the domestic and/or urban scale, addressing five common lines of inquiry:

- What are the particular socio-materialities of inclusion, inequality, decarbonization and post-carbon possibilities?
- Who, and what, are the incumbents, obduracies, narratives or regime characteristics that constitute the problem?
- What promising lines of agency might promote post-carbon inclusion? Using empirical cases or thought experiments, how might they scale out, up, or otherwise become more pervasive and supersede existing obduracies and incumbencies?
- How might potential shifts take place from arrangements typified by unequal high carbon to post-carbon inclusion? What existing systems are amenable to revision so both inclusion and low carbon are central?

- What remaining dilemmas, tensions, paradoxes or problems with aforementioned lines of agency and shifts in arrangements present as priorities for future inquiry and testing?

Structure of this book

The four editors set out to co-author this book, but engaged a number of co-authors over time, leading to our dual role as editors and as authors. The intent is to provide a consistent thematic flow, while engaging with a broader range of topics and material than a traditional authored manuscript would. The result is a mix of empirical, conceptual and narrative work that engages with 13 different, but related, typically urban, phenomena.

Chapter 2 examines urban experiments. The authors compiled a database of such experiments for analysis and selected three cases to demonstrate how such projects morph over time. They argue for the possibilities of bringing to the fore the triple priorities of post-carbon, inequality and inclusive governance in the design and progression of such experiments. Following other work (Evans et al, 2018; Bulkeley et al, 2019) they outline the diversity, unpredictability and contextual nature of urban experiments. A framework is proposed along with a call for more sharing of knowledge about promising and failed experiments, to supplement efforts towards low carbon inclusive transition.

Chapter 3 uses oral histories to chart the impacts of different strategies in domestic energy transitions in the United Kingdom and Sweden. Following the idea of looking back to move forward, it reveals how important affective and relational dimensions are to shaping the fate of transitions. Policy and governance of purposive transitions rarely takes account of these sorts of fundamental everyday experiences, and this chapter sets out insights for would-be transition makers, to inform programme designs.

Chapter 4 sets itself the conceptual task of seeing the city through a temporal, chrono-urbanist perspective, focused on the mass of repeating and cycling rhythms that characterize the dynamic, polyrhythmic patterning of urban life. Recognizing that energy is necessarily implicated in making these rhythms, both through 'natural' rhythmic flows of heat, light and air movement, and through the beats and pulses of energized technologies, leads to engaging with both decarbonizing and de-energizing how cities function. Modes of rhythm-energetic deceleration, reconnection, localization and sharing are all demonstrated to have a role to play but the question becomes whether or not they can be inclusive in how they work out. Making the chrono-urbanist agenda mean more than just the latest plaything of profit-seeking developers, and embedding it more deeply within urban activist and degrowth agendas, is seen as a necessary way forward.

Chapter 5 shows how the just transition idea has roots in particular in post-industrial restructuring following the neoliberal reforms of the 1970s and 1980s, heralding rounds of deregulation, privatization, globalization and financialization. More specifically, as this phenomenon began to merge with initiatives to curtail domestic polluting industries, mining jobs went overseas and industrial towns were left destitute (Abraham, 2017; Pinker, 2020). In the face of a lack of socio-economic planning for such communities, unions and other civil society organizations sought 'just transitions' through compensation, retraining and/or inward investment programmes. The chapter experiments with positioning alternative or complementary virtues as guiding principles for transition, and reflects on the implications of these alternative philosophies, particularly for inclusion.

Chapter 6 aims to form a bridge between contemporary mainstream narratives of housing and radical analyses of a prefigurative nature. It adopts a narratives frame to show how the homeowning hegemony in homeowner-based societies suggests there is no 'Plan B'. It argues for bold imagining of housing models for post-carbon societies, requiring a move away from homeownership and land speculation models. Reflecting on diverse sustainable housing epistemologies (Horne, 2018) and connecting normative ideas of housing as commodity-cum-asset, utility and 'home', the chapter shows how increasing commodification and financialization undermined two other essential dimensions of home, as an affective space and useful domain. Exploring cases associated with eco-collaborative degrowth housing, the authors see post-carbon inclusive housing as necessitating the removal of housing from land price speculation.

Chapter 7 focuses on the fundamental need to breathe air and the consequences of that air being polluted to demonstrate the need to avoid easy assumptions about co-benefits between carbon reduction and air quality improvements. Co-benefits of this form undoubtedly exist, as they do in other parts of the environment–climate nexus. Yet, when viewed through this book's approaches, whether or not co-benefits will be realized evenly and to the advantage of those already most vulnerable or marginalized has to be called into question. The timescales and pace of change of air quality improvement will not be even; investments in 'new tech' will be skewed towards core sites of consumption while 'old tech' will be exported to the 'peripheries' of the Global South; and the urban green liveability agenda carries the risk of gentrification and exclusion. Even if the goal for environmental justice activists has long been to fundamentally reduce and eliminate pollution at source, it is imperative to guard against creating and sustaining enclaves within which continued fossil fuel use, poverty and ill-health remain unchecked.

Chapter 8 mounts a critique of the circular economy idea as currently positioned, steeped as it is in ecological modernization governance and responsibilization borne from New Public Management ideas of pollution control. These approaches are problematic for post-carbon inclusion agendas and, as an antidote, this chapter advances approaches to understanding 'waste' that circumvent dominant narratives where consumers are problematized, but consumption is not. The authors set out social practices and capabilities as useful ways to configure post-carbon inclusion in discard studies, as ways to overcome the traps of circular economy logics.

Chapter 9 explores strong tensions between the move towards post-carbon and the need to sustain life and improve wellbeing in a rapidly changing climate. Attention is particularly focused, unlike most of chapters in the book, on disadvantaged communities in the Global South, where the capability to keep cool in intensely hot conditions is delimited by a whole range of inequalities, including those relating to basic infrastructures of shelter, electricity and water provision. With temperatures increasing in some urban settings beyond the limits of liveability, the just response might well be to actively promote and enable increasing energy consumption to enable the use of cooling technologies, even though, as argued in other chapters, there is a simultaneous need to 'de-energize' much of contemporary economic and social life in order to hold down carbon emissions. The challenge, therefore, becomes one not of blanket judgement and diagnosis but of a careful working through of questions of inclusion that are acutely sensitive to setting, circumstance and patterns of inequality and responsibility.

Chapter 10 presents prefigurative degrowth hybrids, in the form of clusters of degrowth activities ('degrowth formations'), as pointers towards low carbon inclusion. Such hybrids exist within contemporary capitalism but strenuously experiment with degrowth livelihoods and ways of living that are both equitable, minimal, convivial and conform to Earth's limits. Driven by degrowth advocates, many of whom are activist scholars, they offer a research approach and method akin to urban living labs, characterized by collaboration and innovation, and applying both evidence-based and creative approaches to inform and create practices that might consolidate degrowth futures. They can be compared with eco-collaborative housing and ecovillages that address issues similar to degrowth concerns (Nelson, 2018).

Chapter 11 argues for a focus on high consumers of energy – those who constitute the normal professional classes of wealthy westernized countries, who both shape and respond to ramping up of normal everyday consumption, from air travel to meat consumption to larger indoor–outdoor air-conditioned homes. They are deserving of special attention in decarbonization studies due to their direct and disproportionate contribution to the climate crisis, and the ways in which they set new standards and aspirations for others in societies across the world. Using a non-judgemental, empathetic, ethnographic-inspired approach, this chapter provides insights for broader efforts towards post-carbon inclusion. Analysing the relational and social structure of high consumption raises questions and possible agendas for change around shifting meanings, social rules and consumerism itself in order to give permission and, indeed, the public responsibility to consume less.

Chapter 12 again draws upon ethnographic-inspired research into everyday domestic consumption, this time revealing how conventional approaches to energy efficient housing retrofit often don't work and even worsen energy vulnerability. Approaches that might be termed 'decommodified retrofit' are needed. The authors posit ways of understanding and institution building to integrate and centralize post-carbon inclusion in practical policy approaches. Housing retrofit that is configured for universal carbon-free energy-enabled futures draws upon ideas from both socio-technical transitions and degrowth practices.

If prefigurative degrowth hybrids are seen, somewhat simplistically, as micro-scale neighbourhood endeavours, Chapter 13 moves between challenges for individuals and households through to global scale dynamics. Certain degrowth advocates analyse the vast inequities within global production for trade, and flows of trade, to show how such structures conspire to form a typical 'imperial mode of living' (Brand and Wissen, 2021) in the minority world. Minority world activists are continuously frustrated in practising, instead, a solidarity mode of living, which would support post-carbon inclusion at a global scale. Yet, one vehicle that offers a range of opportunities for transformation is eco-collaborative housing models that incorporate aspects of an holistic feminist caring economy. Chapter 13 explores an accessible, affordable and ecologically sustainable best practice model of eco-collaborative housing to reveal avenues for transformation towards a solidarity mode of living or caring commons.

In Chapter 14, we conclude with a discussion of the dangers of decarbonization if they follow current capitalist models. Governing post-carbon inclusion calls for systematic, structured, yet locally responsive and relevant mechanisms for building coalitions, enabled by intermediary functions to share knowledge, connect and mediate across experiments, regions, neighbourhoods and initiatives. This entails solid links between ideas of action/demonstration/living models with activist calls for refocusing forces of capital and reorganizing global resources. This book seeks to contribute both actual living examples and thought experiments, both speaking to each other, in authentic attempts at reflective practice.

References

Abraham, J. (2017) 'Just transitions for the miners: labor environmentalism in the Ruhr and Appalachian coalfields', *New Political Science*, 39(2): 218–40.

Avelino, F. (2021) 'Theories of power and social change: power contestations and their implications for research on social change and innovation', *Journal of Political Power*, 14(3): 425–48.

Benatar, S., Upshur, R. and Gill, S. (2018) 'Understanding the relationship between ethics, neoliberalism and power as a step towards improving the health of people and our planet', *The Anthropocene Review*, 5(2): 155–76.

Bickerstaff, K., Walker, G. and Bulkeley, H. (eds) (2013) *Energy Justice in a Changing Climate: Social Equity and Low Carbon Energy*, London: Zed.

Brand, U. and Wissen, M. (2021) *The Imperial Mode of Living: Everyday Life and the Ecological Crisis of Capitalism*, London and Brooklyn: Verso.

Bulkeley, H., Marvin, S., Palgan, Y.V., McCormick, K., Breitfuss-Loidl, M., Mai, L. et al (2019) 'Urban living laboratories: conducting the experimental city?', *European Urban and Regional Studies*, 26(4): 317–35.

European Commission (2020) *The Just Transition Mechanism: Making Sure No One Is Left Behind*, January. Available from: https://www.citiesforum2023.eu/docs/EU/Just%20Transition%20Mechanism.pdf [Accessed 26 May 2023].

Evans, J., Karvonen, A. and Raven, R. (2018) *The Experimental City*, London: Taylor & Francis.

Geels, F.W. (2010) 'Ontologies, socio-technical transitions (to sustainability), and the multi-level perspective', *Research Policy*, 39(4): 495–510.

Government of Canada (2019) 'Task force: just transition for Canadian coal power workers and communities', Government of Canada. Available from: https://www.canada.ca/en/environment-climate-change/services/climate-change/task-force-just-transition.html [Accessed 23 May 2023].

Halkier, B. and Holm, L. (2021) 'Linking socioeconomic disadvantage to healthiness of food practices: can a practice-theoretical perspective sharpen everyday life analysis?', *Sociology of Health and Illness*, 43(2): 750–63. DOI: 10.1111/1467-9566.13251

Healy, N. and Barry, J. (2017) 'Politicizing energy justice and energy system transitions: fossil fuel divestment and a "just transition"', *Energy Policy*, 108: 451–9.

Horne, R.E. (2018) *Housing Sustainability in Low Carbon Cities*, London: Routledge.

Hui, A., Day, R. and Walker, G. (eds) (2018) *Demanding Energy: Space, Time and Change*, Chippenham: Palgrave Macmillan.

ILO (2015) *Guidelines for a Just Transition Towards Environmentally Sustainable Economies and Societies for All*, Geneva: International Labour Organization.

IPCC (2019) *Global Warming of 1.5°C*. Available from: https://www.ipcc.ch/sr15/ [Accessed 22 January 2024].

IPCC (2022) *Climate Change 2022: Mitigation of Climate Change*, Working Group III contribution to the Sixth Assessment Report of the Intergovernmental Panel on Climate Change. Available from: https://www.ipcc.ch/report/sixth-assessment-report-working-group-3/ [Accessed 22 May 2023].

Janda, K.B. and Topouzi, M. (2015) 'Telling tales: using stories to remake energy policy', *Building Research & Information*, 43(4): 516–33.

Johnstone, P. and Hielscher, S. (2017) 'Phasing out coal, sustaining coal communities? Living with technological decline in sustainability pathways', *Extractive Industries and Society*, 4(3): 457–61.

Lamb, W.F., Antal, A., Bohnenberger, K., Brand-Correa, L.I., Müller-Hansen, F., Jakob, M. et al (2020) 'What are the social outcomes of climate policies? A systematic map and review of the ex-post literature', *Environmental Research Letters*, 15: 113006.

Nelson, A. (2018) *Small is Necessary: Shared Living on a Shared Planet*, London: Pluto Press.

Newell, P. and Mulvaney, D. (2013) 'The political economy of the "just transition"', *The Geographical Journal*, 179(2): 132–40.

Pel, B., Haxeltine, A., Avelino, F., Dumitru, A., Kemp, R., Bauler, T. et al (2020) 'Towards a theory of transformative social innovation: a relational framework and 12 propositions', *Research Policy*, 49(8): 104080.

Pinker, A. (2020) *Just Transitions: A Comparative Perspective*, independent report, 25 August. Available from: https://www.gov.scot/publications/transitions-comparative-perspective/ [Accessed 22 May 2023].

Schlosberg, D. and Collins, L.B. (2014) 'From environmental to climate justice: climate change and the discourse of environmental justice', *WIREs Climate Change*, 5: 359–74.

Scottish Government (2020) *Just Transition Commission*. Available from: https://www.gov.scot/groups/just-transition-commission/ [Accessed 22 May 2023].

Sen, A. (2009) *The Idea of Justice*, London: Allen Lane.

Shove, E., Pantzar, M. and Watson, M. (2012) *The Dynamics of Social Practice: Everyday Life and How it Changes*, London: SAGE.

Sovacool, B.K. (2021) 'Who are the victims of low-carbon transitions? Towards a political ecology of climate change mitigation', *Energy Research & Social Science*, 73: 101916.

Sovacool, B.K. and Dworkin, M.H. (2015) 'Energy justice: conceptual insights and practical applications', *Applied Energy*, 142: 435–44.

Stephens, J.C. and Landsmark, T. (2023) *Diversifying Power: Why We Need Antiracist, Feminist Leadership on Climate and Energy*, Washington, DC: Island Press.

Walker, G.P. (2012) *Environmental Justice: Concepts, Evidence and Politics*, Abingdon: Routledge.

Walker, G. (2013) 'Inequality, sustainability and capability: locating justice in social practice', in Shove, E. and Spurling, N. (eds), *Sustainable Practices: Social Theory and Climate Change*, London: Routledge, pp 181–96.

While, A. and Eadson, W. (2019) 'Households in place: socio-spatial (dis)advantage in energy-carbon restructuring', *European Planning Studies*, 27(8): 1626–45.

Willand, W., Middha, B. and Walker, G. (2021) 'Using the capability approach to evaluate energy vulnerability policies and initiatives in Victoria, Australia', Local Environment, 26(9): 1109–27. DOI: 10.1080/13549839.2021.1962830

Wood, N. (2023) 'Problematising energy justice: towards conceptual and normative alignment', *Energy Research & Social Science*, 97: 102993.

2

Inclusion in Post-Carbon Urban Experiments

Ralph Horne and Louise Dorignon

Urban sustainability experiments of various guises have drawn wide interest among scholars and practitioners of decarbonization. The notion of experimentation 'feeds on attractive notions of innovation and creativity (both individual and collective) while reframing the emphasis of sustainability from distant targets and government policies to concrete and achievable actions that can be undertaken by a wide variety of urban stakeholders in specific places' (Evans et al, 2018: 1). Specifically, urban experiments often envisage community-based, direct forms of exchange that shorten production-consumption chains and provide for human scale decarbonization practice. In prospect then, arguably, the urban scale offers a local antidote to globalized systems of capital accumulation, where production and consumption are remote, and linked by complex supply chains.

Adding to the attraction of urban experiments is the idea that local/city governments are seen as more agile and able to avoid the political quagmire faced by national governments and global agreements. Cities have thus been able to declare 'carbon neutral by 2030' plans and plough ahead seemingly in the vanguard of decarbonization. For urban post-carbon pioneers, experiments are advanced as a tool to find out what works, learn from mistakes and from others' examples. However, the reality is that cities are entangled in globalized systems, whether they be ubiquitous digital technologies or data systems, or cultures and social rules associated with them. Moreover, despite over 40 years of neoliberalism and the rise and rise of private capital, national governments retain significant jurisdictional and financial power over city governments, and multi-level governance of post-carbon cities remains fraught and complex (Karvonen and van Heur, 2014; Bulkeley et al, 2019).

Urban sustainability experiments differ from other urban projects 'by an explicit emphasis on learning from real-world interventions' (Evans et al, 2018: 2). Yet the role of 'community' in urban experiments is contentious, as is the extent to which a community learns from other experiments and passes on learnings. Indeed, the question of whether and how urban sustainability experiments have been able to deliver on inclusion remains largely unanswered (Dickey et al, 2022). A problem at the heart of owner-occupier societies (see Chapters 1, 6 and 12) is that any intervention that improves the quality of urban life in a particular neighbourhood is likely to fuel local house and land price rises. The process of gentrification then unfolds as rents rise and working-class households are forced out while wealthier households move in. Iconic green housing projects, car-free neighbourhood projects, and so on, despite being well-meaning attempts to decarbonize, could in this way unintentionally undermine inclusion in the process of advancing a green agenda.

Furthermore, questions arise about the fate of actual global carbon emissions under urban decarbonization initiatives. With the explicit exception of self-identified degrowth experiments, ways and means to 'undo unsustainability' have received remarkably little attention from policy makers and politicians. Urban experiments such as transition towns, permaculture initiatives and local futures movements have sought to slow down material and economic growth. For the most part, however, urban sustainability centres on new sustainable practices; few initiatives incentivize unmaking, thrift, minimizing, reducing or intentionally *doing without.*

In this chapter, we provide an overview of the diversity of urban experiments and networks that aim at enhancing urban sustainability. Drawing on a database of 80 projects in Australia and internationally, we propose an empirical framework for situating post-carbon urban experiments within the broader field of urban experiments. By our definition, post-carbon urban experiments focus on actions that deliberately aim to achieve inclusion and environmental sustainability, while practising for a post-carbon world. Inclusion that advances justice, rights and universal access to, for example, pollution-free urban environments and services, is thus central. In this regard, we recognize the considerable work done to date on ideas of socio-technical transitions and urban living labs (ULLs). For current purposes, transitions include socio-technical change processes, but also 'just' transitions. ULLs highlight spatiality and scales at play, as well as the central ideas of experimentation and learning.

These ideas are summarized later, prior to the presentation of an empirical framework for understanding the role of inclusion in post-carbon urban experiments. We then illustrate this framework by focusing on three case-study examples. We conclude by reflecting on prospects for urban post-carbon inclusion in practice. In so doing we hope to advance practice so that 'inclusion' and 'low carbon' are put to work jointly, and overtly, in an increasing number and variety of urban projects.

Purposive and just urban transitions

Socio-technical transitions, perhaps most well-known through the multi-level perspective (Geels, 2010), hope for systemic decarbonization through facilitated, managed governance processes. The spatial and urban turns in transitions have produced a burgeoning literature specifically focused on how such socio-technical transition processes might proceed within cities and across urban terrain (Moore et al, 2018). Urban transition labs or ULLs have emerged based on the observation of emission reduction practices in several European cities (Nevens et al, 2013; Evans and Karvonen, 2014; Voytenko et al, 2016).

A managed socio-technical transition, if possible and successful, may 'deliver', for example, a renewable energy-powered city. However, at what cost to inequality? The idea of the just transition starts from the premise that a renewable-energy-powered city is not in itself a sufficient result. Indeed, the just transition movement originated in the United States around the decline of rust belt regions in the face of environmental regulation and global restructuring. A just transition has since been taken up more broadly as a way to focus on disadvantage in decarbonization – and the need to address this (While and Eadson, 2019).

Community participation often features in urban projects, including in the form of distributed governance, cross-sectoral cooperation around shared goals, community co-design and social capital. Such ideas link to foundation concepts of justice and rights to the city. However, practices of participation around plans and enactments that are set within a neoliberal individual-based society – where the starting point is riven with inequalities and uneven capabilities, resources and opportunities – point towards outcomes where the most privileged, eloquent and established are more able to participate to their benefit. Myriad identities or spatially described communities variously engage in othering.

As outlined in Chapter 5, the European Union has adopted the Just Transition Mechanism (European Commission, 2020), which aims at managing the transition towards a climate-neutral economy in a fair way, by putting in place mechanisms to engage, empower and support communities negatively affected by decarbonization. For example, the Canadian government set up a Just Transition Task Force for Canadian Coal Power Workers and Communities (Government of Canada, 2018) and the Scottish government set up the Just Transition Commission (Scottish Government, 2020), aimed at socially just job creation in post-mining communities (Pinker, 2020). The concept of justice has started to be used beyond the specific reference to supporting coal-based communities to make their transition, for example, in discussions about broader geopolitical and inter-generational distributive effects of climate adaptation and mitigation, including about rights to zero-carbon energy sources (Heffron and McCauley, 2018).

While the specific need to support coal-mining communities is clear, this broader arena of just transition is rather less straightforward, yet more interesting for urban post-carbon experiments. It points to broader underlying inequalities in society and, therefore, to their causes (Newell and Mulvaney, 2013). Instead of seeing coal-to-renewables as a 'techno-economic' fix, and related mechanisms designed to minimize backlash from specific coal-mining communities, a broader framing points towards socio-economic structures in western society as both a cause of the climate crisis and of inequality and exclusion in broader society – not just coal-based communities. This links to the calls of Meadowcroft (2011), Avelino and Wittmayer (2016) for a deeper consideration of politics and agency in transitions processes.

Urban living labs

While the idea of the city as a real-life laboratory is not new (Evans et al, 2018), the concept of ULLs has been advanced as a way to understand contingent, spatially situated urban experiments and their governance (Bulkeley and Castán Broto, 2013; Marvin et al, 2018; Rizzo et al, 2021). ULLs have been described as 'a form of experimental governance whereby urban stakeholders develop and test new technologies and ways of living to address the challenges of climate change and urban sustainability' (Palgan et al, 2018: 21), and their many forms and iterations imply such a broad definition. Some cases emphasize the 'living' half of the concept (Karvonen and van Heur, 2014; Bulkeley et al, 2019), emphasizing pilot activities, testbeds, and notions of demonstration and replicability. Others focus on the 'lab' half (Evans and Karvonen, 2011), highlighting the involvement of universities and research centres and the various acts of reflection, evaluation and cross-community sense-making involved. ULLs include geographically bounded spaces and/or intentional programmes or approaches. The role they play or should play in urban governance is inevitably questionable (Palgan et al, 2018).

Sengers et al (2016: 21) talk of 'inclusive, practice-based and challenge-led initiatives designed to promote system innovation through social learning under conditions of uncertainty and ambiguity', with the goal of making innovations 'socially-robust and fair'. This more explicit focus upon inclusion affords distributive justice a more central role, emphasizing alignments with diverse and marginal societal actors. ULLs tend to be initiated and led by relatively elite actors (universities), which inherently limits their inclusivity of diverse and marginal actors. They do, on the other hand, provide research opportunities to reveal how power and agency are orchestrated in order to achieve desired results (Bulkeley et al, 2016; Caprotti and Cowley, 2017). They can be implemented across a range of thematic areas (mobility, energy, information and communication technologies, and so on) and are led by either government, private entities, academic institutions or civil society/not-for-profit actors. Indeed, a key organizing question is the role that urban communities, city governments and urban elites play in shaping or directing socio-technical transitions, rather than being passive recipients of them (Hodson and Marvin, 2016).

Geels and Raven (2006) distinguish between local innovation projects and what they call 'the niche level', which relates to a more systemic intent. The idea is that city actors support niche innovations that gradually emerge to transform urban socio-technical regimes (Geels and Schot, 2007). For instance, using the example of renewable energy again, instead of passively consuming brown energy (say fossil fuel) from a regional grid, cities can institute various measures to incentivize the uptake of local renewable generation to encourage decarbonization within urban boundaries – an urban renewables niche.

Assessing urban post-carbon inclusion

By urban post-carbon experiments, we envisage institutions, practices, discourses and common understandings that might be sustained for periods of time in urban spaces. To approach this empirically, we conducted desktop research and analysis of urban experiments to summarize their nature, scale, scope and ambitions, and undertook five online, semi-structured interviews with stakeholders working in the field of urban innovation, smart cities and social entrepreneurship. Interviewees were selected on the basis of their engagement with relevant networks and existing knowledge and participation in urban experiments. The result was a database of 80 urban post-carbon experiments in Australia, Europe and at a broader international scale.

Keyword searches included urban innovation, integrated precinct, innovative precinct, eco-district, knowledge city, urban lab(oratory), living lab, digital and cities, third spaces, urban think tank, urban experiment(ation), and sustainable precinct. Academic publications and grey/white literature review also supplemented the interview data. Our goal was to develop a diverse database of urban post-carbon experiments that could indicate the evolution of focus and governance of each project over time, noting that geographic spread was rather constrained by language (restricted to English and French) and accessibility of online information, which skewed the cases towards the Global North. Because we undertook this exercise during the 2020 COVID-19 outbreak, experiments in locked down cities relating to health, wellbeing and social sustainability more broadly were included, such as Slow Streets (for example in Oakland and Rotterdam) and outdoor food consumption experiments (for example in Vilnius, Melbourne and London).

The interviews focused on understanding the vision and context behind urban post-carbon experiments and were conducted online. Many case studies were clearly labelled in reference to urban net-zero or carbon-neutral experimentation and inclusion, however, some were less overtly defined. Most of the data collection was completed in September and October 2020, with ongoing revisions to the live database until the writing of this chapter (November 2022). Limitations of internet desktop reviews were balanced by the in-depth knowledge and experience collected in the interviews.

Ten project types were tagged/identified as follows: creative precinct; eco-district; temporary experimentation site; green public space; incubator; infrastructure project; innovation precinct; knowledge network; municipal programme; and urban living lab. Project types were attributed to each project based on their official description and our analysis of their nature and intent. 'Creative precincts' were projects where the arts and/or creativity were a central outcome or activity; 'eco-districts' aimed at combining social, economic and environmental goals; 'temporary experimentation sites' were short/medium-term projects linked to a particular site; 'green public spaces' related to the (re)development of urban green spaces; 'incubators' were focused on supporting the economic development of innovative small and medium-sized enterprises; 'infrastructure projects' were small or large projects around various infrastructure work (health, transportation, and so on); 'innovation precincts' were urban growth projects focused on science and innovation; 'knowledge networks' were material or digital spaces of exchange and collaboration based around knowledge-sharing; 'municipal programmes' were initiatives led by urban governments and municipalities; and 'urban living labs' were places of experimental governance developing and testing new city-related technologies (Palgan et al, 2018). This typology indicates the diverse ways in which urban experiments are conducted, the forms they can take across urban spaces, and the models of elaboration. Other criteria we noted in collecting the case studies were their location, dates of activities, guiding principles, success metrics, main governance model and financing arrangements.

An empirical framework for understanding inclusion in post-carbon experiments

Notwithstanding proponents' framings, we sought to situate each project across three paradigms: climate change; inequality; and inclusive governance. That is to say, we used the material available to estimate the starting point for

Figure 2.1: Framework for understanding post-carbon urban inclusion experiments

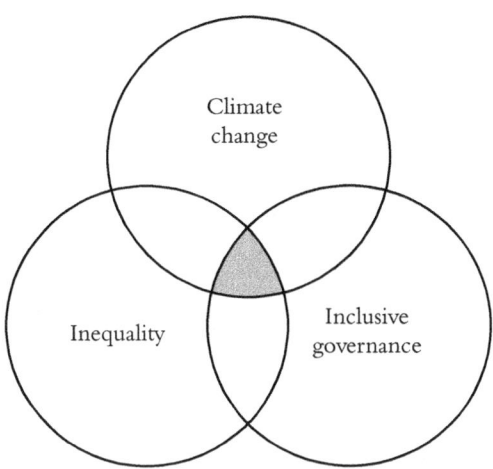

each experiment out of three possible such points: tackling climate change/sustainability; tackling inequality; or practising inclusive or local democratic governance. Of course, it is possible that a given project could be conceived and designed to address two or three paradigms from the outset or as they evolved. In any event, given that all such experiments morph and change over time and have unpredictable trajectories and outcomes, a framework to guide, evaluate and inform the fate of each paradigm in each project was proposed (Figure 2.1).

Conceptually, any given project can be placed at a point within this framework. Over time, it may be actively modified or, in any event, will shift position. The 'ideal' position that a successful 'post-carbon urban inclusion' project will maintain is within the green shaded area, incorporating all three paradigms. In recognition that many of these initiatives get reshaped by actors, relationalities and local political agendas, revealing the often-muddled territories in which low carbon inclusion is designed, produced and/or enacted, the framework could be adopted as an evaluation device, or as an action research tool to guide (re)design as the project proceeds.

Analysis of the database was undertaken to identify cases of real projects where urban experiments appeared to shift from one paradigm to another, or from one paradigm to incorporate a second and/or third paradigm. We found projects that were initiated with the key ambition as addressing carbon reduction/climate change but became more attuned to addressing inequality as they proceeded. Some projects went the other way, from inequality to climate change, beginning with inclusive governance as a central paradigm, and others that incorporated this ambition as they proceeded (Table 2.1).

Table 2.1: Paradigms of post-carbon urban inclusion experiments

Initial or central paradigm	Shift to		
	Climate change	Inequality	Inclusive governance
Climate change • EVA Lanxmeer, Culemborg, the Netherlands • Hammarby Sjöstad, Stockholm, Sweden • Vauban, Freiburg, Germany • BO-01, Malmö, Sweden • Ginko, Bordeaux, France • Audubon Park Garden District, Orlando, US • Project Mint (Triton Square), London, UK • Landschaftspark, Duisburg, Germany • Coulée verte René-Dumont, Paris, France • The Highline, New York City, US • Girondins Development Area, Lyon, France • Parques del Río, Medellin, Columbia • The Lowline, New York City, US • Madrid Río Project, Spain • Hyllie Plaza, Malmö, Sweden • Cheonggyecheon Stream Restoration Project, Seoul, South Korea • Natureandus, Paris, France • Urban Canopée, Paris, France • Roboat, Amsterdam, the Netherlands • One Brighton, UK • Urban GreenUP, EU		• **Lisière d'une Tierce Forêt, Aubervilliers, France (green public space)** • Augustenborg Ekostaden, Malmö, Sweden • Le Champ des Possibles, Lyon, France • La Recyclerie, Paris, France • ShareCity, Dublin, Ireland • Transformative Urban Coalitions Project, Villa 20, Buenos Aires, Argentina • Atelier Énergie and Territoires, France	• BedZED, Sutton, UK • Vulkan, Oslo, Norway • Bankside Urban Forest, London, UK • ATELIER, Amsterdam, the Netherlands; Bilbao, Spain
Inequality • Docks de Saint-Ouen, France • Kalasatama, Helsinki, Finland • New Road Brighton, UK	• **Superblock Barcelona, Spain** • Clichy Batignolles, France		• Architecture et Précarités, international • Les Grands Voisins, Paris, France

Table 2.1: Paradigms of post-carbon urban inclusion experiments (continued)

Initial or central paradigm	Shift to		
	Climate change	**Inequality**	**Inclusive governance**
• Erdre Porterie Development Area, Nantes, France • Queen Elizabeth Olympic Park, London, UK • Confluences, Lyon, France • Fishermans Bend, Melbourne, Australia • Yes we camp!, Marseille, France • Housing Innovation Lab, Boston, US	• Paris-Rive-Gauche, France • Chapelle(s), Paris, France • Marseille Euro-Mediterranée, France		• Oxford Road Corridor, Manchester, UK
Inclusive governance • Ground Control, Paris, France • Agora, Abidjian, Côte d'Ivoire • Villa Itoró, São Paulo, Brazil • Wiki Village Factory, Paris, France • Forum Virum, Helsinki, Finland • Station F, Paris, France • Quayside, Toronto, Canada • Knowledge Quarter London, UK • Clinical Innovation Zone • Smart Cities, San Diego, US • Playable City, Bristol, Oxford, UK; Melbourne, Australia; Austin, US; Seoul, South Korea • Co-Liv, New York City, US; Paris, France • Escenario, Río Cuarto, Holmberg, Las Higueras, Argentina • Hatch, Melbourne, Australia • Start-up-in-Residence, San Francisco, US • Lab Ouishare x Chronos, Paris, France • Sidewalks Lab, New York City, US • CityLab, Melbourne, Australia • Montreal Urban Innovation Lab, Canada	• Catapult Connected Places, London and Milton Keynes, UK • London West End Street Dining conversion, UK • Rotterdam street relocation measures, the Netherlands • Oakland Slow Streets, US • Streetspace for London, UK • One Giant Outdoor Café, Vilnius, Lithuania	• Stapeln Open Makerspace, Malmö, Sweden • Athens' Digital Lab, Greece • Instituto de Vivienda de la Ciudad, Buenos Aires, Argentina • Laboratorio para la Ciudad, Mexico City, Mexico • Sharing.Lab, Copenhagen, Denmark	

Note: terms in bold are discussed later in this section.

For example, UK-based innovation accelerator Catapult Connected Places was created to develop mechanisms for more inclusive governance in cities, transport and place leadership: the network later declared climate action as one of its key imperatives, establishing as its mission to 'convene the markets to spark disruptive innovation and scale up Net Zero and resilience technologies' (Catapult Connected Places, 2023). Similarly, makerspaces, such as Stapeln Open Makerspace in Malmö (Sweden) or Makerspace at the Docklands Library in Melbourne (Australia), were conceived to facilitate encounters, participation and interaction with no costs and restrictions of access. Recently they have been reframed as 'third places' that have the potential to reduce social inequalities. BedZED, a pioneering low-carbon medium-density housing development in Greater London, developed governance tools as a proposed replication strategy for its housing model (Dunster, 2013).

We detail three exemplar case studies – Superblock Barcelona, Lisière d'une Tierce Forêt and Architecture et Précarités (in bold in Table 2.1) – all projects selected to illustrate the various paradigm shifts and urban experimentation types, and to capture how inclusion dynamics have evolved differently across these projects initiated in a top-down manner.

From inequality to climate change: Superblock Barcelona

The Catalan Superblock Barcelona programme proposes sustainable urban transformation at the precinct scale, following smaller local superblock experiments in the Poblenou, Horta and Sant Antoni neighbourhoods in Barcelona. In each case, blocks of buildings were identified, and the space assigned to cars effectively reduced and converted to public space, giving primacy to traffic calming to increase safety, health and liveability.

A superblock typically consists of nine traffic-regulated (3 × 3) city-blocks, including internal and external streets. Inside the superblock, mobility is restricted to pedestrians, residents and essential services, and space is set aside for social interaction and neighbourhood facilities, such as children's playgrounds. Erstwhile through traffic is restricted to outside the superblock. Mini-blocks have also been developed, containing four (2 × 2) blocks, as a smaller-scale strategy to gradually scale up the initiative. The model gained renewed interest during the COVID-19 pandemic during discussions on how to make the city healthier and more liveable, which brought about alternative urban 'hacks' and citizen-led design operations such as tactical urbanism or slow streets. Tactical urbanism here refers to low cost, temporary or DIY activities that aim to slow consumption or advance sustainability. 'Slow streets' is a concept that links to the 15-minute city concept (see Chapter 4). The idea of freeing urban enclaves from motorized traffic follows earlier work in Barcelona in the 1970s and then later embedded in a city-wide mobility programme (the 2013–2018 Urban Mobility Plan) and enacted through Poblenou as a pilot demonstration.

In a physically constrained city that lacks green spaces, the Barcelona superblock project evolved in practice from traffic calming to addressing climate change. Initially guided by the desire to make streets safer and to stimulate active transport as in 'healthy cities', the project evolved into a 'network of green hubs and squares' (Superilla Barcelona, 2023) contributing to reducing greenhouse gas emissions, which would 'gradually spread throughout the city' (Superilla Barcelona, 2023). Superblocks have been progressively built into local climate commitments, including by reducing heat island effects (and thus air-conditioning loads) by enabling water retention and the creation of shade. As Zografos et al (2020: 6) summarize, 'in essence, the superblocks were a vision for transforming the city of Barcelona that both shaped and was shaped by more recent climate adaptation goals'.

With a basis in addressing mobility and urban health inequalities, the Superblock project has assimilated climate change action into its *raison d'être* along the way. The controversies that played out in the early phases have been reshaped as a result. Many of the paradoxes of precinct scale urban retrofit projects also apply to superblocks: too limited and the problems intensify, such as traffic congestion in surrounding remaining thoroughfares; too extensive/successful and gentrification takes hold in and around the superblocks (López et al, 2020). Again, paradoxically, the benefits of the superblock idea (universal social benefits, distributed climate adaptation and action) might only be truly realized when such projects break out of their local areas (or niches, to borrow multi-level perspective language) and the whole city becomes one large superblock project. Health-centred studies also support this idea (Mueller et al, 2020). This in turn challenges the idea of the ULL as an end in itself, and cautions us to think of ULLs as contingent building blocks in the larger post-carbon urban project.

From climate change to inequality: Lisière d'une Tierce Forêt

In 2015, the Lisière d'une Tierce Forêt (Edge of a Third Forest) initiative in Aubervilliers, in the northern suburbs of Paris, was initiated to combat urban heat by revegetation of a parking lot in a disadvantaged municipality. The project was conceived as an ecosystem response to mitigate the urban heat island effect. It consists of passive infrastructure that retains and recycles stormwater to support local biodiversity. Planting was undertaken of various species chosen for their capacity to thrive on disturbed soil engineered for water retention. Rainwater infiltrates the soil and is then stored to supply the trees and provide ambient cooling during periods of heat and drought.

The project initiators were the not-for-profit association Alteralia who already managed the local young workers' hostel, and the planting design was provided by a Parisian landscape architecture practice (Fieldwork). In 2016, these organizations sought the support of Paris&Co, an agency for economic development and innovation in Paris, which includes an 'Urban Lab' team dedicated to supporting urban experimentation projects in connection with the city's strategies in the domains of urban and ecological innovation (Orillard et al, 2020).

The project design did not initially include social sustainability goals other than to provide green amenities and functionality to pedestrians, 250 residents, 50 employees and visitors to the hostel (Parison et al, 2020). At the heart of the project was the transformation of a car park, adjacent to a hostel for young workers in Aubervilliers, into a park and a public/civic square was made car-free. After delivery the project's potential became clear – in addressing social inequality by offering opportunities to young workers living in the centre using the newly developed green space.

The project website states that Lisière d'une Tierce Forêt increases 'territorial resilience'. This new dimension was subsequently brought to the project design. The introduction of trees was treated not as an amenity but rather as essential infrastructure for the contemporary and future city. ADEME, the French government agency, notes that the landscape identity and cooler temperatures provided by the site promote wellbeing and social interactions. The newly planted area was very quickly adopted and used as an extension of living spaces for the inhabitants of the hostel, especially at the end of the afternoon and early evening when the heat was greatest in the tight spaces of the workers' rooms.

In 2021, the association running the centre introduced photography and Meslek Combat workshops aimed at 'helping young people to use their mind and bodies' (Fieldwork Architecture, 2021/2022). According to residents' accounts, the site quickly became a 'friendly' place providing opportunities for social interactions between residents and with the wider neighbourhood (Fieldwork Architecture, 2021/2022). It provided a sheltered place to make tea, smoke, chat, have a picnic, play football, read a book and for 'sharing moments together' (Fieldwork Architecture, 2021/2022). The project is increasingly framed as increasing the visibility of the workers' accommodation association and raising the local populations' awareness of climate change.

Other than the point that the project has shifted from a 'climate change' to a 'climate change and inequality' focus, we note this project was rather muted on initial community co-design, with residents only playing a 'tester' role in the living lab process (Orillard et al, 2020). This raises questions about how different (better or worse?) outcomes might have been if more co-design and intentionality to address inequality had been incorporated in the initial design. In any event, this project offers high potential for reproducibility, given the modest budget and rapid rise in interest in urban greening projects across westernized cities.

From inequality to inclusive governance: Architecture et Précarités

Architecture et Précarités (Architecture and Precariousness) is a collaborative online platform launched in 2022 that aims at rendering visible 'architectural, urban and landscape responses to urban precariousness' (Architecture et Précarités, 2023). The tool is open to all to access and share case studies. Visitors are invited to submit initiatives and projects to enrich the directory and can also leave comments. The site's colour block visuals contribute to its intuitive, user-friendly design, with projects listed according to four fields:

- keywords, which are interconnected (for example – public baths, circular economy, women, waste and land);
- location (through a map of five key types of projects, namely 'spatial transformations', 'research and publications', 'social and artistic actions', 'platforms and collectives', and 'pedagogic experiences');
- actors/instigators/activists (either by name or role);
- projects (by type, title, area of focus, budget, location, year).

A project entry consists of a descriptive article with weblinks accompanied by visual material. The database of projects is downloadable. According to the project website (Architecture et Précarités, 2023), the project was conceived from three key assumptions:

1. Urban policies and change are increasingly marginalizing precarious populations (migrants, homeless people, refugees, the elderly, and so on), including those who face mobility inequalities.
2. However, there are many initiatives to counter these marginalizing forces and to create new places of hospitality and welcome.
3. These initiatives are not visible.

Financial support to develop the website included Caisse des Dépôts et Consignations (a French public sector financial institution and public investor), Ipraus (a local architectural and urban research institute) and the ENSA Paris-Belleville architecture faculty. The primary aim is to make cases visible to a variety of stakeholders, including local authorities, planning professionals, groups and associations, designers (architects, urban planners, designers and landscape architects), citizens, teachers, students, and researchers from architecture and landscape schools. A secondary aim is to create a 'social museum of the 21st century', a place for archiving, transmitting and discussing knowledge of the fate of these initiatives (Architecture et Précarités, 2023). The project declares a political/polity ambition by choosing to list examples that 'constitute plural, localised, multi-situated and most often collective responses' and 'contribute to the existence of the city's public in all its diversity' (Architecture et Précarités, 2023).

Intending to highlight architectural, urban and landscape solutions to inequality, in its various forms, Architecture et Précarités gradually morphed into a tool for inclusive governance based on its very method: a collaborative catalogue of interventions that are expanded by shared knowledge, and that can be downloaded for educational or policy-making efforts. Limitations include the relatively slow growth of the project, given its reliance on open-source, unpaid contributions by collaborators around the world, and its primary language, French, which may discourage submissions, dissemination and consumption from outside the francophone world.

Conclusion

We propose three paradoxes and associated dilemmas that arise from the cases. However, first it is important to acknowledge the limits and ambition of this work. We do not seek to advance a theory, rather, a heuristic tool. The meanings and boundaries of our three paradigms are necessarily contested and imprecise, open to challenge. Also, we have no consistent longitudinal data, and rely on web and verbal accounts. Data collection was constrained in time, so we do not claim an accurate dynamic account. The retrospective nature of our work is designed to make sense of projects that we feel in any event have merit as bold and well-intentioned urban experiments towards sustainability, inclusion and/or collective governance. Our heuristic is, thus, predicated on the idea that illuminating and giving space for each paradigm is an important and indeed necessary contribution to post-carbon urban experiments.

All three cases, we contend, started with a bias towards a particular aim, in other words, one of the three paradigms. Then this aim evolved in association with various dynamic shaping factors associated with contingent relations, orientations and adaptations in each case project. Context-based priorities often led to focused actions towards specific goals, such as converting a parking lot conducive to increasing urban heat into an environmentally enhanced public space. Relationalities and local political agendas acted variously to enable or constrain aspects of low carbon inclusion. In Superblock Barcelona, local contestations and traffic management issues have complicated the transformation of street space into public squares and potentially slowed down the generalization of superblocks to a wider urban area; a condition, we argue, for this experiment to counter gentrification and realize broader aims for inequality reduction and climate action.

Paradox 1 is that a local urban experiment can only 'succeed' when it is no longer a local urban experiment. If it 'succeeds' in improving the urban realm, but remains local, then political-economic structures will inevitably promote forms of extraction that result in gentrification or some related form of new uneven urban relations – that is, exacerbating pre-existing inequalities. However, as local experiments become more widely adopted or proposed, they encounter new oppositional actors and forces that alter their course, often problematically according to their original aims. An associated dilemma exists between testing locally bounded projects and scaling them across broader urban areas.

Initial guiding principles and success metrics shed light on how projects and their outcomes evolved across paradigms. Emerging and secondary paradigms arose in various ways through subtle power relations. Our observations of the financing arrangements of the projects predictably highlighted the ethical and paradigm orientations of each project, as well as potential limitations, but also acted as a predictor of the project evolution across paradigms. For example, the fact that the originator of Lisière d'une Tierce Forêt ran a hostel for local young workers is germane to the project's evolution from an urban climate greening project to a local inclusion project.

This leads to Paradox 2, that a local urban experiment can only 'succeed' in extending across paradigms when it is open to change and sufficiently configured to allow such change to evolve. Yet, projects insufficiently grounded in their design and aims are also open to capture by extractive forces. This leads to a dilemma over project contingency and obduracy. Those that become ingrained and embedded run increasing risks of becoming captured or otherwise bogged down in contemporary political-economic struggles, while those that remain independent and 'outside' are precarious and short-lived almost by nature.

Paradox 3 is around the curation, design and performative work of recognizing, sharing and interrogating urban experiments. Links between experiments are needed, as are associated curatorial and cataloguing activities. A further need is to create accessible, comprehensive, up-to-date and dynamic global databases of urban projects, with open source, common or consistent independent contextual and evaluation material. Sufficient funding should be allocated to such cataloguing efforts, to ensure there are no language and accessibility barriers, and to maintain regular contributions, peer-review and software maintenance. Yet, the act of creating official and comprehensive databases excludes 'unofficial' projects and brings with it the inevitable risk of succumbing to funders' interests. It also masks the legitimacy of deliberately underground and 'non-projects', creating a dilemma of legitimacy. Architecture et Précarités is an open-source collaborative model, that is primarily public/government funded, making the experiment transparent and relatively accessible. But the relatively small scale of resources available may prevent regular input into the platform and potentially limit its outreach.

This is not a flippant point. There is a serious question about how to amplify the potential that 'non-projects', such as ordinary, banal tactical urbanism (Lydon and Garcia, 2015; Silva, 2016) or outcomes of 'quiet activism' (Steele et al, 2021), may have on low carbon and inclusive transformation. Surely the less talked about ordinary good planning, cognizant of inclusion and decarbonization imperatives, is as powerful as media-conscious, innovative urban experiments? Mid-rise housing renewal in working-class Getafe, in Madrid (Spain) includes well-connected, highly efficient buildings with shared equity arrangements, thoughtfully designed shared amenities, with ample shared open space facilities, shops at street level on the outside, shared courtyards with play areas and vegetable gardens on the inside, and rooms for rent for family visits. In one example, a two-bedroom duplex sells for €115,000 at 2016 prices (approximately AU$180,000). This is not an urban experiment; it is well-planned, thoughtful urban development, largely uncelebrated but apparently effective.

In conclusion, the work that we hope to do by proposing a schema containing three paradigms of post-carbon urban inclusion experiments is to highlight particular facets of urban processes in action. As Evans et al (2018) and Bulkeley et al (2019) have illustrated, urban experiments are not undertaken in a vacuum. They are not predictable, they reflect their protagonists, they morph over time, and they bridge the formal and informal. To this list we would add that the evolution of project objectives is particularly important to the interplay of carbon-inclusion-governance considerations. Thus, Superblock Barcelona was originally focused on pedestrian safety and access to public spaces at a local level, and progressively became a leading climate change mitigation exemplar for municipality-led urban action. Lisière d'une Tierce Forêt started off as a micro-local solution to urban heat and subsequently evolved to become a site for locals seeking active exercise and/or artistic space – addressing inequalities and promoting social cohesion in an economically disadvantaged neighbourhood. Architecture et Précarités was conceived as a collaborative online platform with the goal to bring visibility to a range of architectural solutions to social precarity around the world.

The outcomes of these experiments unfold over time in unknowable and unpredictable ways. They are examples of a plethora of innovations, from new municipalism to inclusive economies and decarbonization projects, that challenge the brutality of neoliberal cities and the plundering of the global commons. Without them, decarbonization faces grave consequences of widening inequality. Following earlier ideas of ULLs (Bulkeley and Castán Broto, 2013), dilemmas about appropriate scope, scale, planning, stakeholder arrangements and official legitimacy or informality are inevitable and indeed important. This point supports the value of a curated meta-bank of urban projects where post-carbon inclusion is critically and openly centred, deliberately countering the current problem that post-carbon and inclusion are rarely addressed conjointly. A key point of a framework, such as that proposed here, is the possibility to draw attention to unintended consequences or design parameters that might be avoided, and to render visible the hitherto taken-for-granted parameters of urban projects. While we make no claim that consideration of this framework as a heuristic design tool would necessarily guarantee improved outcomes, it would serve to elevate and make more transparent those key factors in urban sustainability transitions in cities, while leaving each experiment necessarily open to social ingenuity.

References

Architecture et Précarités (2023) *Architecture et Précarités* [authors' translation]. Available from: https://architecture-precarites.fr/ [Accessed 23 May 2023].

Avelino, F. and Wittmayer, J.M. (2016) 'Shifting power relations in sustainability transitions: a multi-actor perspective', *Journal of Environmental Policy and Planning*, 18(5): 628–49.

Bulkeley, H. and Castán Broto, V. (2013) 'Government by experiment? Global cities and the governing of climate change', *Transactions of the Institute of British Geographers*, 38(3): 361–75.

Bulkeley, H., Coenen, L., Frantzeskaki, N., Hartmann, C., Kronsell, A., Mai, L. et al (2016) 'Urban living labs: governing urban sustainability transitions', *Current Opinion in Environmental Sustainability*, 22: 13–17.

Bulkeley, H., Marvin, S., Palgan, Y.V., McCormick, K., Breitfuss-Loidl, M., Mai, L. et al (2019) 'Urban living laboratories: conducting the experimental city?', *European Urban and Regional Studies*, 26(4): 317–35.

Caprotti, F. and Cowley, R. (2017) 'Interrogating urban experiments', *Urban Geography*, 38(9): 1441–50. DOI: 10.1080/02723638.2016.1265870

Catapult Connected Places (2023) 'Climate action'. Available from: https://cp.catapult.org.uk/imperatives/climate-action/ [Accessed 22 May 2023].

Dickey, A., Kosovac, A., Fastenrath, S., Acuto, M. and Gleeson, B. (2022) 'Fragmentation and urban knowledge: an analysis of urban knowledge exchange institutions', *Cities*, 131: 103917.

Dunster, B. (2013) 'BedZed community near London', in Voss, K., Musall, E. and O'Donovan, J.R. (eds), *Net Zero Energy Buildings: International Projects of Carbon Neutrality in Buildings*, Munich: Institut für Internationale Architektur-Dokumentation, pp 103–7.

European Commission (2020) *The Just Transition Mechanism: Making Sure No One is Left Behind*. Available from: https://ec.europa.eu/info/strategy/priorities-2019-2024/european-green-deal/actions-being-taken-eu/just-transition-mechanism_en [Accessed 22 May 2023].

Evans, J. and Karvonen, A. (2011) 'Living laboratories for sustainability: exploring the politics and epistemology of urban transition', in Bulkeley, H. (ed), *Cities and Low Carbon Transitions*, New York: Routledge, pp 126–41.

Evans, J. and Karvonen, A. (2014) '"Give me a laboratory and I will lower your carbon footprint!": Urban laboratories and the governance of low-carbon futures', *International Journal of Urban and Regional Research*, 8(2): 413–30.

Evans, J., Karvonen, A. and Raven, R. (2018) *The Experimental City*, London: Taylor & Francis.

Fieldwork Architecture (2021/2022) *Tertiary Forest* [authors' translation]. Available from: https://vimeo.com/649433738 [Accessed 22 May 2023].

Geels, F. (2010) 'Ontologies, socio-technical transitions (to sustainability), and the multi-level perspective', *Research Policy*, 39: 495–510.

Geels, F. and Raven, R. (2006) 'Non-linearity and expectations in niche-development trajectories: ups and downs in Dutch biogas development (1973–2003)', *Technology Analysis & Strategic Management*, 18(3–4): 375–92.

Geels, F. and Schot, J. (2007) 'Typology of sociotechnical transition pathways', *Research Policy*, 36: 399–417. 10.1016/j.respol.2007.01.003

Government of Canada (2018) *A Just and Fair Transition for Canadian Coal Power Workers and Communities*, Gatineau: Environment and Climate Change Canada.

Heffron, R.J. and McCauley, D. (2018) 'What is the "Just Transition"?', *Geoforum*, 88: 74–7.

Hodson, M. and Marvin, S. (2016) *Retrofitting Cities: Priorities, Governance and Experimentation*, London: Taylor & Francis.

Karvonen, A. and van Heur, B. (2014) 'Urban laboratories: experiments in reworking cities', *International Journal of Urban and Regional Research*, 38(2): 379–92.

López, I., Ortega, J. and Pardo, M. (2020) 'Mobility infrastructures in cities and climate change: an analysis through the Superblocks in Barcelona', *Atmosphere*, 11(4): 410.

Lydon, M. and Garcia, A. (2015) *Tactical Urbanism: Short-Term Action for Long-Term Change*, Washington, DC: Island Press.

Marvin, S., Bulkeley, H., Mai, L., McCormick, K. and Voytenko Palgan, Y. (2018) *Urban Living Labs: Experimenting with City Futures*, London: Routledge.

Meadowcroft, J. (2011) 'Engaging with the politics of sustainability transitions', *Environmental Innovation and Societal Transitions*, 1: 70–5.

Moore, T., de Haan, F., Horne, R. and Gleeson, B. (2018) *Urban Sustainability Transitions: Australian Cases – International Perspectives*, Singapore: Springer.

Mueller, N., Rojas-Rueda, D., Khreis, H., Cirach, M., Andrés, D., Ballester, J. et al (2020) 'Changing the urban design of cities for health: the superblock model', *Environment International*, 134: 105132.

Nevens, F., Frantzeskaki, N., Gorissen, L. and Loorbach, D. (2013) 'Urban transition labs: Co-creating transformative action for sustainable cities', *Journal of Cleaner Production*, 50: 111–22.

Newell, P. and Mulvaney, D. (2013) 'The political economy of the "just transition"', *The Geographical Journal*, 179(2): 132–40.

Orillard, F., Fautrerob, V. and Puel, G. (2020) 'Les Urban Living Labs, une solution innovante pour le renouvellement de la fabrique des services urbains?' [Urban Living Labs, an innovative solution for renewing the fabric of urban services], *Géographie, Economie, Société*, 22(3–4): 453–76.

Palgan, Y.V., McCormick, K. and Evans, J. (2018) 'Catalysing low carbon and sustainable cities in Europe?', in Marvin, S., Bulkeley, H., Mai, L., McCormick, K. and Voytenko Palgan, Y. (eds) *Urban Living Labs: Experimenting with City Futures*, London: Routledge, pp 21–36.

Parison, S., Chaumont, M., Kounkou-Arnaud, R., Bernik, A., Silva, M.D. and Hendel, M. (2020) *'Tierce Foret': Greening a Parking Lot*, Paris: Interdisciplinary Energy Research Institute (LIED).

Pinker, A. (2020) *Just Transitions: A Comparative Perspective*, report. Available from: https://www.gov.scot/publications/transitions-comparative-perspective/ [Accessed 22 May 2023].

Rizzo, A., Habibipour, A. and Ståhlbröst, A. (2021) 'Transformative thinking and urban living labs in planning practice: a critical review and ongoing case studies in Europe', *European Planning Studies*, 29(10): 1739–57.

Scottish Government (2020) *Just Transition Commission*. Available from: https://www.gov.scot/groups/just-transition-commission/ [Accessed 22 May 2023].

Sengers, F., Berkhout, F., Wieczorek, A. and Raven, R. (2016) 'Experimenting in the city: unpacking notions of experimentation and sustainability', in Evans, J., Karvonen, A. and Raven, R. (eds), *The Experimental City*, London: Taylor & Francis, pp. 15–31.

Silva, P. (2016) 'Tactical urbanism: towards an evolutionary cities' approach?', *Environment and Planning B: Urban Analytics and City Science*, 43(6): 1040–51.

Steele, W., Hillier, J., MacCallum, D., Byrne, J. and Houston, D. (2021) *Quiet Activism: Climate Action at the Local Scale*, Place: Palgrave Macmillan.

Superilla Barcelona (2023) *Superblocks, Green Hubs and Squares*. Available from: https://www.barcelona.cat/pla-superilla-barcelona/en/superblocks-green-hubs-ans-squares [Accessed 25 May 2023].

Voytenko, Y., McCormick, K., Evans, J. and Schliwa, G. (2016) 'Urban living labs for sustainability and low carbon cities in Europe: Towards a research agenda', *Journal of Cleaner Production*, 123: 45–54.

While, A. and Eadson, W. (2019) 'Households in place: socio-spatial (dis) advantage in energy-carbon restructuring', *European Planning Studies*, 27(8): 1626–45.

Zografos, C., Klause, K.A., Connolly, J.J.T. and Anguelovski, I. (2020) 'The everyday politics of urban transformational adaptation: struggles for authority and the Barcelona superblock project', *Cities*, 99: 102613.

3

Histories of Heating: Looking Back, Moving Forwards

Aimee Ambrose, Jenny Palm, Stephen Parkes and Beth Speake

Introduction

The way we heat buildings is a major source of carbon emissions (38 per cent across the European Union) (IEEE European Public Policy Committee, 2018). We must rapidly shift from heating via high carbon fuels (such as gas, oil and coal) to lower carbon heat sources (such as air or ground source heat pumps) if we are to meet legally binding carbon reduction targets by mid-century or sooner.

Current high carbon systems contribute to great inequality and exclusion across Europe in terms of access to adequate, affordable warmth in the home, with certain socio-demographic groups (such as single parent households, women, children and key workers) and countries (such as Bulgaria, Lithuania, Portugal and Greece) being disproportionately affected by an inability of households to afford to heat the home to a safe and comfortable level ('energy poverty') (Aizarani, 2023). The transition to lower carbon systems provides an opportunity to redress these inequalities and end or ease energy poverty for those currently affected, if it is designed around a detailed appreciation of who is affected and the difficulties they experience. Transitions to low carbon heating systems need to speed up, but inclusivity and opportunities to redress injustices inherent in the current system cannot be sacrificed in the hurry to decarbonize.

This chapter forwards two core arguments, first arguing that, although mundane, changes to the way we heat our homes are deeply personal and can be life-altering. If the transition to low carbon heating is to avoid disadvantaging anyone then care must be taken to understand how different groups within society, and even different individuals within a household, are differentially affected by changes to home heating. Second, drawing on data from an Anglo-Swedish study, we argue that we have transitioned from one approach to home heating to another before, so opportunities exist to learn from experiences of past heating transitions (and how they have played out over time) to inform a fairer and more inclusive transition this time around. Learning from past heating transitions requires the introduction of historical methods to the field of energy studies and we also reflect on the merits of oral histories in this context.

This chapter comprises four sections in addition to this one. The next section outlines the case for combining past and future oriented analysis in the context of domestic energy transitions. We then describe our own attempt at this with reference to an Anglo-Swedish oral history project. We then share some findings before discussing what they reveal about the ways that domestic heating transitions impact domestic life and can also deepen existing injustices and create new ones. The conclusions return to the starting premise of this book, aiming to draw out the key considerations to emerge from this chapter regarding the rapid attainment of inclusive, post-carbon heating provision.

Grand narratives versus lived realities

Over the last 70 years, most European countries have already undergone one or more transitions in home heating provision. Moving first away from burning solid fuels (that is, coal and wood) in the home and towards communal or individual systems (for example, district and gas central heating) and now towards low carbon, digitalized electric heating systems. Domestic heating transitions have huge potential to impact unevenly and to deepen or create inequalities between different groups within society and within and between households and countries. Energy transitions offer hope for more equitable access to adequate energy but only if we understand and can anticipate how they are likely to play out in the everyday lives of a diversity of citizens. One way to achieve this is to examine the genealogy of the problem (Garland, 2014).

Narratives around heating transitions tend to operate as grand narratives (Darby, 2017), overlooking varied experiences, and social and cultural impacts, and focusing on simple narratives centred around the benefits. An example of a grand narrative might be that no longer burning coal in the home improved health through better air quality (Hernández, 2016). Or, the comfort and cleanliness of central heating improved all of our lives (Hernández, 2016; Hanmer et al, 2019). Grand narratives tend to gloss over the disruption, unevenness, injustice and also the joy (or loss of joy) resulting from technological change. They also neglect personal stories capable of revealing more complex and nuanced individual realities. Such personal stories are 'more than peripheral to the serious business of energy policy and transition', revealing how high-level energy policies and technological change play out in daily life (Darby, 2017).

Personal stories about the past are a form of oral history. Oral histories offer multiple benefits as a research method and enable the construction of 'effective histories', which prioritize detail and complexity over neat narratives (Veyne, 1997). Effective histories are an important antidote to established approaches to energy research that reflect biases towards the present as the dominant system of rationalization (Mahon, 1992). Unlike other qualitative methods, oral histories reveal previously undocumented phenomena in the private world of the home, somewhere technologists and policy makers do not typically see (Goodchild et al, 2017).

Several studies demonstrate the potential associated with the application of oral histories to the study of home heating. For example, Goodchild et al (2017) and Butler et al (2014) reveal strong relationships between experiences of home heating during childhood and present practices and preferences, alluding to the long-term influence of home heating practices and technology – wearing multiple layers to bed, rationing heating use regardless of wealth, and preferences for open fires all stemmed from early experiences (Goodchild et al, 2017).

Methods capable of revealing personal and granular experiences of energy policies are gaining increasing attention, as reflected in the rise of 'energy biographies' (Butler et al, 2014; Groves et al, 2016; Darby, 2017), which draw out overlooked influences on how energy use changes across the life course and between contexts. Here, a historical approach provides an alternative to the snapshots of one point in time, which result from the dominant methods of surveys and semi-structured interviews typically used in energy research (Ambrose et al, 2017). Such historically sensitive approaches are favoured for revealing complex interactions between ever-shifting social, cultural and political conditions, technological change and life stages and events, as well as revealing the richness of human experience, and the unintended or untold consequences of energy policies.

Can looking back help us to progress fairer low carbon transitions?

We aim to distil lessons that are instructive for fairer, more inclusive domestic energy transitions. While analyses of past transitions cannot provide exact synergies with current transitions, several sources show how an understanding of historical processes can inform future pathways. Within energy studies, 'transition' is employed analytically to assess major historical shifts in energy systems. While the focus is mostly on national and global scales (Allen, 2012; Fouquet and Pearson, 2012; Arapostathis et al, 2013), the domestic sphere also features. Energy historians have provided insight into social and political impediments to energy plans, as well as the social context in which people create, deploy and use technologies. For instance, Hirsh and Jones (2014) highlight the benefits of historical analysis for understanding the challenges of contemporary energy transitions, contending that the comparison of earlier events and contemporary challenges can identify forgotten considerations, still pertinent today.

Research approach

The oral histories presented in this chapter were gathered as part of a larger study: an Anglo-Swedish project focused on how, in the Global North, our relationship with energy is growing more distant and less tangible. The project involved experimentation with participatory methods to (re)engage citizens with the sources of their everyday energy (in this case, energy from waste and nuclear energy were used as examples). In part, we focused on exploring the historical roots of our progressive disengagement from where our energy comes from (Ambrose, 2020), prompting a sub-study focused on oral histories of heating. To this end, a set of 26 oral histories were gathered between 2016 and 2019 across case studies of Sheffield (United Kingdom [UK]) and Lund (Sweden), based around participant's memories of keeping warm at home since childhood. The exercise represented an attempt to understand in more detail how, over time, we have become progressively more detached from practices of home heating as technology has advanced and networked heating (in these cases reticulated gas networks in the UK and district heating in urban areas of Sweden) has replaced more individual systems (in these cases open fires and stoves or ranges). We also hoped to explore the consequences of this detachment from heating systems for, among other things, experiences of the home, family life and affordability.

The oral history interviews conducted in Sweden took place in 2019 with residents of a sheltered housing scheme in the historic city of Lund (South Sweden): four men and seven women participated aged between 73 and 95 years. The ten interviews conducted in England were conducted in 2016 to test the application of oral histories to the study of home heating. The results were put forward for re-analysis and supplemented with five further interviews with volunteers recruited through a workshop in a public library in Sheffield. Recruitment of participants in both countries was largely opportunistic and, as such, did not aim to be representative. Given that home heating is a concern for everyone at higher latitudes, anyone could contribute (Ong, 2012).

Participants in England tended to be younger than those in Sweden and were aged between 45 and 75 years and represented an even split of men and women. Most were living in Sheffield, an ex-industrial city in the north of the country, but snowballing techniques (where one participant recommends another to speak to) led us to participants from other parts of the UK. Many participants had moved around and recounted memories of homes in various locations around the UK.

Oral history seeks to be agentic in nature, allowing the interviewee to recount their own story in their own way (Maye-Banbury, 2021). As such, the researcher only occasionally posed questions to keep the account moving, seek clarification or probe. The interviews began with an open question about participant's earliest memories of keeping warm at home.

Analysis of the oral histories followed a hermeneutic circle, involving interpretation of the data on two levels (Goodchild et al, 2017). The first level involved understanding the accounts as life stories of the individual, the second level as thematic stories that go beyond the immediate intentions of the respondent (Rosenthal, 1993) and linking the account to the broader socio-technical changes and exogenous events reflected in the individual trajectories. As life stories, analysis must allow respondents' accounts to speak for themselves and, therefore, involved inductive manual open coding based on the researcher's first reading of the oral histories. The second level of interpretation involved shaping this into a written narrative, looking for synergies and divergences between accounts. Here we present this narrative, with data from the UK (specifically England) and Sweden presented together.

Heating transitions across place and time: findings

The universality of cold homes

Participants who grew up in the UK universally recounted draughty housing with basic heating infrastructure (open fires or free-standing heaters), including those in more affluent households. Participants made frequent reference to draughts, damp and condensation:

> 'It was single glazing so every morning it would be dripping wet with condensation in the winter. I remember my mum leathering [wiping with a leather cloth] the front window every single morning because it was so wet.' (David, 52, UK)

> 'I think there were a few winters where there were quite prolonged periods of being cold and that was quite hard actually. There were times when we did actually have the gas stove and the open fire on at the same time in the one room and we would do things to try and stop draughts coming in.' (Peter, 52, UK)

> 'The problem with the flat was that it was damp and it was pokey. It wasn't particularly comfortable and took quite a bit of warming.' (John, 63, UK)

Despite expressing dissatisfaction with the warmth and comfort of their childhood homes from their current vantage point, most older participants acknowledged that they would not have questioned these conditions at the time. It was "just how it was", "you never really thought about it". However, those, such as Nadia (45), who recalled feeling cold at home in the 1980s, by this point had reference points in friends and neighbours with gas central heating and the means to use it, leading her to feel less accepting of being cold and feeling left behind. "By the 80s everyone around me had central heating but we didn't. We had never really questioned using one gas fire and sitting in front of it together on a rug to eat dinner. But gradually we were left behind and I started to notice how cold we were" (Nadia, 45, UK).

It was not the case that people did not mind being cold, but more that there was no expectation of being warm. Cold homes were not generally viewed or experienced as hardship, and it appears that cultural attitudes to heating and warmth might have prevented those with the means to heat their homes well from doing so: "It was a bit of a social–cultural shift and an expectation around the warmth of the home. There's just been a shift in the notion of what is reasonable and expected so I don't think it was a financial calculation" (Richard, 66, UK).

Early memories of keeping warm at home had a different starting point among participants in Sweden, where most people started their account at the point of the Second World War. This period was memorable, not least because Sweden experienced severe winters during this period while at the same time everything (including fuel) was in short supply. Several participants recalled using blackout curtains, which were connected with avoiding bomb attacks, but also providing insulation: "Yes, it was the blackout curtains … you had to hang blackout curtains on the windows so it [the house] would not be visible … but then it would be warm inside too and the warm air did not leak" (Anna, 89, Sweden). This quote also suggests that homes in Sweden during this period were, as in the UK, also draughty.

Cold water

A strong theme within the accounts of participants in Sweden (not raised by those in the UK) concerned access to warm water. For many respondents in Sweden, this seemed to represent a bigger challenge than heating the home, and washing in cold water was remembered with discomfort:

> 'We froze, but it was due to the cold water. Everyone used cold water, you know. You did not have hot water. … On the kitchen stove we had, next to a water reservoir, you had a copper tank with a tap and when you set a fire underneath it, the water became hot. So you had

hot water when you cooked something on the stove. But when you washed in the morning you had no hot water.' (Alice, 85, Sweden)

'The biggest difference between now and then is the warm and cold water. It is such a difference to when I grew up, you cannot compare it. You had to boil all water.' (Lena, 95, Sweden)

'You did not wash so often either, but you often avoided washing or doing laundry when it was the coldest outside. It had to lie unwashed until it got warm outside and then you had to wash a lot at once. And you could not wash so often, it was much dirtier than it is today.' (Anna, 89, Sweden)

The data suggest that the cold indoor environment was easier to manage through strategies like putting on more clothes, while the lack of warm water was more difficult and energy intensive to solve. Water could be boiled to warm it up, but this would place additional pressure on fuel supplies.

The era of solid fuels – wood and coal

All participants, with the exception of the youngest, Nadia (45, UK) and Will (40, UK), recalled a reliance on coal and/or wood during childhood, and the labour related to moving and storing it and cleaning and maintaining fires: "Mum and Dad had to do a lot of making the fire every evening, and chopping kindling, and dragging coal in and out. It's what everybody did in those days" (Jane, 74, UK). There were also clear memories among UK respondents of periodic deliveries of fuel and careful management of it was required: "You had to manage your coal supply carefully, you weren't going to order more before the next delivery was scheduled" (Elizabeth, 70, UK).

By contrast, those who grew up in rural areas of Sweden recounted having access to woodland, where there was common access to fuel. Urban dwellers, on the other hand, relied on deliveries of wood (sometimes just once a year) in the same way that households in the UK received deliveries of coal. Fathers were generally recalled as responsible for fetching wood from the forest but the whole family would be involved in chopping, storing and drying it.

'We bought firewood once a year, up to three cubic metres. We put a huge tarpaulin on the lawn when it was still winter. Then you had to devote yourself to chopping, sawing and more chopping. Then it would lay and dry somewhere inside before you could use it.' (Maria, 79, Sweden)

City dwellers in Sweden were more likely to recall a scarcity of wood and coal due to rationing during the war. This was not the case for those living in the countryside, who had access to forests.

Gendered roles

In the UK, as in Sweden, women were responsible for domestic labour, and keeping the family warm by maintaining fires but also (primarily in the UK) by knitting jumpers and blankets. As David (UK) put it, "I recall a regular production line of jumpers being knitted by my mum." "It was the women who would get up first and get everything ready so it was warm for when the kids got up and also when the man woke up" (Maria, 79, Sweden). "Even if he got up first, it was her job" (Alice, 85, Sweden).

Peter described fire maintenance and washing as a "real slog" for his mother, and both he and Elizabeth recalled the purchase of a washing machine as a liberating event. The increasing affordability of labour saving appliances, combined with the advent of central or district heating, appeared to help free up women's time, creating opportunities for them to participate in paid employment: "I think it was the combination of central heating and things like washing machines that allowed my Mother to get a part time job in a greengrocer, which was good for her and good for us all financially and otherwise" (Jane, 74, UK). In Sweden, fathers tended to be responsible for heavier manual tasks such as insulating the house by shovelling snow up against the walls. In the UK, there was much more evidence that women and children would take on responsibility for the management of the fuel supply.

The move away from solid fuels

For participants growing up in the 1960s and 1970s across both countries, there was a clear sense that throughout their lives, home heating became progressively less tangible and more convenient. After the era of wood and coal, respondents in Sweden recalled a period where oil was used, which was cleaner and more convenient. This era was short-lived and district heating soon became the norm in urban areas (where many dwellings are heated via a network of pipes fed by a single communal heat source). During the 1950s and 1960s urbanization accelerated in Sweden and many interviewees previously living in the countryside moved into city flats where there was district heating.

Driven by the Clean Air Act (1956), which legislated against domestic coal fires in smog prone areas, the transition away from open fires in the UK began for some before gas central heating became widespread (from the late 1960s onwards). This was evident in the increase in 'free-standing' heating such as paraffin heaters, electric heaters, gas fires and even electric blankets reported during the 1960s. Yet, plug-in heat sources did not address the problems of uneven warmth throughout the home that were common in the era of the coal fire. For example, Nadia's childhood home was heated by free-standing gas fires, but use of them was rationed due to affordability. It was, therefore, only possible to heat one room, which became the nucleus for family life: "The gas fire was almost like a focal point, we used to lay a cloth on the floor and then we would put our food out on it and we used to sit around it" (Nadia, 45, UK).

As gas central heating covering the whole home became more common (but not universal) in the UK in the 1970s and 1980s, with billing for usage undertaken quarterly, Elizabeth, Jane and Elaine all reported a fear of using it too much. This fear was distinct from earlier concerns about the coal or wood supply not lasting, because it was harder to estimate how much was being used. Use of such systems was seen as "new-fangled" (Elizabeth, 70, UK), or "a treat" (Jane, 74, UK). Jane recalls how gas was never a cheap option and always felt like a bit of a luxury: "Obviously these things had to be rationed because they consumed gas, which was never cheap" (Jane, 74, UK). For some respondents, like Elaine (60, UK), the financial impact of the transition away from coal was felt more acutely because her family had been entitled to free coal as part of her father's employment by the National Coal Board.

The culture of frugality, which began during the era of solid fuels and intensified with the advent of gas central heating, appeared entrenched. For example, Elaine still worried about using the central heating too much even though she was now able to afford it: "I never put the heating on unless I'm really, really desperate." This related to the sense that it is difficult to know how much is being used, whereas with "a heat source which you can hold in your hands, you knew where you were". The anxiety driving this behaviour seems to be less about fear of running out of fuel and more around the lack of control over the cost of it.

The situation was different in Sweden where, from the point that district heating became widespread, households rarely had to think about heating or the associated costs. Heat was in plentiful supply, charged at a flat rate and was felt to be inexpensive. "We got central heating. We had no worries about the heat. We received the bill twice a year, but it was not so much money" (Simon, 81, Sweden). "This came in the 50s, since then it has been like this. It is something you take for granted, it has been an obvious, less reflected part of your life. Not much thought is given to it" (Anna, 89, Sweden).

Lost practices

In Sweden, the transition to district heating led to the loss of old (manual) heating practices, such as chopping and drying wood, building fires, or reducing heat demand by putting on clothes, putting wadding in window frames, gathering around the stove, shovelling snow around the house, or putting up thick curtains.

A common technique in Sweden and in the UK before district and central heating was to seal off at least one room to avoid heating it, a practice that endured until the 1970s and 1980s:

> 'It was the "fine room", it would just stand there. You could not be in that room. The "fine room" was not allowed to be used. It was always cold. I do not really understand how you could have it so cold because it must have destroyed the wallpaper and everything. Perhaps it simply cost too much to fire up the whole apartment.' (Nancy, 90, Sweden)

It appears that this act of reserving a 'fine room' was not just about energy saving, as these rooms were off limits all year round. It was speculated by respondents in Sweden that this practice may also have been aimed at demonstrating that a family could afford to have a room reserved for 'best' or to maintain cleanliness in at least one room, away from the soot and grime of the fireside.

In Sweden many of these practices were consigned to memory, but participants in the UK clung tighter to practices mastered during the pre-central heating period, such as building fires, rationing fuel (even when affordability was no longer an issue) and only switching on the heating when the temperature became unbearable.

A return to tangibility?

While participants in Sweden continued to benefit from a plentiful and affordable heat supply, and perceived no need to change their heating arrangements, there is a discernible trend in the UK back towards more tangible forms of heating. Around half of those interviewed had installed wood or multi-fuel burners, albeit usually as a supplementary heat source in addition to central heating. This was primarily an aesthetic choice that brought them pleasure, but for some this brought a partial return to a sense of control in relation to heating; Elaine, John, Nadia and Richard described portioning out wood supplies to ensure they lasted the winter. Elaine described how she liked the discipline and the tangibility of buying two bags of coal per week and making it last, and had returned to a similar system with her wood-burning stove:

> 'It was much more efficient and I liked it, two bags of coal, I knew where I was. In the summer I would still buy two bags of coal to save it up for the winter. So, I used to buy the same the whole year

round so that I knew I'd got enough. Then again for me it was about knowing I've got enough money to pay the bill. But even now we've got central heating and a wood burner, and we use our own wood from the garden.' (Elaine, 60, UK)

Despite satisfaction with the current arrangements in Sweden, participants spoke wistfully about the fireside and tried to recreate it. The residential home we visited played a video of an open fire constantly on the TV.

Discussion
Technological change and diverging heating pathways

Cold homes appear universal in the pre-central/district heating era, seemingly regardless of social class, but those living in rural Sweden were less likely to recall anxieties around heating costs and rationing fuel due to common access to forests for fuel. As households transitioned to central/district heating, accounts across the two countries start to diverge.

In the UK, the drive to carefully manage fuel consumption has not gone away, even among the more affluent. There was less evidence of this in Sweden, where most urban households do not have to worry about comfort or heating costs and their practices for managing the cold are rendered obsolete, something also identified by Sherriff et al (2019) in relation to passive cooling practices in Australia. Heating appears to have disappeared from the consciousness in urban Sweden and it appears that grand narratives around the success of district heating ring true. The picture may be more complex in rural areas.

UK households, on the other hand, reveal the transition to gas central heating to be less consistent, with grand narratives hailing the virtues of technological advancement. Many still experience discomfort and actual or feared affordability issues despite gas central heating. Home heating remains in their consciousness, as do coping strategies like Elaine's rationing of firewood, her reluctance to use the heating, and the broader trend towards installation of stoves. Partly the endurance of these practices might be attributed to the strong influence of things learnt in childhood (Butler et al, 2014; Goodchild et al, 2017). Yet, comparison with experiences in Sweden suggests that these practices are more easily relinquished when affordable warmth is assured for the majority. The risk here is that the suffering of the vulnerable minority in Sweden may be overlooked, whereas in England those in energy poverty are at least advocated for by a wide range of charities and lobbying organizations.

There is also evidence within participants' accounts that, when the change being proposed (that is, district heating) offers and delivers substantial benefits for the household compared to the status quo, transitions can unfold rapidly.

Fouquet and Pearson (2012) observe that such private benefits are less compelling for low carbon energy sources and devices today, hence efforts to decarbonize heating in Sweden aim to decarbonize the heat supply at source, maintaining current (generally very satisfactory) arrangements in urban homes.

Our interviews also reveal how the achievement of thermal comfort depends on more than space heating in the sense that washing in cold water was recalled with particular discomfort. In this vein, there is a strong suggestion that it was perhaps no single change in heating technology alone that was responsible for some of the transformations recalled. For example, it appeared to be the combination of central heating and labour saving devices (that is, washing machines) that proved emancipatory for women, suggesting that the most far-reaching changes in our domestic lives occur when multiple labour saving technological innovations combine.

Interactions with wider socio-economic change

It appears that later urbanization in Sweden compared to the UK and, linked to this, a more modern urban housing stock, coupled with the greater efficiency and lower costs of district heating, combined to liberate participants from the labour, discomfort and anxiety of cold homes. We therefore see how broader socio-economic change (that is, urbanization) combined with energy policy responses to the growing urban population (that is, district heating) continue to positively influence the comfort and financial circumstances of urban households in Sweden today. By contrast, in the UK, a new heating technology (central heating) applied to a largely ageing, uninsulated housing stock brought about significant change but produced less transformational results. In this sense, we are reminded of how opportunities to maximize the positive impact of transitions can be missed.

Divisions of labour

In participants' accounts, we see evidence of all the temporal levels of change identified by Goodchild et al (2017) – the relatively long-term influence of technological change (central/district heating), changes in line with the life cycle (that is, starting a family, retirement and so on) and the impact of shocks (that is, war). Missing from this framework are the gradual but profound shifts within the labour market and how they interact with the gendered nature of home heating and comfort management. There was clear evidence within both sets of interviews of the binary division of labour in the pre-central/district heating era whereby women occupied the role of comfort manager (Sánchez et al, 2020; Petrova and Simcock, 2021). Fathers, on the other hand, were depicted as undertaking less routine labour in relation to heating, that is, shovelling snow or fetching wood. As previously discussed, technological innovation appears to have been (at least partly) emancipatory for women. This is likely to have been transformational in terms of the labour market but also undoubtedly heightened the enduring 'double burden' whereby women absorb responsibility for both paid employment and household management (Petrova and Simcock, 2021).

Still, both Darby (2017) and Rohse et al (2020) highlight how transitions away from solid fuel heating can contribute to economic obsolescence and attendant struggles to re-establish collective and individual identity. These issues are most notable for men in communities formed around fuel extraction. This was not a prominent theme within our interviews, but is noteworthy in the context of discussions about the profound and personal consequences of energy transitions. In essence, improvements in comfort, cleanliness and associated gains for health, wellbeing and women's inclusion in the labour market can come at a cost to male employment and identities linked to fuel extraction and the communities built around it (Daggett, 2018).

In discussing the family dynamics of domestic heating, it can be easy to overlook the perspective of children. Most participants begin their story during childhood – a time when their energy experiences are heavily mediated by their parents. Parents, in turn, are hostage to their housing conditions, available technology, their financial means, tradition and social expectations. We know that these early experiences can shape practices and attitudes towards home heating for life, yet the child's perspective is rarely explicitly sought (Gonzalez-Pijuan et al, 2023).

Unevenness and getting left behind

In trying to build a coherent narrative around these individual accounts, it is easier to focus on commonalities than divergences and to overlook outlying accounts that reveal a different perspective. This is how grand narratives take hold, extrapolating the stories of the few to the broader population. Careful attention must be paid to accounts that reveal a different experience of history. Nadia's story provides an example here. While her story is set against the mass transition to gas central heating in the UK during the 1970s, her recollections highlight the socio-economic fault lines which meant that lower income households benefited much later than their wealthier counterparts. For Nadia, not having access to gas central heating at a time when her peers did awakened her to her family's exclusion and led her to acknowledge the hardship of living in a cold home. Her family life was structured differently to her peers as a result of their heating arrangements, and she did not benefit from the same level of comfort. Nadia's story provides a pertinent example of why the current policy mantra of 'leaving no one behind' in the transition away from fossil fuels must be realized (European Commission, 2019).

Conclusion

Important considerations are prompted by the deep, personal accounts of transition shared by respondents, which (if heeded) undoubtedly complicate the task for the policy makers, practitioners and technologists charged with driving the transition to low carbon heating at pace. In essence, the oral histories illustrate how technological innovations in home heating solve some problems (that is, problems of convenience, thermal comfort and freeing up women's time) for some groups (those who can afford adequate energy) at the same time as creating new ones, including feelings of a lack of control over fuel consumption, higher costs and reduced family togetherness. They highlight how transitions can be a source of social and cultural loss and economic hardship for communities and households (Daggett, 2018; Rohse et al, 2020), as well as a source of hope and opportunity for a fairer future.

It seems likely that many of the complications associated with changes to heating technologies and fuel sources recollected in the oral histories may not have been anticipated or were underestimated by those designing and implementing the policies and interventions underpinning the transitions that respondents lived through. Therein lies a key risk associated with implementing technological change without explicit consideration of the likely social and cultural transformations and injustices that may be triggered.

Certainly, it is difficult to anticipate all the possible ways that such changes may impact financially, socially and culturally, especially given how (as the oral histories attest), the impacts of technological change can vary substantially across place, between demographic groups and between different life stages. However, the emerging methodological turn within the field of energy studies (towards biographical and historical approaches) is helping to address this lacuna, encouraging us to look beyond grand narratives that present transitions as following a neat, techno-economic success story. A growing body of evidence is drawing out the messier lived realities and the less obvious, longer term, intangible impacts of energy system change, which can be harnessed to support a fairer transition today. But is this shift going far enough and fast enough and is the evidence reaching decision makers? Will a more humane, less presentist approach to thinking about the implications of heating transition ever gain equal status to dominant techno-economic policy rationales?

Of course, the accounts featured in this chapter provide only a flavour of the diversity of experiences of energy transitions that exist in the world, and many of those interviewed had experienced significant social mobility over their life courses, enabling progressively more privileged energy circumstances as time went on. There are many groups and places within which energy transitions will impact more heavily than it did on our participants. As such, priority should be given, in research and policy, to those in the most precarious energy circumstances, such as Global South households, children in low-income families, single parents, women, those with disabilities, those in precarious housing circumstances, the elderly, those tied to fossil fuel industries and so on. For these types of households in these locations, it is imperative that we anticipate, as far as possible, the full range of impacts (good and bad) that are likely to play out over time as a result of transitions to low carbon heating and from there work towards improving their circumstances through transition.

One aspect of the challenge faced by decision makers is to rapidly effect the vital shift to post-carbon heating systems. The other aspect of the challenge, which is equally vital, is to do so in a way that prioritizes those currently excluded from accessing adequate, affordable warmth while also being alert to the sometimes unintended ways that changes to heating systems also reshape and reorganize lives, cultures and societal and geographical inequalities. Care must be taken to draw previously excluded populations and places into more just energy circumstances (reaping the attendant benefits for health, wellbeing and social and economic inclusion), without – at the same time – taking it beyond the reach of others.

One of the most promising routes to a heating transition that is both post-carbon and inclusive is to not just rely on relatively niche bodies of research (such as this one) to illuminate diverse experiences of transition but to rapidly diversify the characteristics of those who are writing and designing our heating futures. Only when we do this will a much broader range of socio-demographic, socio-economic, cultural and place-based perspectives truly be factored into decision making.

References

Aizarani, J. (2023) 'Energy poverty in the EU by country 2020', *Statista*, 21 January. Available from: https://www.statista.com/statistics/1260733/eu-energy-poverty-by-country/ [Accessed 25 May 2023].

Allen, R. (2012) 'Backward into the future: the shift to coal and implications for the next energy transition', *Energy Policy*, 50: 17–23.

Ambrose, A. (2020) 'Walking with energy: challenging energy invisibility and connecting citizens with energy futures through participatory research', *Futures*, 117: 102528.

Ambrose, A., Goodchild, B. and O'Flaherty, F. (2017) 'Understanding the user in low energy housing: a comparison of positivist and phenomenological approaches', *Energy Research & Social Science*, 34: 163–71.

Arapostathis, S., Carlsson-Hyslop, A., Pearson, P., Thornton, J., Gradillas, M., Laczay, S. et al (2013) 'Governing transitions: cases and insights from two periods in the history of the UK gas industry', *Energy Policy*, 52: 25–44.

Butler, C., Parkhill, K.A., Shirani, F., Henwood, K. and Pidgeon, N. (2014) 'Examining the dynamics of energy demand through a biographical lens', *Nature and Culture*, 9(2): 164–82.

Daggett, C. (2018) 'Petro-masculinity: fossil fuels and authoritarian desire', *Millennium*, 47(1): 25–44.

Darby, S.J. (2017) 'Coal fires, steel houses and the man in the moon: local experiences of energy transition', *Energy Research & Social Science*, 31: 120–27.

European Commission (2019) 'A European Green Deal', *European Commission*. Available at: https://commission.europa.eu/strategy-and-policy/priorities-2019-2024/european-green-deal_en [Accessed 28 May 2023].

Fouquet, R. and Pearson, P. (2012) 'Past and prospective energy transitions: insights from history', *Energy Policy*, 50: 1–7.

Garland, D. (2014) 'What is a "history of the present"? On Foucault's genealogies and their critical preconditions', *Punishment & Society*, 16(4): 365384.

González-Pijuan, I., Ambrose, A., Middlemiss, L., Tirado-Herrero, S. and Tatham, C. (2023). 'Empowering whose future? A European policy analysis of children in energy poverty', *Energy Research & Social Science*, 106, 103328.

Goodchild, B., Ambrose, A. and Maye-Banbury, A. (2017) 'Storytelling as oral history: revealing the changing experience of home heating in England', *Energy Research & Social Science*, 31: 137–44.

Groves, C., Henwood, K., Shirani, F., Butler, C., Parkhill, K. and Pidgeon, N. (2016) 'Energy biographies: narrative genres, lifecourse transitions, and practice change', *Science, Technology, & Human Values*, 41(3): 483–508.

Hanmer, C., Shipworth, M., Shipworth, D. and Carter, E. (2019) 'How household thermal routines shape UK home heating demand patterns', *Energy Efficiency*, 12(1): 5–17.

Hernández, D. (2016) 'Clean heat: a technical response to a policy innovation', *Cityscape*, 18(3): 277–82.

Hirsh, R.F. and Jones, C.F. (2014) 'History's contributions to energy research and policy', *Energy Research & Social Science*, 1: 106–11.

IEEE European Public Policy Committee (2018) 'Heating and cooling future of Europe and interactions with electricity: a position statement', *IEEE*, 16 January. Available from: https://www.ieee.org/content/dam/ieee-org/ieee/web/org/about/heating_and_cooling_future_of_europe_25_january_2018.pdf [Accessed 25 May 2023].

Mahon, M. (1992) *Foucault's Nietzschean Genealogy: Truth, Power, and the Subject*, Albany: Suny Press.

Maye-Banbury, A. (2021) 'All the world's a stage: how Irish immigrants negotiated life in England in the 1950s/1960s using Goffman's theory of impression management', *Irish Journal of Sociology*, 29(1): 32–53.

Ong, B.L. (2012) 'Warming up to heat', *The Senses and Society*, 7(1): 5–21.

Petrova, S. and Simcock, N. (2021) 'Gender and energy: domestic inequities reconsidered', *Social & Cultural Geography*, 22(6): 849–67.

Rohse, M., Day, R. and Llewellyn, D. (2020) 'Towards an emotional energy geography: attending to emotions and affects in a former coal mining community in South Wales, UK', *Geoforum*, 110: 136–46.

Rosenthal, G. (1993) 'Reconstruction of life stories: principles of selection in generating stories for narrative biographical interviews', *The Narrative Study of Lives*, 1(1): 59–91.

Sánchez, C.S.G., Fernández, A.S. and Peiró, M.N. (2020) 'Feminisation of energy poverty in the city of Madrid', *Energy and Buildings*, 223: 110157.

Sherriff, G., Moore, T., Berry, S., Ambrose, A., Goodchild, B. and Maye-Banbury, A. (2019) 'Coping with extremes, creating comfort: user experiences of "low-energy" homes in Australia', *Energy Research & Social Science*, 51: 44–54.

Veyne, P. (1997) *Foucault Revolutionizes History*, Chicago: University of Chicago Press.

4

Inclusive Rhythms: Chrono-Urbanism and De-Energization

Gordon Walker

Introduction

Cities are routinely characterized in spatial terms, understood as produced through geographically structured processes and with planning oriented towards the better organization of urban space. Less commonplace is a focus on the temporal dimensions of cities, seeing the urban as full of patterns that reproduce in time as well as in space, and considering the possibilities of a temporal perspective on city organization. In this chapter, I approach questions of post-carbon inclusion and the transformations needed to strip carbon-heavy techno-energies out of urban life through a temporal lens, drawing specifically on rhythmanalytic thinking and on recent moves towards a 'chrono-urbanism' perspective in urban planning (Henckel et al, 2013; Moreno et al, 2021; Pozoukidou and Chatziyiannaki, 2021). While there is much in technology-oriented decarbonization that can be examined through a temporal and rhythmic orientation (Walker, 2021), my focus here is towards modes of 'de-energization', or the more fundamental taking out of techno-energies from the reproduction of everyday life. I work through how the urban can be conceived in both polyrhythmic and poly-energetic terms before outlining four general principles for rhythm oriented de-energization: decelerating urban processes; reconnecting social, environmental and biological rhythms; localizing polyrhythmic relations; and enabling the shared synchronization and sequencing of rhythms of activity and infrastructure. Rhythm is broadly understood here as a pattern of repetition which can be variously regular or irregular and be observed in diverse entities and phenomena (Lefebvre, 2004 [1992]).

I argue that, while working with these principles has the potential to contribute to the transformations that are needed in moving to a post-carbon world, close attention also has to be paid to inclusion and to the distribution of the direct and indirect benefits of temporally oriented de-energization strategies. To centre on a practical example, the challenges of advancing the emblematic case of contemporary chrono-urbanism – the '15-minute city' – are considered. As a superficially appealing objective, under closer examination this highlights both the possibilities but also the tensions involved in temporally as well as spatially reorganizing the reproduction of everyday life, while advancing inclusion across differentiated social groups. To begin, I outline how urban settings can be conceptualized in rhythmic terms and the intimate relations urban rhythms have with energy and carbon emissions.

Urban rhythms and urban energies

Urban settings are inherently full of patterns in time, both human and non-human. They have temporal structure, rhythms that repeat day to day, that beat with various schedules and timetables, that are different between weekday and weekend or that have a structure over the seasons, over the year, or over multi-year periods. These diverse beats and pulses interconnect, interweave and interact, creating complex polyrhythmic patterns that are fundamental to how the urban functions, to how people get on with their lives and anticipate what is to be expected as city life plays out over time. In their foundational writing on rhythmanalysis, Lefebvre and Regulier (2004: 102) approach cities in such terms, as 'the site of a vast staging where all these relations with their rhythms show and unfurl themselves'. Others taking up their rhythmanalytic approach have characterized the rhythms and 'chronotopes' of particular urban settings (for example, Lehtovuori and Koskela, 2013; Osman and Mulicek, 2017; Nkooe, 2018) and provided rhythmized accounts of experiences of urban mobility, tourism, shopping and leisure (for example, Schwanen et al, 2012; Jones and Warren, 2016; Edensor and Larsen, 2018). Within this literature some urban spaces are characterized as more rhythmically involved, more densely animated, some made up of rhythms that clash and conflict, others more symphonic or harmonious. Certain rhythms, such as those of economy, capital accumulation and infrastructure, are seen to dominate, producing and reproducing differentiation and inequality in temporal as well as spatial terms, and shaping how urban space is experienced.

Rhythms are spatio-temporal but also essentially energetic phenomena, as made clear in Lefebvre's definitional statement that 'everywhere where there is interaction between a place, a time and an expenditure of energy there is rhythm' (Lefebvre, 2004 [1992]: 15). The material animations that rhythms constitute necessarily mean that an energy expenditure, flow or conversion is involved. Crucially this encompasses the energies of bodies, ecologies and environments, and the 'techno-energies' of powered technologies, and the infrastructures that support them. Cities are, therefore, both intensely polyrhythmic, but also intensely poly-energetic spaces, full of diverse forms of energy flow, running through city atmospheres, ecologies and environments, making and enabling things to happen, powering up machines and generating movement from place to place of people, things and flows of information. All of which we can then appraise as instances of rhythmic repetition.

Understood in techno-energetic terms, cities account for around 70 per cent of global primary energy consumption (Creutzig et al, 2015), with much of the carbon emitted through the long history of fossil fuel dependency also centred on cities and the energy systems that support them. As urbanization has progressed and cities have grown and developed over time, they have become more intensely energetic and carbon emission-generating spaces, part of a broader co-evolution between energy, time and society (Walker, 2021). This makes them both deeply immersed in the climate crisis, and a key setting for contemporary energy and climate action.

Through a rhythm lens, forms of rhythm modification and recalibration can be seen in various ways within ongoing urban energy transition processes, including in cities becoming 'smart' (Bulkeley et al, 2016) and subject to forms of 'algorhythmic governance' (Coletta and Kitchin, 2017). Such temporal 'techno-fixes' have a role to play, but there have for some time been calls for city planning to incorporate temporal thinking more fundamentally into progressing sustainability objectives. Jalas (2005: 73), for example, argues that bringing the environment into 'spatial planning implies nothing less than temporal planning'. Recent debates about chrono-urbanism connect into such arguments, without being driven primarily by a climate or environment orientation. For example, an otherwise excellent collection of work on the 'space-time design of the public city' (Henckel et al, 2013), while emphasizing questions of justice and quality of life, does not foreground elements of the wider sustainability or climate agenda. Chrono-urbanism does, however, have a contribution to make to moving towards a post-carbon future, if cast in broader terms and recognizing the important interrelations between the rhythms of social and environmental systems. Thinking temporally, or rhythmically, also does not have to be limited to formal urban planning processes but can also be about how other stakeholders and groups, often with more radical orientations, act with intent to make cities both fundamentally more sustainable and better places for habitation.

Principles for de-energization

So how might, in principle, an orientation to rhythm contribute to stripping both energy and carbon out of the reproduction of urban life? As noted earlier, the addition of 'de-energization' here is a deliberate counterweight to the dominant, often technology-oriented, focus on decarbonization that runs through much climate mitigation discourse. As I have argued at greater length elsewhere (Walker, 2021: 162–5), even if the old carbon dominated energy orders are eventually overturned (including through instigating fundamentally new rhythmic relations within how they operate), this will still be insufficient as a response to the climate emergency. There is a need rather to go further into our entanglement in rhythms and energies to address not only the carbon that is released, but also the techno-energetic expenditures and dependencies that continue to evolve and reproduce in energy intensive contexts in the Global North, and crucially to do so in ways that can build justice within transition processes (Bickerstaff et al, 2013). Approached from a rhythmanalytic perspective this poses a series of questions. How can energy intensive societies live with and through social rhythms that are less entangled with and dependent on techno-energies? How can connections and dependencies be rebuilt with rhythm-energies *outside* of energy systems? How can better synchronizations be formed with times, temporalities and rhythms that have the capacity to counter patterns of fracture, dissonance and injustice in human and ecological life?

Some guiding principles can be identified as a starting point within the long-standing body of writing on sustainability, green development, low energy societies and similar. Little of this discourse engages directly with rhythm, but there are strands of thinking concerned with time and temporality. These include Adam's (1990; 1998) extensive writing on timescapes and social-natural temporal relations, and work on temporalities in relation to sustainability (Held, 2001: Aldrich, 2005) and environmental research, policy and politics (Szerszynski, 2002; Jalas, 2006). Research approaching sustainability and energy demand through a social practice perspective has also drawn on various temporal frameworks and concepts (Strengers and Maller, 2015; Hui et al, 2018). Activist discourses and grassroots initiatives also provide inspiration, including those focused on low carbon communities and transition towns; as well as in deep ecology and – as in Chapters 10 and 13 – radical frameworks for degrowth and alternatives to dominant capitalist models of economy and development (Demaria et al, 2013). Importantly, such thinking is often focused on alternative ways of evaluating wellbeing, alongside stripping out pollution and ecological damage from economic activity. Four general principles, understood in rhythmic terms, can be identified across this body of work, without seeking to present this as a definitive systemization.

Decelerating rhythms: slowing the energetic tempo

Many writers and analysts have diagnosed and critiqued manifestations of the increasing speed of social, economic and cultural phenomena, with accelerations associated with various phases of industrialization, urbanization and/or globalization (Adam, 2004; Aldrich, 2005; Rosa, 2015; Wajcman and Dodd, 2017). In rhythmic terms, speeding up can mean either a rhythm having a shorter duration or a higher tempo of repetition, or both combined; a slowing down, therefore the reverse. Often (but not necessarily) the outcome of more energetic expenditure, or more intense thermodynamic conversions, has been an increase in speed in these terms. For Rosa (2015: 73), social acceleration includes 'the more rapid production of goods, the speedier conversion of matter and energy'. Rosa, along with many others, also critiques the increasing tempo of material, social and cultural obsolescence and the speed with which shifts in energy-enabled consumption take place. In the face of such accelerations of many types of rhythms and their knock-on consequences, slowing down is widely advocated as a response to socio-ecological crisis, as well as to the observation that faster ways of living are not obviously happier ones. Slow design, 'more time less stuff' (Jalas, 2006), slow travel and slow food (Hsu, 2014) are examples of slogans advocating forms of deceleration.

However, some caution is needed in applying deceleration as a general principle, particularly given that acceleration has not taken place everywhere or been a common experience, with its pace and manifestation strongly differentiated across geographies, social groups and aspects of social experience. For Rosa (2015: 21), 'forces of acceleration and deceleration do not balance out, but are instead very unequal in distribution', meaning that there is no one common starting point for change, or simple way in which less speed necessarily means more equality, as Illich (1978) rather deterministically argued. Deceleration as a principle, therefore, has to be approached with some care and differentiation.

Reconnecting rhythms: social and natural coupling

As with social acceleration, the disconnection of the rhythms of society and everyday life from the rhythms of natural cycles, ecologies and organisms has also been the subject of much critique. Adam emphasizes the essential rhythmicity of nature, in all its forms, arguing that clock time represents 'a technological time created to human design' (1990: 74) in which 'the variable times of nature – of day and night, seasons and change, growth and ageing, birth and death – are objectified, constituted independent of life and cosmic processes, of human activity and social organisation' (Adam, 2004: 4). Others have focused on how various forms of disconnection from 'natural clocks' have harmful consequences for health and happiness (Prance, 2005), or on how the imposition of industrial rhythms on agricultural production clashes with the natural times of animals and ecologies (Held, 2001). For Rosa (2015), there are links to social acceleration, given that speeding up implies discordances with the slower times of natural systems. Advocacy for reconnecting to the times of nature emerges from such critique, including in relation to living more harmoniously with energy, weather and climate. A compelling ethical question at a time of climate crisis is to ask what work *really* needs to be done by techno-energies, and what can be achieved in other ways (see also Chapter 9, in relation to energy use for cooling). This includes drawing far more directly and substantially on the vast energetic flows *outside* of energy systems, flows that were doing agentive rhythm-energetic work – warming, illuminating, flowing, eroding – long before artificial technologized energies came into being. This brings into critical focus substitutions between natural and techno-energetic energies, ways of achieving valued outcomes without techno-energetic expenditures, and ways of recalibrating social and bodily rhythms to the timings of natural energetic beats and pulses.

Here again though, close attention must be given to the practical workings of a general principle of reconnection to natural rhythm-energies. There can be an over-romanticized view of being close to the rhythms of natural processes that can manifest in brutal, dangerous and unreliable forms, and to an idea of doing without techno-energies through frugality that can be blind to the realities of living in poverty (Walker, 2013). Making reconnections with care, in context, and with awareness of different circumstances, is therefore necessary.

Localizing rhythms: proximity and attunement

Closely aligned to discourses of reconnection are those that, in various ways, seek to make life more local. This is a strong theme in much environmental activism – although not without critique (North, 2010) – with various groundings, including resistance to the 'distances travelled' by commodities in global production networks, and the search for place-based communality in local environmental action (Schlosberg, 2019). In rhythm terms, localization can be most obviously about simplifying and radically shortening the sequential chains and pulses of movement between points of production and points of consumption, by making in situ or sourcing products from the local area. The energy implicated in the rhythms of extended transnational movement is, therefore, stripped out, although different modes of movement over distance (for instance, digital versus shipping versus air travel) can also entail quite different energy demands. Localization can also in more polyrhythmic terms be about attuning the interaction of social, bodily and ecological rhythms to those of place and situation. This can include recognizing how landscapes and places are poly-energetic in which rhythms of different natural energy flows intermingle, exchange and interact, varying over space and time, in both regular and more chaotic patterns of repetition. Attunement to local poly-energetic landscapes matters to making ways of life which are less dependent on techno-energies, and more aligned with rhythms of natural light, heat, air movement and other aspects of environment and ecology embroiled in making places energetically what they are. This has been an important theme, for example, of building design, for some time, in both vernacular and more high-tech forms, and for some versions of place-making and city planning. Critiques centred on green gentrification and the creation of exclusive sustainable enclaves have also accompanied such strategies, and will figure again later in the chapter.

Sharing rhythms: synchronizing and sequencing

Sharing is connected quite directly to localization, and has recently emerged as a general principle of sustainability, often with an urban focus (Leismann et al, 2013; McLaren and Agyeman, 2015) and aligned with degrowth perspectives (Jarvis, 2019). Sharing in rhythmic terms encompasses both sharing 'in synchrony' and 'in sequence'. Synchronized sharing involves activities being performed together with other people, with a common rhythm in space and/or time, often involving a collective orchestration of using an infrastructure of some form. Such synchronizations are entirely routine, arguably an 'evolutionary trait' (McLaren and Agyeman, 2015: 323). However, there has been much critique of the loss of rhythms of 'doing things together', for example in relation to trends towards more people living alone, the fragmentation of family life and greater social differentiation in access to public spaces. For de-energization, the synchronization of shared social rhythms matters because of how the outcomes of the energetic-rhythmic work of technologies can have an economy of scale and of spatio-temporal concentration (Isaksson and Ellegård, 2015). In simple terms, energized technologies, in principle, will support the energy-demanding practices of a collective of people at a lower level of energy use than an individualized and asynchronous pattern of similar performances. Public transport for enabling mobility is an obvious example.

Sharing of material things can also include sharing in sequence, a type of sharing which is again quite familiar. In rhythmic terms this means something being in use in a sequential pattern that links to the rhythms of multiple 'users' and, therefore, being used at a higher tempo or frequency, or over a greater longevity than would otherwise be the case. For example, a (power) tool that is borrowed from a collective tool store, rather than individually purchased to sit idle most of the time, or a bicycle or car that is available through a mobility sharing scheme.

As with deceleration, reconnection and localization, we have to exercise some caution in following rhythmic sharing as a general principle. Yates (2016: 449) argues that 'what counts as doing something together with somebody else is far from straightforward, encompassing a mosaic of different forms of communality', meaning that working out its energetic implications can be particularly complex. There is also a necessary critique of some high-profile manifestations of sharing in sequence (such as Airbnb) being seen as productively aligned with sustainability objectives (Voytenko Palgan et al, 2017). As Martin (2016: 159) argues, the sharing economy has 'the paradoxical potential to: promote more sustainable consumption and production practices; and, to reinforce the current unsustainable economic paradigm'.

The 15-minute city, inclusion and temporal injustice

As is clear in laying out these four principles, they can be readily linked to examples of specific types of actions being undertaken in pursuit of carbon transition objectives. Seeing these through a rhythm lens makes lines of connections that foreground their temporal dimensions and opens up their relevance to a broader understanding of what a chrono-urbanism agenda might entail and achieve. An initial indication has also been given of the type of inclusion questions that can be raised in relation to each principle, and the risks of social exclusion that they might each harbour. To explore these further, in this section I focus on the '15-minute city' as the emblematic case of contemporary chrono-urbanist discourse.

The concept of the 15-minute city is credited to Carlos Moreno, who in 2020 was particularly influential in shaping the re-election campaign of the Mayor of Paris, Anne Hildago, at a time when the COVID-19 lockdown was presenting many challenges for city governance and urban living. Moreno's proposition was for an 'urban set up where locals are able to access all of their basic essentials at distances that would not take them more than 15 minutes by foot or by bicycle' (Moreno et al, 2021: 100), therefore giving a temporal metric a key role in city governance. In his scheme a set of six 'essential social functions to sustain a decent urban life' are identified as needing to be accessible in terms of living, working, commerce, healthcare, education and entertainment. Figure 4.1 provides a visual representation as applied to Paris.

This is not the first instance of a temporal accessibility metric. There have been previous formulations of 20-minute and 30-minute city principles – including accessibility by public transport, walking and cycling – that have been applied in a number of contexts including in Australia, the United

Figure 4.1: Diagrammatic representation of the '15-minute Paris' (*Le Paris du ¼ Heure*)

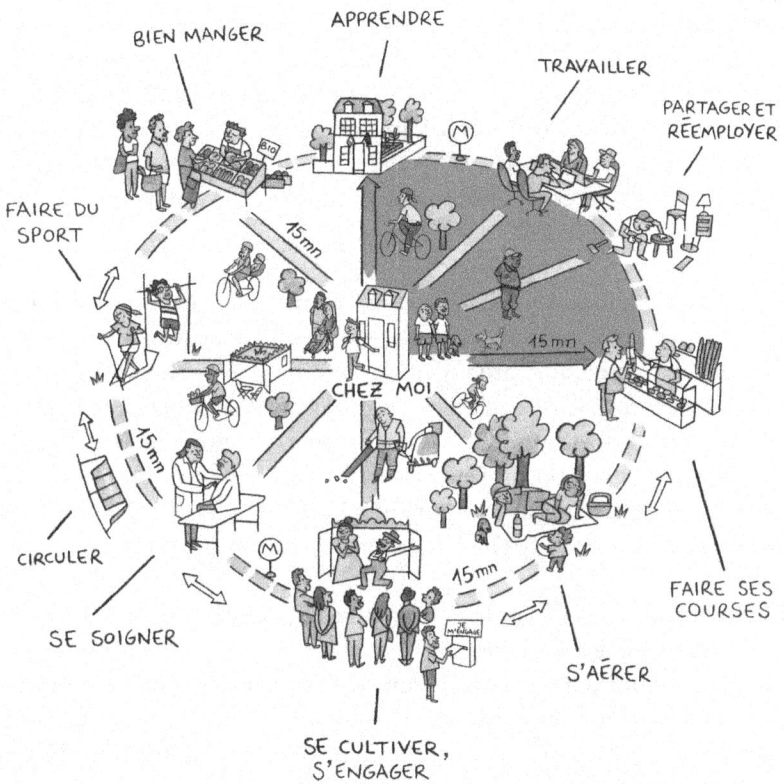

Notes: translations: *appendre* (learn); *travailler* (work); *partager et réemployer* (share and reuse); *faire ses courses* (go shopping); *s'aérer* (enjoy the outdoors); *se cultiver, s'engager* (be engaged in your community); *se soigner* (take care of yourself); *circuler* (get around); *faire du sport* (play sports); *bien manger* (eat well); *chez moi* (home).

Source: Micaël Dessin (reproduced with permission)

States and Italy (Henckel et al, 2013; Capasso Da Silva et al, 2019; Levinson, 2019; Pozoukidou and Chatziyiannaki, 2021). While there are also close ties to many other long-standing planning principles, such as the compact city (Burton et al, 2003), Moreno and colleagues argue that the 15-minute city concept has some distinctive objectives and characteristics, including in terms of social inclusion, participation and community cohesion. It is argued, for example, that pursuing its temporal metric through urban restructuring requires 'the urban social fabric becoming even more closely knitted and with residents made to interact and participate more in activities that ultimately strengthen their social bonds, building character and trust, which ultimately leads to the building of more healthy urban landscapes' (Moreno et al, 2021: 100–1).

Environmental and ecological gains, alongside accessibility and liveability, are also seen to be intrinsic:

> [S]aving on community time also saves the urban environment through the reduced emissions from both vehicles and power plants when fuels are extracted and processed. In addition to reducing time, the transformation that is to take place to ensure that all basic amenities are accessible within reach must ensure that the available urban space is optimized, hence promoting novel land uses, which is also critical in reconciling human liveability pursuits aligning with the urban ecology. (Moreno et al, 2021: 101)

In this and other accounts of the concept, there is little explicit engagement with its energy implications, beyond references to 'reduced emissions', and the language of rhythm is not typically applied in how it is understood. However, it does provide a planning proposition within which the relationship between rhythm and energy can be foregrounded, and elements of the four principles of de-energization previously discussed can be drawn out.

The most fundamental transformation the 15-minute city embodies is one of conceiving mobility in terms of the rhythms of the energized body rather than those of carbon-powered mobility. In walking and cycling the rhythmic repetitions of muscles of the body replace the rhythmic repetitions of cylinders, axles and wheels. Rhythmic work powered by hydrocarbon fuels is replaced by rhythmic work powered by calories, meaning that the corporeal rhythms of bodies – of muscles, heart and lungs – are (re)activated, making good use of ingested calories and improving the eurhythmic qualities of bodily ensembles. The rhythms of mobility become restructured around the speed and duration capabilities of bodies – set notionally at 15 minutes per trip – enabled by infrastructures that provide for effective walking and cycling based route-making. The hegemonic domination of road traffic, that acts to segregate public space (Spinney, 2010) and discipline the key temporal beats of urban life, is broken. Embodied rhythms take their place and carbon emissions integral to techno-energy powered mobility are eliminated.

This central shift in rhythm-energy terms plays directly into the first principle of de-energization – of decelerating rhythms – but, as summarized in Table 4.1, all four principles of de-energization through rhythm governance are to varying degrees enrolled in the 15-minute city proposal. Localizing rhythms is directly part of the proximity and density logics integral to its accessibility focus. Sharing rhythms can be found in the synchronous and sequential use of public space given over to walking and cycling and 'retrieved' from the needs of cars, in bike sharing schemes which are envisaged as part of enabling a cycling culture, and in the 'share and reuse' included in Figure 4.1. Reconnecting rhythms, in terms of making use of the rhythms of energetic flows in the environment, is not strongly aligned, but figures in the expectation that greenspace provision (and therefore the rhythms of the natural environment) will be part of enabling local exercise and creating an active local community.

The 15-minute city concept certainly has relevance to the focus on rhythm and de-energization in this chapter, and to imagining how aspects of the temporality of post-carbon cities might be structured. However, practical obstacles to its realization can be readily identified. Some cities, such as Barcelona, have been shown to already largely satisfy the 15-minute city criteria (Ferrer-Ortiz et al, 2022), at least for access to education, healthcare, commerce and entertainment. However, many others around the world have an urban structure that follows a very different pattern, of sprawl and high separation between residences and services, often also having weak urban governance that displays little ability to determine or restructure development processes.

Managing urban space to ensure that work as a 'basic essential' is available for all is a particularly difficult goal (Pozoukidou and Chatziyiannaki,

Table 4.1: Rhythmic de-energization principles within the 15-minute city concept

De-energization principle	Relevance to 15-minute city concept
Decelerating rhythms	Rhythms of walking and cycling are prioritized as generally slower modes of mobility
Reconnecting rhythms	Encounters with rhythms of nature both in local greenspace and in engaging in active mobility
Localizing rhythms	Shortening rhythms of movement through proximity, supply chain rhythms locally structured
Sharing rhythms	Rhythms of synchronized and sequential sharing of public space and bicycle infrastructure

2021). Relevant considerations include the specialization of skills and wide range of forms of employment that people have experience in or aspire to; the insecurity of precarity of much contemporary employment; and the market driven processes that typically dominate the geography of both housing provision and job availability. Taking such matters into account, it is clear that governing the spatial and temporal-rhythmic relation between home and work faces severe challenges. As Mullen and Marsden (2018: 161) argue more broadly, 'housing and employment precarity present a substantial challenge to attempts to reduce energy intensive transport and related emissions' serving to encourage car ownership because of the flexibilities in trip-making that enables. Some images of and writings about the 15-minute city focus on digitalization and home working (as apparent during COVID-19 lockdowns), which inherently enable the compression of home–work relations in space and time. However, this is a particular and largely privileged, middle-class view of contemporary employment practices and opportunities, especially when viewed with a global reach.

Such a privileged view connects to broader questions about who the 15-minute city is for, under what imagined conditions of everyday life and circumstance, and with what openness to diversity and recognition of inequality. So-called 'green gentrification' accompanying the application of sustainability principles into local planning and design (Gould and Lewis, 2016; Anguelovski et al, 2018) has been recognized as having potentially corrosive effects on low income, minority and disenfranchised neighbourhoods. Critiques of the 15-minute city have seen it as having this gentrification potential. Glaeser, for example, has argued that:

> The basic concept of the 15 min city is not really a city at all. It's an enclave – a ghetto – a subdivision. ... I am very worried that a focus on enabling upper-middle income people to walk around in their nice little 15-min neighbourhood precludes the far larger issue of how we make sure our cities once again become places of opportunity for everyone. (Glaeser, 2021)

While the 15-minute city discourse asserts that equality, diversity and cohesion will be ensured, including through bottom-up participatory planning processes, the fact that in a short time it has already become part of the rhetorical vocabulary of property developers does not encourage such optimism. As Luscher (2022: 1) comments, 'it now seems mandatory for property developers to include a "15-minute city" reference in their marketing. It's urbanist "virtue signalling"'. A substantial set of inclusive community planning and 'anti-displacement' tools and policies have been proposed in order to resist green gentrification processes (Oscilowicz et al,

2021), but implementing these in the face of the often intensely market-driven politics of urban investment is a challenging task.

If 15-minute neighbourhoods are *not* able to provide inclusivity, then the notion that the rhythms of movement in everyday life will be equalized and de-energized (to a large degree) will not be achieved. However, even if they *are* able to be diverse across various dimensions of social and demographic difference, then equalizing the accessibility of basic needs for all can still be problematic. The reliance on muscle energy and the rhythmic capabilities of bodies to enable movement has clear scope to exclude those whose bodies have limited energetic power, or are constrained in how this can be deployed in terms of age, disability and chronic illness. Shorter-term illness or life events, such as having a baby, can also interrupt established patterns of mobility. How concerns about safety when walking and cycling refract across gender, race and age also raise questions about how inherently 'just' the 15-minute concept might be. As Verlinghieri and Schwanen question in relation to walking:

> If this practice becomes for some people in certain situations – e.g., in unfamiliar neighbourhoods or on streets deemed 'risky' because of who might be encountered – heavily dependent on smartphone apps tethered to near-planetary digital systems, is it still 'good' or desirable given its connection to carbon consumption and the socio-spatial coding of bodies in terms of, for instance, physical strength, gait or skin colour? (Verlinghieri and Schwanen, 2020: 4)

It is clear from the rhythmanalysis literature that urban lives are rhythmically complex and diverse. There are broad rhythmic structures that can be observed at an aggregate level, but people can live within these with quite different spatio-temporal structures, constraints and freedoms. While the 15-minute city concept seeks to bring more equality into the rhythms of making a decent life in the city, there are a number of reasons why it may fail to do so unless close attention is paid to such spatio-temporal differentiation.

Conclusion

In this chapter I have argued that the conjunction between rhythm and energy is intrinsically embedded both in the deeply problematic form of the techno-energized and carbon-heavy city, and in transitioning towards a de-energized, post-carbon future. What the simultaneously polyrhythmic and poly-energic profile of the post-carbon city should be is a crucial question, which extends beyond just thinking about the rhythms of the city as movement and pathways in space and time. A set of principles for approaching this question have been laid out, which in various ways seek to de-energize the reproduction of urban living. Modes of rhythm-energetic deceleration, reconnection, localization and sharing all have a role to play, including through mobilizing environmental and bodily energies and their rhythmic profiles, instead of, and in relation to, those of energized technologies.

Giving more explicit attention to temporality and rhythm in urban responses to the climate crisis has been neglected to date but holds much potential. As Held (2001: 356) argued some time ago, 'if we ignore climatic and other relevant context-variables with their rhythms and *eigenzeiten* [embedded times], as we have done for a long time in planning our settlements, architecture and construction, we cannot be on a sustainable energy path'. I have though made clear that there are evident risks of reproducing or exacerbating patterns of existing urban exclusion and injustice that have to be foregrounded within the transition of urban rhythms into post-carbon forms. It follows that acting to counter these risks has to be part of a broadly conceived chrono-urbanist agenda. While the 'in-fashion' chrono-urbanist concept of the 15-minute city productively aligns with moves towards de-energizing city rhythms, I have argued that its co-option may well lead to it becoming little more than the latest rhetorical slogan to give a green gloss to urban development projects. Chrono-urbanism needs to resist such capture by urban elites and align more with the discourses and agents of just transition and degrowth. Engaging with and further developing the notion of 'temporal justice' (Mallet, 2014) may also be productive, taking it beyond just a focus on inequalities in the 'right to time' in everyday life, towards a broader set of concerns with how urban times and environmental and climate justice intersect.

References

Adam, B. (1990) *Time and Social Theory*, Cambridge: Polity Press.

Adam, B. (1998) *Timescapes of Modernity: The Environment and Invisible Hazards*, London: Routledge.

Adam, B. (2004) 'Of metaphors, morals and memories: reflections on socio-environmental action from a temporal perspective', *Working Paper Series 68*, School of Social Sciences, Cardiff: Cardiff University.

Aldrich, T. (ed) (2005) *About Time: Speed, Society, People and the Environment*, Sheffield: Greenleaf.

Anguelovski, I., Connolly, J.J.T., Masip, L. and Pearsall, H. (2018) 'Assessing green gentrification in historically disenfranchised neighborhoods: a longitudinal and spatial analysis of Barcelona', *Urban Geography*, 39(3): 458–91.

Bickerstaff, K., Walker, G. and Bulkeley, H. (eds) (2013) *Energy Justice in a Changing Climate*, London: Zed.

Bulkeley, H., Mcguirk, P.M. and Dowling, R. (2016) 'Making a smart city for the smart grid? The urban material politics of actualising smart electricity networks', *Environment and Planning A*, 48(9): 1709–26.

Burton, E., Jenks, M. and Williams, K. (2003) *The Compact City: A Sustainable Urban Form?*, Abingdon: Routledge.

Capasso Da Silva, D., King, D. and Lemar, S. (2019) 'Accessibility in practice: 20-minute city as a sustainability planning goal', *Sustainability*, 12(1): 129.

Coletta, C. and Kitchin, R. (2017) 'Algorhythmic governance: regulating the "heartbeat" of a city using the Internet of Things', *Big Data & Society*, 4(2). DOI: 10.1177/2053951717742418

Creutzig, F., Baiocchi, G., Bierkandt, R., Pichler, P.-P. and Seto, K.C. (2015) 'Global typology of urban energy use and potentials for an urbanization mitigation wedge', *Proceedings of the National Academy of Sciences*, 112(20): 6283–8.

Demaria, F., Schneider, F., Sekulova, F. and Martinez-Alier, J. (2013) 'What is degrowth? From an activist slogan to a social movement', *Environmental Values*, 22(2): 191–215.

Edensor, T. and Larsen, J. (2018) 'Rhythmanalysing marathon running: "a drama of rhythms"', *Environment and Planning A*, 50(3): 730–46.

Ferrer-Ortiz, C., Marquet, O., Mojica, L. and Vich, G. (2022) 'Barcelona under the 15-minute city lens: mapping the accessibility and proximity potential based on pedestrian travel times', *Smart Cities*, 5(1): 146–61.

Glaeser, E. (2021) 'The 15-minute city is a dead end – cities must be places of opportunity for everyone'. Available from: https://blogs.lse.ac.uk/covid19/2021/05/28/the-15-minute-city-is-a-dead-end-cities-must-be-places-of-opportunity-for-everyone/ [Accessed 9 September 2022].

Gould, K.A. and Lewis, T.L. (2016) *Green Gentrification: Urban Sustainability and the Struggle for Environmental Justice*, Abingdon: Routledge.

Held, M. (2001) 'Sustainable development from a temporal perspective', *Time and Society*, 10(2–3): 351–66.

Henckel, D., Thomaier, S., Könecke, B., Zedda, R. and Stabilini, S. (eds) (2013) *Space–Time Design of the Public City*, Dordrecht: Springer.

Hsu, E.L. (2014) 'The slow food movement and time shortage: beyond the dichotomy of fast or slow', *Journal of Sociology*, 51(3): 628–42.

Hui, A., Day, R. and Walker, G. (eds) (2018) *Demanding Energy: Space, Time and Change*, Chippenham: Palgrave Macmillan.

Illich, I. (1978) *Energy and Equity*, New York: Pantheon.

Isaksson, C. and Ellegård, K. (2015) 'Dividing or sharing? A time-geographical examination of eating, labour, and energy consumption in Sweden', *Energy Research & Social Science*, 10: 180–91.

Jalas, M. (2005) 'Sustainability in everyday life – a matter of time?', in Reisch, L. and Ropke, I. (eds), *The Ecological Economics of Consumption*, Cheltenham: Edward Elgar, pp 151–73.

Jalas, M. (2006) *Busy, Wise and Idle Time: A Study of the Temporalities of Consumption in the Environmental Debate*, Helsinki: Helsinki School of Economics.

Jarvis, H. (2019) 'Sharing, togetherness and intentional degrowth', *Progress in Human Geography*, 43(2): 256–75.

Jones, P. and Warren, S. (2016) 'Time, rhythm and the creative economy', *Transactions of the Institute of British Geographers*, 41(3): 286–96.

Lefebvre, H. (2004 [1992]) *Rhythmanalysis: Space, Time and Everyday Life*, London: Continuum.

Lefebvre, H. and Regulier, C. (2004) 'Attempt at the rhythmanalysis of Mediterranean cities' in Lefebvre, H., *Rhythmanalysis: Space, Time and Everyday Life*, London: Bloomsbury, pp 93–106.

Lehtovuori, P. and Koskela, H. (2013) 'From momentary to historic: rhythms in the social production of urban space, the case of Calcada de Sant'Ana, Lisbon', *Sociological Review*, 61(1): 124–43.

Leismann, K., Schmitt, M., Rohn, H. and Baedeker, C. (2013) 'Collaborative consumption: towards a resource-saving consumption culture', *Resources*, 2(3): 184–203.

Levinson, D. (2019) *The 30-Minute City: Designing for Access*, Sydney: Network Design Labs.

Luscher, D. (2022) 'The 15-minute city as marketing slogan'. Available from https://www.15minutecity.com/blog/marketing [Accessed 8 September 2022].

Mallet, S. (2014) 'The urban rhythms of neoliberalization', *Justice Spatiale-Spatial Justice*, 6: 1–19.

Martin, C.J. (2016) 'The sharing economy: a pathway to sustainability or a nightmarish form of neoliberal capitalism?', *Ecological Economics*, 121: 149–59.

McLaren, D. and Agyeman, J. (2015) *Sharing Cities: A Case for Truly Smart and Sustainable Cities*, Cambridge MA: MIT Press.

Moreno, C., Allam, Z., Chabaud, D., Gall, C. and Pratlong, F. (2021) 'Introducing the "15-minute city": sustainability, resilience and place identity in future post-pandemic cities', *Smart Cities*, 4(1): 93–111.

Mullen, C. and Marsden, G. (2018) 'The car as safety-net: narrative accounts of the role of energy intensive transport in conditions of housing and employment uncertainty', in Hui, A., Day, R. and Walker, G. (eds), *Demanding Energy: Space, Time and Change*, Chippenham: Palgrave Macmillan, pp 145–64.

Nkooe, E.S. (2018) 'A Lefebvrian analysis of public spaces in Mangaung, South Africa', *Urban Planning*, 3(3): 26–39.

North, P. (2010) 'Eco-localisation as a progressive response to peak oil and climate change: a sympathetic critique', *Geoforum*, 41(4): 585–94.

Oscilowicz, E., Lewartowska, E., Levitch, A., Luger, J., Hajtmarova, S., O'Neill, E. et al (2021) *Policy and Planning Tools for Urban Green Justice: Fighting Displacement and Gentrification and Improving Accessibility and Inclusiveness to Green Amenities*, Barcelona: Barcelona Laboratory for Urban Environmental Justice and Sustainability.

Osman, R. and Mulicek, O. (2017) 'Urban chronopolis: ensemble of rhythmized dislocated places', *Geoforum*, 85: 46–57.

Pozoukidou, G. and Chatziyiannaki, Z. (2021) '15-minute city: decomposing the new urban planning eutopia', *Sustainability*, 13: 928. DOI: 10.3390/su13020928

Prance, G. (2005) 'Natural clocks', in Aldrich, T. (ed), *About Time: Speed, Society, People and the Environment*, Sheffield: Greenleaf, pp 26–38.

Rosa, H. (2015) *Social Acceleration: A New Theory of Modernity*, New York: Columbia University Press.

Schlosberg, D. (2019) 'From postmaterialism to sustainable materialism: the environmental politics of practice-based movements', *Environmental Politics*, 8 March. DOI: 10.1080/09644016.2019.1587215

Schwanen, T., Van Aalst, I., Brands, J. and Timan, T. (2012) 'Rhythms of the night: spatiotemporal inequalities in the nighttime economy', *Environment and Planning A*, 44(9): 2064–85.

Spinney, J. (2010) 'Improvising rhythms: re-reading urban time and space through everyday practices of cycling', in Edensor, T. (ed), *Geographies of Rhythm: Nature, Place and Mobilities*, Farnham: Ashgate, pp 113–27.

Strengers, Y. and Maller, C. (eds) (2015) *Social Practices, Intervention and Sustainability: Beyond Behaviour Change*, London: Routledge.

Szerszynski, B. (2002) 'Wild times and domesticated times: the temporalities of environmental lifestyles and politics', *Landscape and Urban Planning*, 61: 181–91.

Verlinghieri, E. and Schwanen, T. (2020) 'Transport and mobility justice: evolving discussions', *Journal of Transport Geography*, 87: 102798.

Voytenko Palgan, Y., Zvolska, L. and Mont, O. (2017) 'Sustainability framings of accommodation sharing', *Environmental Innovation and Societal Transitions*, 23: 70–83.

Wajcman, J. and Dodd, N. (eds) (2017) *The Sociology of Speed: Digital, Organization and Social Temporalities*, Oxford: Oxford University Press.

Walker, G. (2013) 'Inequality, sustainability and capability: locating justice in social practice', in Shove, E. and Spurling, N. (eds), *Sustainable Practices: Social Theory and Climate Change*, London: Routledge, pp 181–96.

Walker, G. (2021) *Energy and Rhythm: Rhythmanalysis for a Low Carbon Future*, London: Rowman & Littlefield.

Yates, L. (2016) 'Sharing, households and sustainable consumption', *Journal of Consumer Culture*, 18(3): 433–52.

5

Alternatives to Justice for a Thriving Transition

Aimee Ambrose, Alvaro Castano-Garcia and Yael Arbell

Introduction

The moral discourse around low carbon transitions currently favours justice as its main virtue, often highlighting injustice within the current system and ways to avoid it in future. When we aim for justice, our focus is on what is lacking rather than what might be possible. Low carbon transitions represent an opportunity to reinvent our systems and ways of life but also the associated virtues and values that guide and shape them. The transition must exclude no one and must prioritize those most in need and most disadvantaged by the current system. In this context, the concept of justice – transitioning away from fossil fuels in a way which promotes a fairer world – feels very relevant and provides a helpful guide. But is justice all we should be aiming for?

In this chapter, we experiment with positioning alternative or complementary virtues as guiding principles for the transition and reflect on the implications of these alternative philosophies, particularly for inclusion. Ultimately, we put forward the beginnings of an alternative framework, which does not ignore justice but promotes the virtues of generosity and care as foundations of justice or complements to it. These virtues and the alternative values they uphold have the potential to shape low carbon transitions from the starting point of genuine concern for the wellbeing of others.

We begin by taking a critical look at the specific concept of just transition that has come to dominate the academic and policy rhetoric around the shift to a lower carbon society. We go on to explore two new, alternative concepts based around alternative virtues, namely: a generous transition and a caring transition. We reflect on what sort of policies might emerge under each framework, or combination of frameworks, and the inclusion dynamics that may be fostered under these different scenarios.

Unpicking justice

Justice is a broad concept with many different interpretations and applications, including, in the context of low carbon transitions, environmental justice, climate justice and energy justice. Each of these concepts has a different genesis, emphasis and objective. Environmental justice can be traced back to the Civil Rights Movement in the United States (US) in the 1950s and 1960s. The movement strives for the fair treatment of all people regardless of race, colour, origin or income in the context of environmental quality and governance (Lehtinen, 2009). Climate justice focuses on human rights and social inequality and, in particular, the injustice that emissions generated by developed nations in growing their wealth are driving the climate crisis, the effects of which are felt most acutely by developing nations. The movement contends that developed nations should take responsibility for emissions reductions and should compensate the developing world for the impacts they are suffering. Energy justice is a newer research agenda seeking to apply justice principles to energy policy, practice and research, challenging us to view energy provision not just as a technical challenge but a question of equity and calling for greater inclusion of citizens in energy related decision making.

There are examples of where each of these concepts have penetrated policy and political discourse. For example, several federal governments of the US, including the current Biden–Harris administration, have used the language of, and committed to deliver, environmental justice. Moreover, climate justice has been a guiding concept within climate negotiations since the 1990s, including the recently concluded 27th meeting of the United Nations Framework Convention on Climate Change (UNFCCC) Conference of the Parties (COP). Despite these promising examples, justice arguably has not come to dominate environmental policy discourse in any meaningful way. The related concept of 'just transition', however, has.

The just transition concept is favoured for its apparent ability to promote greater justice for people and planet without calling into question the dominant economic paradigm of perpetual economic growth (Newell and Mulvaney, 2013; Pinker, 2020). It has gained considerable traction, becoming pervasive within flagship (often Global North focused) policy frameworks and national transition policies across many countries. For example, the International Labour Organization and the United Nations have both adopted the language of just transition and released guidance on how countries might operationalize the concept. The European Commission (EC) has also heavily subscribed to the concept, as exemplified in their Green Deal (2019) and Just Transition Mechanism. The concept is now percolating down to individual countries that are adopting the philosophy of just transition within policy to try and ensure that the prioritization and compensation of those most affected by, and vulnerable to, transition forms a prominent consideration in policies relating to economy, energy, transport, housing and so forth.

In some countries, initiatives aimed at a just transition have a very specific focus on particularly vulnerable sectors, such as the Canadian coal industry (Government of Canada, 2019). In others, for example Scotland, the concept is used in a more generalized way but with an economic leaning, espousing the ambition to create a fairer, more climate resilient economy (Scottish Government, 2021). This economic focus reflects the origins of the just transition movement in the US during the 1980s and 1990s, as an attempt by workers within threatened industries to demand fair treatment in the dismantling of their sectors (Pinker, 2020). As environmental regulations threatened jobs dependent on fossil fuels, unions tried to achieve a 'just transition' for their workers through programmes that guaranteed new jobs or early retirement packages for those affected (McCauley and Heffron, 2018).

Although there is no single definition of just transition, there is a degree of international consensus that it reflects an intention to combine environmental protection with the creation of decent, high-quality work for all (UFCCC, 2020). The emphasis on universality of access to decent, less environmentally damaging work suggests that inclusion is central to notions of a just transition. Yet this focus on universality also has the clear potential to undermine more nuanced understandings of who is most vulnerable and who must, therefore, be protected and prioritized for support and compensation, a vital prerequisite of inclusion.

Bare minimums versus opportunity

The tone of the discourse within policies informed by just transition suggests that a just transition, as operationalized within policy, is not aiming at a reversal of fortunes for those disadvantaged by a high carbon society, offering them the opportunity to thrive and perhaps, to borrow from the language of degrowth, to redefine what represents a 'good life' to them (D'Alisa et al, 2014). Instead, the aims relate to the avoidance of stranding among communities on the frontline of high carbon economies (Di Chiro, 2016), via compensation for the impact of the transition on the economic aspects of their lives and efforts to find them a place in the new economy. This narrow focus on recompense to economic disruption overlooks the wide-ranging pressures placed by a fossil fuelled society on health, wellbeing, enjoyment, quality of life and hope for our children's futures.

Surely the low carbon transition, a necessarily colossal reorganization of the way we live and how we organize societies and economies, provides the best opportunity in at least 500 years – the point at which Trentmann

(2016) argues that our obsession with growth and global trade began in earnest – to emancipate the 'worker bees' that have kept our 'empire of things' functioning (Trentmann, 2016: 76) and afford them an opportunity to thrive through transition, rather than merely survive.

Critiques of just transition as interpreted in a policy context are well established within the academic literature. Some point to the top-down nature of policies aimed at a just transition whereby bureaucrats and industry leaders (often from privileged backgrounds) determine who is most vulnerable and how they should be compensated (Banerjee and Schuitema, 2022). This dehistoricizes the concept, distancing it from the 'grassroots' origins of the movement, spearheaded by workers on the verge of obsolescence (Castano-Garcia, forthcoming). Top-down solutions, it is logical to argue, run greater risk of misunderstanding or underestimating the impacts associated with transition, misidentifying and mis-prioritizing those most affected and compensating them in the wrong ways. Other critiques include the risk of misappropriation and exploitation of the concept for greenwashing, the lack of an agreed definition, a skewed focus on the economic aspects of transition, and a focus on addressing or offsetting the symptoms of injustice rather than their structural causes (McCauley and Heffron, 2018).

Considering these wide-ranging critiques, we might legitimately question whether it is the right concept to adopt in guiding us equitably through the transition and securing the best possible outcomes for those most affected by the climate crisis and the transition away from fossil fuels.

Exploring alternatives to justice

A key objective of this chapter is to challenge and explore alternatives to concepts, such as just transition, that can be seen to set low expectations or aspirations for the transition. Where adherence to the principles of a just transition can ameliorate some of the huge potential for new or deepened injustice associated with energy transitions, other virtues such as generosity (with its emphasis on thriving and wellbeing) and care (with its emphasis on nurturing and reciprocity) emphasize the opportunities presented by the transition for transformation and a better life. In the following sections, we focus first on generosity, then care, as alternative or complementary guiding virtues for low carbon transitions, and consider the potential implications they have for the form and fate of the transition.

A generous or altruistic transition

What if the emphasis of the policy and academic rhetoric around the transition to a low carbon society centred around a generous or altruistic, rather than (or in addition to) a just transition?

Aristotle argues that those who suffer from generosity deficiency are either more frugal with their resources than they ought to be, or greedy because they take too much. Here we explore the notion that generosity can be located at the beginning of an alternative 'ethical chain' (Castro, 2021), which could play an important role in driving just transitions. Generosity could guide action towards what Aristotle (1908) defined as the noble and appropriate mean between the two opposing extremes of stinginess and wastefulness. Generosity is also a 'productive virtue' (Castro, 2021) with the potential to resonate across and bring together people and communities with different interests.

When distinguishing generosity from extravagance or wastefulness, Aristotle highlights that extravagance is characteristically self-destructive, since it wastes resources essential for living. In an international development context, Global North nations can be seen to exemplify the characteristics of extravagance that will ultimately, if left unchecked, become self-destructive as the Earth is rendered uninhabitable. Generosity deficiency is also evident in the inadequacy of Global North gestures towards Global South countries who experience some of the most intense impacts of climate change, driven by high carbon lifestyles in the Global North (James et al, 2014).

In relation to this point about the self-destructive nature of extravagance, this may be where generosity is misunderstood and perhaps rejected as a virtue, on the basis that it may be misconstrued as omitting self-interest. Generosity does not demand selflessness but instead requires that one gives to others to the degree that giving does not damage one's own material health (Allen, 2018). This is where generosity can be seen as distinct from altruism, which involves acting to promote someone else's wellbeing even at cost to ourselves (Allen, 2018). As we will go on to discuss, recent gestures on the part of Global North countries towards Global South nations have not been without their benefits for the giver, suggesting they are closer to acts of generosity than altruism. In this context, Singer (2015) suggests that effective altruism should be focused on donating resources only after careful reasoning to decide how best to provide support and to which causes. Singer's arguments remind us that both generosity and altruism can be ineffective if they are not carefully considered, effectively targeted, and aligned with the needs of recipients, not just those giving. Understanding the needs of the intended beneficiaries has the potential to transform an act of apparent generosity from one that is done to the recipients to one that is inclusive of them.

In this vein, commentators such as Gabriel (2017) rail against the notion that altruism could represent the key to increased global justice, highlighting the risks associated with donor-centrism and how a reliance on altruism reinforces existing tendencies for the decision-making power to reside with the wealthy who are out of touch with the complex injustices faced by those they ostensibly seek to help. In essence, under this model, the very structures that created the injustice in the first place are relied on to address it.

In this section, we have been careful to distinguish between the more conditional and perhaps less habitual nature of generosity and the more fundamental nature of altruism as a philosophy or way of life. As will be discussed, generosity might represent a more viable and realistic first step towards justice in the context of low carbon transitions than altruism, and one which is already being enacted to some degree.

Loss and damage: an act of generosity?

If global society is to meet all of its needs within the resources provided by one Earth, Global North countries will need to reduce resource consumption considerably to enable more even consumption globally. Responsibility squarely rests on Global North nations, given that the US, the European Union and China together produce just under 60 per cent of global emissions, compared to – for example – just 3 per cent of global emissions emanating from African nations combined (Ulgen, 2021). Although vital for our collective survival, such a reduction in resource consumption could be considered an act of generosity or even altruism towards citizens elsewhere and future generations everywhere, given the absence of any legal obligations to redress resource inequality. In this context, distinctions between generosity and justice can be subtle and blurred. However, a key contention of our argument concerns how acts of generosity or altruism could be seen as a prerequisite or enabler of greater justice. For example, once everyone benefits from their fair share of Earth's resources in perpetuity, then justice has arguably been achieved. But what is necessary to trigger this is greater generosity on the part of Global North countries, especially the most privileged among them, who must compromise their existing lifestyles to enable others (both within their own unequal societies and those of the Global South) to survive and thrive. Generosity will result in limited compromises, whereas altruism might lead to much greater concessions on the part of the Global North.

We currently see an example of what might arguably constitute generosity at the state level in the form of Denmark's proactive commitment to paying 'loss and damage' to the most climate-vulnerable areas of the world. In announcing the intention, the Danish Development Minister used the language of justice and fairness, stating that 'It is grossly unfair that the world's poorest should suffer the most from the consequences of climate change, to which they have contributed the least' (Volcovico, 2022). Given that there is currently no obligation placed on Global North countries to offer such compensation, this act can be understood as a generous act undertaken in pursuit of greater justice for the world's poorest, worst affected regions. Justice is the motivation, generosity is the action.

This is useful in highlighting how, when justice feels idealistic and a remote prospect that would involve seismic shifts in the current world order, an act of apparent generosity can feel like a tangible starting point. However, as Castro (2021) points out, generosity can only lead to justice if we give the right amounts to the right people at the right time. The idea of giving the right amount feels fundamentally at loggerheads with the concept of generosity, which involves giving only what you can.

A gesture such as that undertaken by Denmark, although symbolically important, is not likely to be significant enough (in its scale and monetary value) to represent a significant step along the path to justice. However, it does fulfil important functions in the sense that giving (to a point where it doesn't harm the giver but does help the receiver) arguably boosts wellbeing, strengthens relationships and builds bridges (in this case between countries and regions), promotes a sense of global community, supporting countries producing many everyday goods, and quietening consciences through a practical act (Huffington, 2014). Yet, to return to the title of this chapter, this act on the part of Denmark is undertaken at a high level by way of apology and reparation, to help a little with the struggles faced by the most affected regions, not to enable communities within them to thrive and determine their own future. The amount given is unlikely to impact the abundance enjoyed by countries like Denmark, nor will it move recipient nations towards abundance, with research identifying that countries in receipt of such payments spend it all on adaptation (James et al, 2014). Certainly Denmark's actions appear to echo the critiques advanced by Gabriel (2017) by reinforcing the dominance of developed nations and the reliance of Global South nations on their charity, which is likely to be based on a flawed understanding of their needs.

This act alone does not amount to justice across global society and remained an isolated act of charity until recently when, during the COP 27, a historic deal was struck to compensate developing nations for their vulnerability within the climate crisis and to help them adapt. It is intended that those most vulnerable in the context of the climate crisis will be prioritized, yet definitions of vulnerability in this context remain moot. This agreement can be viewed, arguably, as less an act of generosity and more of a response to the pressure associated with sitting around a table with representatives of nations deeply affected by the current and historic actions (and inaction) of the developed world. The adequacy and effectiveness of this agreement, which is not legally binding, will hinge on whether the amount available is determined by how much contributing nations are willing to provide or what affected nations really need. Moreover, the inclusivity of the agreement will be determined by the extent to which the beneficiaries are permitted to define the extent and nature of their own vulnerability and what they need from the fund.

Generosity as prerequisite to justice

Generosity has never been systemically adopted and enshrined in policy and legislation in the same way as justice is, possibly because justice is aspired to as a basic minimum expectation whereas generosity remains something that is 'nice to have' across many modern cultures. However, the arguments we forward here propose that these virtues might be more interrelated and interdependent than they might first appear – in the sense that routinized generosity, which is correctly targeted and built around nuanced understandings of the needs of recipients, could perhaps take us closer to the attainment of justice, over time. Yet, in the context of low carbon transitions, there is no time left for cultures of generosity to slowly develop, which may further underline why justice remains our 'back stop' virtue under crisis conditions. Altruism, in our view, remains a more distant prospect given that it involves giving in a more unbridled way that would, for example, in a global context, involve giving Global South nations all they need regardless of Global North needs. The impact of such a philosophy would be seismic, if undertaken sensitively and democratically, but feels a distant prospect despite the promising developments associated with the COP 27.

A caring transition

Generosity can be seen as driven, in part, by care. A small number of scholars have begun examining where care and caring sit in relation to justice, in much the same way as we have considered the concept of generosity and altruism in this context. In this section we focus specifically on ethics of care, which has been the focus of the academic debate surrounding the notion of a caring transition. Ethics of care is a theory that prioritizes inter-personal relationships and our interdependence on one another, and overlaps with generosity and altruism through an emphasis on benevolence.

Where generosity suggests that we should only give where it will not be to the detriment of our own material health, ethics of care promotes the idea that our primary duty is to the community and others (Damgaard et al, 2022), a notion closely allied to altruism. Approaches informed by ethics of care are considered to weaken individualistic and consumerist impulses, putting communities at the centre of economic life as opposed to corporations and individuals (Grubby, 2019).

Prioritization and contextual specificity

There is an important emphasis within ethics of care on prioritization and identifying who is most affected by the consequences of our choices. In addition, the philosophy promotes the prioritization of individuals and groups according to their level of vulnerability. Within this approach, there is no scope for 'blanket policies', with responses and solutions instead situated in a deep and nuanced understanding of context.

Implicit within this philosophy is a focus on fairness or justice achieved through treating everyone differently in order to achieve greater equality. This manifests as an emphasis on understanding the needs of and caring for those most affected and also most in need. The language of opportunity and thriving is not explicit within ethics of care and is also very different to that of justice, focusing on relationships and community as opposed to individuals and rights. Damgaard et al (2022) find that the language of care, relationships and community better reflect people's ethical feelings about low carbon transitions than the language of justice and individual rights. Ethics of care is also distinct from generosity in the sense that it assumes a routinized prioritization of, and care for, the most vulnerable, rather than potentially limited, isolated or periodic acts of generosity.

To start to understand how ethics of care might operate in the context of climate change and low carbon transitions, we return to the example of loss and damage. We do not draw on this example as a demonstration of ethics of care, but more as a means of illustrating how a caring transition would need to operate quite differently to a financial payment.

Calling once more on this example enables us to see how the virtues of justice, generosity and care might coexist and interact within one climate policy. Certainly, this policy can be seen as being motivated, at least in part, by ethics of care. This is apparent in the recognition, within the policy, of our global interconnectedness in the context of environmental damage and climate change, by prioritization (or at least greater recognition) of and attempts at safeguarding the most vulnerable at a global scale. It can also be interpreted as an attempt at promoting friendship through repairing or building better relationships between Global North and South. It will not, however, achieve the contextual sensitivity and lasting impact espoused by ethics of care if it relies on limited financial payments determined by the donor without consultation with the recipient nations on the form and amount of compensation. The likely financial limitations of the policy place it more in the realms of an act of generosity while the official discourse around it is one of improving fairness (justice).

Leaving no one behind or deciding who is brought along first

The emphasis within ethics of care on safeguarding may not perfectly complement the idea reflected in the title of this chapter – that transition can present an opportunity to promote thriving where currently there is struggle. However, as a guiding philosophy, it can make an important contribution to securing better outcomes for everyone by ensuring care for the most affected and vulnerable (where correctly identified) through its emphasis on prioritization. While the notion of leaving nobody behind has been widely espoused in connection with the concept of just transition, an ethics of care perspective reminds us that we need to consider who should be brought along first, otherwise we are left with the established convention that those who can pay benefit first.

An extensive review of existing evidence conducted by Sovacool (2021) identified 24 distinct groups as vulnerable in the context of climate mitigation, with non-human species, farmers, the rural poor, labourers, Indigenous communities and future generations receiving the greatest proportion of coverage within the literature and disabled people, victims of modern slavery, coastal homeowners, prostitutes, children, local businesses, refugees, alcoholics and suburban homeowners among those receiving the lowest proportion of coverage, despite their obvious vulnerability. This suggests that we have some understanding about who is most vulnerable in relation to low carbon transitions and who needs our care because their lives are being made more difficult or even ruined by the transition. We at least have some idea whose lives we should be aiming to turn around at this moment of great change. Although it is also clear that there are multiple blind spots, within the research community, regarding the plight of a wide range of other vulnerable groups who are, for whatever reason, being overlooked or inadequately considered.

Sovacool (2021) also highlights how, perhaps unexpectedly, some of those most vulnerable in the context of the transition are also those heavily embroiled in delivering the transition, for instance, those manufacturing technology for the transition (such as photovoltaic panels) and enduring slavery and poor health as a consequence, communities hosting wind farms, or those sacrificing food producing land for biofuel production. In essence, many of those whose work might be construed as care or sacrifice for the environment (whether by choice or not) are left uncared for by the transition that they are helping to facilitate.

Of course, our impression of who is most vulnerable will depend greatly on whose plight has been highlighted through research, journalism, or made an example of by politicians or other influential figures. The work of González-Pijuan et al (2023) provides an example of a highly vulnerable group (children) who are known to be disadvantaged by the status quo but are not being recognized or prioritized within transition policy that has the potential to improve their circumstances. She highlights ample existing evidence of the ways that children are impacted heavily, and in distinct ways, by unaffordable heating and poorly insulated homes (energy poverty), resulting in poor physical and mental health and reduced educational attainment, yet energy policies aimed at decarbonization and the resolution of energy poverty across Europe fail to recognize their needs, instead making broad and vague references to 'families'.

These examples highlight some of the difficulties in accurately identifying who is most vulnerable and in most need of safeguarding, as would be required by a transition guided by ethics of care. They also underline the need for the philosophy of ethics of care to extend to the research community, encouraging the prioritization of the most vulnerable, and careful consideration of whose plight is spotlighted through research and publication.

Care, justice and thriving

Prioritization and understanding who is most vulnerable is a fundamental principle of ethics of care and is also vital to the attainment of justice, in the sense that we cannot meaningfully pursue justice if we do not know who we are seeking it for. We therefore see complementarity between the concepts of care and justice. Moreover, care and greater responsiveness to differential needs can also be argued to provide a foundation for a better life and, in this sense, adopting ethics of care as a guiding principle in the context of low carbon transitions can be seen to transcend justice in its ability to promote thriving over merely surviving.

Conclusion

This chapter highlights an additional and fundamental level of complexity associated with responses to the climate crisis that has not previously been considered. In a world that appears to have widely subscribed to the notion of just transition, there seems little appetite for debate, which calls our focus on justice into question. Yet, it is our hope that this chapter has gone some way to demonstrating that virtues matter and that conscientious consideration of the virtues framing our approach to transition should not be sacrificed in the (necessary) haste to shift to a post-carbon society.

Virtues tend to operate on a subconscious level. It is, therefore, entirely possible that those designing low carbon transitions or other responses to the climate crisis are not even conscious of which virtues they are promoting or channelling through their work. However, we argue that the virtues associated with low carbon transitions are important because they can produce very different sorts of policies and actions and impact the extent to which they are inclusive and avoid deepening existing or creating new inequalities and injustices.

To avoid a myopic focus on justice, it seems beneficial for transition policies to be informed by multiple perspectives and philosophies, opening up the possibility of promoting greater wellbeing and abundance through transition, especially for the victims of the high carbon world. In this sense, we conclude that there is complementarity and interdependency between the different perspectives explored here (justice, generosity, care) and value in using them in combination. In arguing for this, the chapter lends support to the argument put forward by Castro (2021) that generosity may sit at the start of an ethical chain reaction that leads to justice. Consideration of the principles of ethics of care within this context might feel like a complication too far, but introduces important new dimensions to the debate, reminding us to identify and prioritize those most in need in order to achieve justice. Combining notions of generosity or even altruism with ethics of care can help to negate some of the risks associated with donor-centrism (Gabriel, 2017), by instilling that the decision to act generously must be quickly followed by prioritization of beneficiaries, based on a detailed understanding of their needs, ensuring that the generosity is well placed.

We do not propose dispensing with the concept of a just transition in the context of low carbon transitions, but to see it as one of a number of key concepts that together might produce transition policies promoting the best possible outcomes for human and non-human stakeholders and effectively prioritizing the most vulnerable within the current high carbon world order and also within the future low carbon world order and at all stages in between.

This chapter also highlights how language matters. Commitments such as the EC's pledge to 'leave no-one behind' in the move away from fossil fuels (EC, 2019) may seem difficult to fault, yet such statements discourage consideration of who needs to be prioritized. As Damgaard et al (2022) allude to, the language we use in connection with transitions matters and will impact both the level of public support for transition policies and the extent of our ambitions for them. Discourse focused on justice leads us to strive to avoid making anyone's situation worse through transition and fighting for rights and recognition. The language of generosity conjures visions of benevolence, magnanimity and grand gestures, while the language of care feels supportive, nurturing and reciprocal. As the crisis grows deeper and more urgent, there has never been a greater need to strike a more aspirational tone and in doing so to raise our ambitions and expectations around what the transition should do for us and our non-human counterparts. In this context, the language of generosity and care feels like a vital addition to the discourse.

References

Allen, S. (2018) *The Science of Generosity*, White Paper prepared for the John Templeton Foundation, Berkeley: Greater Good Science Center at University of California, Berkeley.

Aristotle (1908) *Nicomachean Ethics*. Available from: http://classics.mit.edu/Aristotle/nicomachaen.4.iv.html [Accessed 6 January 2022].

Banerjee, A. and Schuitema, G. (2022) 'How just are just transition plans? Perceptions of decarbonisation and low-carbon energy transitions among peat workers in Ireland', *Energy Research & Social Science*, 88: 102616.

Castano-Garcia, A. (forthcoming) 'Transitions for zero carbon futures: from just to generous', *Futures*.

Castro, E. (2021) 'Hacia una ética de la generosidad', IV Encuentro de Filosofía Intercultura, 28 May, Instituto Hamalgama Métrica, Las Palmas de Gran Canaria, Canary Islands. Available from: https://www.youtube.com/watch?v=FjNwR1n1eSY [Accessed 28 May 2023].

D'Alisa, G., Demaria, F. and Kallis, G. (eds) (2014) *Degrowth: A Vocabulary for a New Era*, London: Routledge.

Damgaard, C.S., McCauley, D. and Reid, L. (2022) 'Towards energy care ethics: exploring ethical implications of relationality within energy systems in transition', *Energy Research & Social Science*, 84: 102356.

Di Chiro, G. (2016) 'Environmental justice', in Adamson, J., Gleason, W.A. and Pellow, D.N. (eds), *Keywords for Environmental Studies*, New York: New York University Press, pp 100–5.

EC (2019) 'A European Green Deal', *European Commission*. Available from: https://commission.europa.eu/strategy-and-policy/priorities-2019-2024/european-green-deal_en [Accessed 28 May 2023].

Gabriel, I. (2017) 'Effective altruism and its critics', *Journal of Applied Philosophy*, 34(4): 457–73.

González-Pijuan, I., Ambrose, A., Middlemiss, L., Tirado-Herrero, S. and Tatham, C. (2023) 'Empowering whose future? A European policy analysis of children in energy poverty', *Energy Research & Social Science*, 106: 103328.

Government of Canada (2019) 'Task force: just transition for Canadian coal power workers and communities', *Government of Canada*. Available from: https://www.canada.ca/en/environment-climate-change/services/climate-change/task-force-just-transition.html [Accessed 23 May 2023].

Grubby, E.C. (2019) 'Responsible generation: how care ethics can activate a just energy transition', Master's Thesis, Environmental Arts and Humanities, Corvallis: Oregon State University. Available from: https://ir.library.oregonstate.edu/concern/graduate_thesis_or_dissertations/w95055636 [Accessed 28 May 2023].

Huffington, A. (2014) *Thrive: The Third Metric to Redefining Success and Creating a Life of Well-Being, Wisdom, and Wonder*, New York: Harmony Books.

James, R., Otto, F., Parker, H., Boyd, E., Cornforth, R., Mitchell, D. et al (2014) 'Characterizing loss and damage from climate change', *Nature Climate Change*, 4(11): 938–9.

Lehtinen, A.A. (2009) 'The environmental justice movement in the USA', in Kitchin, R. and Thrift, N. (eds), *International Encyclopedia of Human Geography*, Amsterdam: Elsevier.

McCauley, D. and Heffron, R. (2018) 'Just transition: integrating climate, energy and environmental justice', *Energy Policy*, 119: 1–7.

Newell, P. and Mulvaney, D. (2013) 'The political economy of the "just transition"', *The Geographical Journal*, 179(2): 132–40.

Pinker, A. (2020) *Just Transitions: A Comparative Perspective*, Scottish Government. Available from: https://www.gov.scot/publications/transitions-comparative-perspective/ [Accessed 28 May 2023].

Scottish Government (2021) *Just Transition – A Fairer, Greener Scotland: A Scottish Government Response*, Scottish Government, 7 September. Available from: https://www.gov.scot/publications/transition-fairer-greener-scotland/ [Accessed 28 May 2023].

Singer, P. (2015) *The Most Good You Can Do*, New Haven: Yale University Press.

Sovacool, B.K. (2021) 'Who are the victims of low-carbon transitions? Towards a political ecology of climate change mitigation', *Energy Research & Social Science*, 73: 101916.

Trentmann, F. (2016) *Empire of Things: How We Became a World of Consumers, From the Fifteenth Century to the Twenty-First*, London: Penguin.

Ulgen, S. (2021) 'How deep is the north–south divide on climate negotiations', Carnegie Europe. Available from: https://carnegieeurope.eu/2021/10/06/how-deep-is-north-south-divide-on-climate-negotiations-pub-85493 [Accessed 26 October 2023].

UNFCCC (2020) *Just Transition of the Workforce, and the Creation of Decent Work and Quality Jobs*, United Nations Framework Convention on Climate Change. Available from: https://unfccc.int/sites/default/files/resource/Just%20transition.pdf [Accessed 7 October 2022].

Volcovico, V. (2022) 'Denmark becomes first to offer "loss and damage" climate funding', *Reuters*, 21 September. Available from: https://www.reuters.com/world/denmark-becomes-first-offer-loss-damage-climate-funding-2022-09-20/ [Accessed 28 May 2023].

6

Housing Narratives for Post-Carbon Inclusive Societies

Ralph Horne, Anitra Nelson and Louise Dorignon

Current dominant models of housing in homeowner societies, such as in Western Europe, North America and Australia, are not by and large producing post-carbon inclusive housing that is affordable, accessible and regenerative, and free of fossil fuels in their production and operation (see Chapter 1). Instead, what is unfolding is a growing crisis of climate change, energy poverty and housing affordability. The climate emergency and COVID-19 have brought fresh urgency to both housing and home as building blocks of societies, raising questions about decarbonizing housing and the suitability of a variable housing stock inhabited by diverse and disconnected households.

The current housing stock in predominantly homeowning societies is ageing and in need of renovation and retrofit, largely comprising suburban lower density detached dwellings, with isolated pockets of mid-20th-century modernist high-rise public housing and, in larger cities, post-millennium high-rise apartment blocks produced in the financialization boom. Land is at a premium, just as people are under relentless pressure to relocate to city regions for employment and services. The mass of lower density suburbia presents millions of privately owned parcels in a splintered urban landscape resistant to accommodating new demand by densification squeezing in more people and dwellings. Greenbelts and peripheral regional areas are targeted to satisfy this demand. Too often, the result is dormitory settlements, supporting working people who have long commutes and limited local infrastructure. Improving mobility infrastructure is inevitably complicated by private land ownership arrangements from within suburbs through to the central city. Where mobility upgrades are achieved, the stock becomes unaffordable as pent-up demand ensures that such housing is snapped up by wealthier homeowners, and rents spiral upwards around transport hubs. Thus, the seemingly eternal housing affordability crisis is a perennial feature of policy agendas, all set within a 'gathering storm' of climate change.

In this chapter we argue that realizing post-carbon inclusive housing in many such cities and societies will require overcoming the problems of inequality and unsustainability associated with homeownership-based systems and emerging systems of financialized housing. These systems are characterized by an urgent need to advance affordability, decommodification and democratization (Kadi et al, 2021). We assess prospects for the proliferation of inclusive housing in the post-carbon era. This is not only a technical matter of fiscal settings and policy change. It is also a matter of confronting the idea that owner-occupied housing is the only or best option, and that a growth model of economic development is the route to achieving this. It involves debunking widely touted assumptions that any alternative is impossible, delusional, naïve or idealistic. As Davoudi (2022: xvii) puts it: 'These taken-for-granted assumptions, dressed up as realities, have colonized our social imaginaries to the extent that it is easier to imagine the end of the world than to contemplate the end of capitalism and neoliberalism.'

Hence, the aim of this chapter is to form a bridge between contemporary mainstream narratives of housing and radical analyses of a prefigurative nature. We start by outlining the central problems of housing inclusion, inequality and decarbonization in the context of the development of Western homeowner-based housing systems. We reflect on housing studies as a diverse field, connecting normative ideas of housing as a three-part social construct: a commodity-cum-asset (homeownership, housing markets, investments and capital accumulation); housing with use values offering spaces (shelter), services and comforts (such as climate control and locational convenience); and housing as 'home' where affective dimensions of dwellings connect to subjective meanings, emotions, memory and ontological security. Housing studies itself spans a range of epistemologies and different narratives drawn from physical sciences, social sciences and humanities (Horne, 2018).

Mata et al (2020) argue that reductions in carbon and energy demand associated with changing practices have greater potential than current techno-behavioural options. Engaging with broader socio-material structures, political economy, institutional alignments, and emerging practices, discourses and understandings of housing and energy justice is critical in advancing post-carbon housing inclusion. We acknowledge the development of distinct narratives that relate to environmental sustainability, inclusion and governance at household, neighbourhood or urban scales. In so doing we build on the work of Weber (2016) and of Brill and Durrant (2021), who show how discourse and narratives are shaped by, and then reshape, the limits of decisions and possibilities in the housing system.

We present examples to illustrate prospects for more just and sustainable housing models to supersede existing housing obduracies and incumbencies. We view illustrative cases as a prelude to speculating on prospects for more just and sustainable housing forms and models to establish post-carbon inclusion.

Origins of westernized housing

Prior to the industrial revolution, the housing systems in Western Europe were mainly functional (Vance, 1971). Two of the aforementioned three social values of housing were evident, namely the utility of shelter and connection to place as home. Generally, as industrialization proceeded, the most desirable new zones were on the urban periphery, while worn-out areas and housing were passed down successively to those on lower incomes. The focus for fledgling speculative housebuilders was outer suburban, better-off areas. This led to a shortage of housing and a sharp drop in quality of life for working-class urban dwellers. This early 19th-century period saw reinforcing processes of speculative housebuilding and private landlording alongside an expansion of broader loans and credit to drive housing consumption.

As Ball (1981) explains, in the United Kingdom (UK) this led to an inefficient building industry with the working class paying the price. Meanwhile, settler societies with their 'Wild West' and individualized pasts embraced and extended homeownership ideals and aspirations, connecting the idea of commandeering land parcels through invasive land-owning histories. The UK, United States (US) and Australia were at the vanguard of driving homeownership through a range of tax incentives for the construction industry and homeowners.

Eventually, the housing situation deteriorated to the point where governments stepped in, in other ways. In the early- to mid-20th century, as two world wars centred on Europe, large national projects of slum clearance and reconstruction heralded a relatively short-lived era of a state-supervised filling of market gaps. Housing market regulation and non-market provision of public housing led to some decommodification. However, this was short-lived. Homeowner incentives continued to grow and were reinforced, widening the gap between homeowners and renters. By the 1970s, housing construction had become a key driver of economies, providing the conditions for a major shift in housing commodification.

Transition 1: From housing and home to financial asset

Deregulation through the 1980s, alongside offloading the vestiges of public housing stock, added fuel to the flames of financialized housing systems. North America and Australia exemplified the consequences of financialization with housing as a commodity-cum-asset coming to dominate social value. These entrenched private property regimes are characterized by the most excessive, oversized, carbon-emitting housing alongside unequal access in the western world. Genuine crises typify these regimes – house prices keep rising in the long term despite cycles of bust and boom in the real-estate market. These challenges are central both to increasing inequities and to prohibiting householders from making rational sustainability changes to their housing and households.

The post-millennium high-rise boom in many Western cities became far detached from ideas of housing as home or even utility as real estate became a central place for dumping international capital. By 2008, the global financial crisis demonstrated the central importance of housing in western financial systems (Guironnet et al, 2016). Now, the cart leads the horse as much housing is determined by financial markets and, despite the global financial crisis, there is little evidence that widespread definancialization of housing is in sight (Aalbers, 2017). Indeed, some have observed the 'planned' abandonment of urban neighbourhoods, through deliberate immobilism of areas of housing by private homeowners while municipal services remain powerless (Nussbaum, 2015).

Although the idea of housing as a tradeable asset is relatively new, it took around a couple of centuries to produce these arrangements. During this transition, the collective imaginary of housing shifted from one of utility, place, memory and belonging, to one of financial risk, competition and speculation. As the house became a citizen's location of their financial security, land occupied by housing became a gold-standard traded asset; a commodity that dwarfs others, commands the attention of governments, investors, usury businesses and, of course, all the intermediaries of property.

Today, people often obtain loans to purchase properties that are in the wrong configuration and location for their housing and sustainability needs. In fear of missing out on price speculation, they either live in substandard arrangements or they rent out their home and rent their actual abode in a place and configuration that works for them. In Australia, investments in housing are made all the more 'lucrative' by negative gearing, a form of financial leverage that provides generous tax breaks on mortgage costs of rented housing. This enables 'mum and dad' owners of rented out properties to participate in the housing market from a position of strength over those who do not have negative gearing benefits. Negative gearing is an inequitable arrangement that deprives certain people of the chance at homeownership and makes housing more unaffordable (Blunden, 2016), driving open the gap between 'haves' and 'have nots'. A financialization logic frames these tax breaks as investments that drive housing supply and, thereby, place downward pressure on rents (Pawson, 2018). The fact that such 'trickle down' economics singularly fail to materialize is somewhat muted in this narrative. In his analysis of the role of think tanks on housing policy in England, Foye (2022) points out how the dominance of a selective causal narrative and policy agenda can be attributed to the influence of capital interests behind these organizations.

Contemporary narratives of low carbon housing and inclusion

Housing seen as a series of use values for its occupants is now relegated to a secondary consideration. The hegemony of financialization in housing dictates that land price speculation trumps all other considerations, including property condition, preparedness for climate change, decarbonization and, of course, inclusion and access based upon need or human rights. The global model of a bourgeois home is described primarily in financial terms, rather than for utilitarian purposes, while affect and connection are left dangling. Home as a place with accumulated memories, meanings, emotions and the possibility of ontological security presents as outdated, naïve and frivolous compared to the serious business of securing an accumulative asset. Home is thus reframed and compounded with ideas of lifestyles, housing arrangements and investments that are transient, hypermobile and 'flexible' (Grisdale, 2021.

How has this heavy influence of financialization shaped studies and understandings of low carbon housing and inclusion? The seminal call from Jim Kemeny (1992) for housing research to engage with social theory has arguably led to more critical housing scholarship, yet Clapham (2017: 163) observes a 'growing schism between researchers who focus on policy relevancy and those that pursue more theoretical work'. In these circumstances, narratives – stories that offer simplified, accessible and believable accounts of processes and change (Herman, 2009) – have become tools for particular actors to advance particular outcomes (Crawford and Flint, 2015). Social constructivist approaches provide a means to reveal such narratives, as in the case of rental housing policy change (Bierre and Howden-Chapman, 2020).

Through discourse analysis, Heslop and Ormerod (2019) show how UK narratives of the housing crisis are shaped to emphasize supply constraints due to over-regulation, by actors whose interests lie in the removal of such regulation. When housing supply is hastened by deregulation, this crisis worsens, as it actually resides in deregulation and raises inequality. They note how such dominant narratives can shift over time and, in particular moments, such as following the Grenfell Tower inquiry, which examined the circumstances surrounding the 2017 fire at Grenfell Tower in London.

Certain narratives present urban renewal as a way to tackle housing shortages through releasing seemingly underutilized land (Gurran and Ruming, 2016). Such projects are founded in financialized structures,

Table 6.1: Underlying narratives of low carbon housing and inclusion

	Inclusion	Low carbon
Housing	Supply constraints, regulation, homeownership	Behaviour, homeownership, automation, consumption
Urban scale	Urban renewal, land supply	Smart, walkable, private vehicles

necessitating a slice of the action for developers in social housing (Byrne and Norris, 2019). In this narrative, somehow it seems reasonable to tackle urban poverty and underfunded social housing through large financial transfers from the public purse to the private sector, given that some of it will go into affordable housing.

Selzer and Lanzendorf (2019) show how low carbon narratives for urban mobility are optimistic regarding a shift towards sustainability while being shaped by norms around car ownership and private transport. Similarly, the low carbon housing narrative is shaped by optimistic assumptions about home automation, ownership and capabilities, just as environmental sustainability narratives intersect with routines and aspirations in low carbon retrofit. Ultimately, many assumptions about consumption remain largely intact through this process (Maller et al, 2012).

Contemporary narratives of low carbon housing and inclusion are thus dualistic, contradictory and contested, with superficial discourses of energy efficiency and affordability, and more muted but highly pervasive underlying narratives that reinforce dominant logics of ownership, supply and demand, and consumption (Table 6.1). These underlying narratives constitute key logics and assumptions that allow the status quo to perpetuate financialized housing and, thus, perpetuate unaffordability and delays in tackling climate change impacts in inclusive ways.

Emerging cross-cutting narratives of low carbon and inclusive housing

As Table 6.1 shows, there are (at least) four distinct underlying narratives that reproduce housing financialization across housing and urban scales in the direction of inclusion and/or low carbon. However, as these housing financialization narratives are increasingly challenged, they adapt, giving rise to the emergence of cross-cutting narratives, or the 'multiple logics' combination (Wainwright and Demirel, 2023). Hitherto separate narratives about affordable housing crises are, thus, increasingly engaging with low carbon agendas, and vice versa. Similarly, narratives about urban inequalities and development are increasingly engaging with urban scale, low carbon narratives. We explore both the emerging logics of cross-cutting narratives and some challenges and opportunities for the emergence of low carbon inclusion in the following sections.

Housing inclusion meets low carbon

The unaffordability 'crisis' dominates Australian housing inclusion debates, focusing on households in the lowest two quintiles of income who spend over 30 per cent of their income on housing (Gabriel et al, 2005). However, rather than a bounded crisis, since the 1970s there has been a continuously worsening situation tied to financialization processes – pre-dating both the global financial crisis (Beer et al, 2007) and the COVID-19 pandemic (Wetzstein, 2017). Perversely, the term 'crisis' has been a handy means to justify providing more land to be released into the housing market, which fuels the flames of housing unaffordability arising from financialization (Cook and Ruming, 2021; O'Callaghan and McGuirk, 2021).

This crisis logic has permeated debates on supply, intersectionality and disadvantage, directing social housing policy makers and landlords – presiding over a diminishing public housing stock and unregulated private rental market – towards the prospect of more supply by any means possible. Social housing remedies are invariably presented as urban renewal projects (Troy, 2017) involving mixed ownership, including shared equity and right-to-buy. In other words, the idea of crisis allows for the default homeownership narrative to dominate, and the perpetuation of petty landlordism and hoarding of stock. It dangles the illusion of allowing more people to enter a property-owning middle class, but inevitably results in increasing financialization and inequality, and 'accumulation by dispossession' (Cooper et al, 2020).

These debates have taken place largely separate from those about retrofit and decarbonization. However, a cross-cutting narrative is now advancing where stock replacement projects are projected as a solution to the poor condition of both social and private rental stock in terms of energy efficiency and climate proofing. Just as housing advocates point out the compounding effects of spiralling energy bills and poor design on housing affordability, the 'solution' presented involves extending financialization, under the guise of providing new, energy efficient stock to replace old inefficient stock.

Urban inclusion meets low carbon

The dubious promise of urban renewal comes with the formidable social price tag of removing people from their homes, land clearing, significant greenhouse gas emissions, and if 'successful', accelerating gentrification and spatial segmentation. The low carbon narrative was largely absent from such debates until it became another rationale for urban renewal, a way to meet carbon commitments via financialization in the form of energy-efficient new urban renewal, aka 'low carbon gentrification' (Bouzarovski et al, 2018). This is a growing feature of the more recent housing financialization vehicle build-to-rent (BTR). Thus, BTR has been carefully positioned through discourse and narratives (Brill and Durrant, 2021) as a new way to meet housing needs with a façade of homeownership, substituting a speculative developer with an institutional landlord and adding green credentials into this novel, rentier model, 'Financialization 2.0' (Wijburg et al, 2018).

This additional element is superficially logical. Long-term institutional landlords have some incentive to invest in durable, sustainable design for their buildings as they intend them to last so that they can extract rent for an extended period. Put another way, their longer tenure means more exposure to operating carbon emissions. This contrasts with the obvious split incentives of build-to-sell models, playing a role in opening up space for BTR as a new asset class facilitating new financial vehicles within housing and real estate. It opens calls for investigation into how building specification and design are undertaken on such projects, and the prospects for aligning interests on advancing low carbon design and operation (Nethercote, 2020).

In their optimistic account of BTR, Abidoye et al (2022) propose that 32 factors determine their implementation, dominated by regulatory settings, alignment of interests around planning affordances, incentives for investors, and industry capacity and positioning. Carbon targets enter as a factor in municipal and state buy-in, enabling the manufacturing of consent. Strategies of market making and the technical, political and discursive knowledge required both point to key roles of intermediaries in integrating decarbononization narratives, planning, capacity, and finance with BTR to forge a new frontier of financialization (Brill and Durrant, 2021; Goulding et al, 2023; Nethercote, 2023).

Consequently, we caution against simply welcoming the intersection of urban inclusion and low carbon narratives. Rather, this has provided renewed opportunities for rent extraction. Notably, large-scale social housing retrofits involve less loss of embodied carbon, and better outcomes for residents in situ. This intersection holds the possibility of a post-carbon inclusive outcome largely free of financialization (Chatterton, 2013). Perhaps unsurprisingly, large scale social housing retrofit is widely considered complex, expensive and barely worthwhile; it does not easily incorporate private housing provision and, therefore, runs counter to capitalist production processes (Hodson et al, 2016) and their underlying narrative.

Low carbon housing meets inclusion

In the upper right-hand quadrant of Table 6.1, we find sustainability advocates, regulations, policy frames and businesses focused on low carbon housing – primarily for owner-occupier housing. Here, political economy discourse is notably muted (Knuth, 2019). Imaginaries have aware consumers choosing smart energy, digital and automatic systems within dwellings ideally produced through high-tech factory-prefab construction using 'biophilic' materials. The cutting-edge jargon escalates from 'energy efficient' and 'sustainable' to 'low carbon', 'bill-neutral', net-zero or positive-energy – increasingly centred on automation and management devices that predict or detect people and demand, configurable and increasingly harnessing algorithms, using technologies of artificial intelligence. These techno-futures for low carbon housing are constructed by the same logics that seek to drive up demand by raising standards of comfort, cleanliness, convenience and security – automating and controlling spaces and bodies, such as outdoor heaters in winter, coolers in summer, windows and blinds, switches and lighting, nutrition and health devices.

This low carbon construction and retrofit narrative, largely separate from housing inclusion milieu, lacks critical scholarship on financialization (Maalsen, 2023). Thus, ecological modernization logics abound with environmental goods monetized and internalized through taxes and carbon markets, and receipts used to fund rebates and fresh innovation into low carbon alternatives. As indicated in Chapter 12, such approaches have succeeded in delivering domestic photovoltaic (PV) systems almost exclusively among households fortunate enough to participate in such schemes, while increasing the price of electricity for those already in energy poverty and least able to pay.

In the realm of ultra-engineered timber, prefabrication, indoor environments loaded with controls and design innovations, charging points in the garage, and a battery and heat pump, there is little space for the diversity and individuality of ordinary homemaking. In this housing-centred low carbon imaginary, ideas of home – emotional ties to place – are relegated to secondary, domestic considerations, behind rationalities about paybacks, efficiencies and return on investment in green technologies.

For low carbon narratives to deliver inclusive housing, new skills and technologies emerging around low carbon housing would need to be centred within social housing organizations and institutions. Even where tenants would benefit from lower bills and better health outcomes of low carbon homes, often the funding settings and prioritization processes for social housing provision prevent these being realized (Baker et al, 2023). Once again, we observe that, while this intersection holds the possibility of a post-carbon inclusive outcome largely outside of financialization, it is placed silently in the too hard basket.

Urban low carbon meets inclusion

In the lower right-hand quadrant of Table 6.1, we see the green-tech behavioural logics of low carbon housing extended to the urban scale through walkability, micro-grids and green urban design. Again, a significant reliance on hopeful applications of 'smart' technology to make life more efficient, this time in locational terms, through automated mobility systems and shared infrastructure such as micro-grids. As with the individual home scale, a utilitarian primacy is given to ideas of choice, efficiency, convenience and comfort. The market is a given, embraced as an enabler, with little space for considering who and what capabilities are enabled, and whose are comparatively or decisively disabled and excluded.

This techno-green narrative is not the only imaginary in the low carbon housing and communities segments. There is also an eco-niche oriented more towards co-housing, eco-communities and self-reliance. Here, DIY or community-driven DIO (do-it-ourselves) projects use materials and designs with low embodied energy construction, coupled with PV solar connected to hot water. Off-grid systems present as low impact, low consumption housing options for committed and intentional 'green' housing communities or households, with more-or-less intents to limit or exclude the market and financialization from the model. This eco-niche is notably different from the techno-green narrative in as much as certain models eschew homeownership deliberately in an attempt to avoid land speculation (detailed later in this chapter).

In this context, we turn to four demonstrative cases to form a bridge between, on one hand, contemporary mainstream narratives of (a) low carbon and (b) inclusive housing and urbanism and, on the other hand, radical analyses of a prefigurative nature, where efforts to overcome land price speculation and financialization are more overt. We view such cases as a prelude to speculating on prospects for more just and sustainable housing forms and models to establish post-carbon inclusion.

Demonstrative cases of mainstream low carbon, inclusive housing experiments

BedZED

Constructed in 2002, BedZED (Beddington Zero Energy Development) is a widely publicized green housing development whose aim is to use energy only from renewable sources generated on site. It has attracted many visitors and considerable attention from built environment professionals (Oktay, 2022), informing both subsequent social housing and the UK government's introduction of the 2016 carbon target.

The development includes 82 houses, 17 apartments, office spaces, a college and community facilities. The project emerged from a collaboration between architect Bill Dunster, BioRegional Development Group and Peabody Trust (a social landlord). The London Borough of Sutton provided brownfield land at a reduced price. Bespoke technologies include a central woodchip heat/power plant, shared electric cars and PV panels attached to the conservatories of every unit (Dunster, 2013). Designs highlight common greenspace, insulation, airtightness, ventilation (using the distinctive rooftop wind cowls) and passive solar heating (Oktay, 2022). The project promoted sustainable transport, and construction materials were sourced locally, including reclaimed timber to reduce the embodied carbon footprint (Tang et al, 2011).

However, the planned ecological footprint of residents has not been realized due mainly to some technologies not working, the low occupancy rate (2.2 per dwelling), and resident practices of shopping, working and socializing in a carbon-intensive city. Nevertheless, a new ambition was developed, to become a leader in the field through inclusive governance of low carbon projects, the One Planet Framework, and an accreditation procedure, which has subsequently become 'an international brand' (Williams, 2017: 199). Negotiating a range of housing market conditions around the world, Williams concludes that 'the translation of socio-technical systems to new spatial contexts is a highly fluid process' (2017: 202), and that multiple pathways and influences are at play where BedZED-like projects are enacted.

Half the BedZED apartments are split between social rental housing and shared equity, in an effort to cater for lower income households. This further entrenches homeownership as the ideal. Far from detaching the model from the market, housing unaffordability and gentrification, it provides new access for financialization. Indeed, the development is well-liked by residents apparently. It has promoted a heightened sense of place compared to the nearby neighbourhood of Hackbridge (Oktay, 2022). Thus, 20 years after its establishment as 'the UK's first major zero-carbon community', its founders celebrate a dubious achievement, namely that it has 'continued above-market sale prices' (Bioregional, 2023).

Nightingale (Baugruppen)

Nightingale developments in Melbourne (Australia) draw upon the German Baugruppen model. Criticized there for unintentionally reinforcing some housing inequalities while addressing others (Hamiduddin and Gallent, 2015), the Nightingale model advocates a means to provide medium density 'sustainable' development that avoids the excesses of speculative market-based housing.

Referred to as 'deliberative developments' to differentiate them from speculative and intentional community developments, the Nightingale model incorporates communal design aspects, such as shared laundries and gathering spaces, that also aim to economize by reducing necessary private spaces and cut carbon emissions as a result. Novel in reducing car parking, and designed to be more energy efficient than building code requirements, they lead developer best practice. Nightingale apartment living attracts an enlightened clientele seeking association with such practices. Design criteria encouraging communal practices include a 40-apartment limit per development, and up-front negotiation of expectations to participate in committees, regular communal dinners and activities designed to promote cohesion.

A core idea is for architects to partner in their development and act as developers on behalf of future residents, who purchase lots prior to construction, arguably reducing capital costs and cutting out the developer's profit (Sharam, 2020). Attempting to deter investors and encourage community, covenants are placed in dwelling contracts to restrict resale prices to an indexed amount based on median prices locally, and to prioritize buyers already accepted on the waiting list. Nightingale has also developed smaller apartments to appear more accessible to all-comers. However, as gentrification impacts multiply within local areas – arguably partly due to the attractive Nightingale model – their covenants do not escape heightening, exclusionary prices. Moreover, the covenant system has not been rigorously tested through legal challenge. Tying resale prices to median rates does not detach Nightingale housing from the market, although it is likely to deter those who are purely investors otherwise attracted to what remains (in 2023) to be a popular model.

Households purchase into the model within a market context, making an agreement with the developer – distinct from community-driven co-housing with processes for community formation and formal entry and exit. Nightingale-like models are unlikely to represent a diverse community or eschew gentrification pressures. Indeed, with specific demographic, class and cliques, the idea of creating community this way can be readily critiqued – just as developers have been critiqued for master-planning new estates as if they were co-developing communities in green outer suburbs.

The Nightingale entity has recently transitioned from a social enterprise to a not-for-profit, ostensibly due to the lack of ability to scale the original model. Now, the model is to partner with institutional landowners, often faith-based organizations, to develop buildings with an agreed portion of affordable housing managed by the provider. As yet, in mid-2023, Nightingale has no social housing provision nor low-income affordances, and its covenant scheme, ultimately, does not remove housing from the market, consequently becoming part of the 'problem' of housing unaffordability, albeit with a green and stylish hue.

Degrowth housing models

In contrast to tweaking mainstream commercial housing models, many degrowth (or postgrowth) housing models challenge private ownership, consciously withdraw housing from the conventional market, and practice post-carbon living. Typically, residents take up less dwelling space per capita and live in more tightly knit self-governing but outward-looking communities. Here, we simply point to key features in three existing models and refer readers to more detailed studies of the same.

Nelson and Chatterton (2022) identify two postgrowth examples, first a mutual home ownership financial model of just 20 households in a cooperative eco-cohousing project in West Leeds (UK), the Lilac (low impact living affordable community). Residents purchase a mutual share capped in value, specifically to ensure affordability to all potential members of their cooperative society. Self-governance and reciprocity are at the core of the model, every resident leasing their homes via a member charge of one-third of their net income. The members thus increase their equity which, however, is linked to average UK wages rather than average UK house prices, effectively decoupling the cost of their housing from the market (Chatterton, 2015). Although they have private dwellings designed for environmental sustainability, they economize on cars, and share common facilities, spaces and activities.

Second, is the Zürich (Switzerland) model of radical 'young housing cooperatives', such as Kraftwerk 1 and Kalbreite (see Chapter 13). Lilac developed against the odds in a disabling regulatory and financial environment, whereas these Zürich cooperatives developed out of an enabling environment due to the city's unique century-long history of facilitating housing cooperatives. Indeed, a target of around one-third of Zürich's apartments (set by a 2011 referendum) belong to housing cooperatives. Radical young housing cooperatives stretch the conventional model – integrating low carbon building and design features, and simple living cultures directed at minimizing dwellers' ecological footprints. They aspire to a footprint commensurate with 10 billion humans living within planetary limits and satisfying all their basic needs.

Both cases demonstrate mutualism and practices pointing to commoning to support mundane ecological practices and enhance inclusion. Zürich apartment housing cooperatives must be able to prove to the city authorities that they reflect the diversity of the city's demographic, including non-Swiss and so on. Cooperative members co-own their land and buildings through shares offering permanent, full and equitable rights, in effect securing affordable rental tenancies, alongside co-governing their cooperatives in transparent and responsible ways. They include social housing tenants. Given the scale and diverse internal plans of apartments, households can readily shift housing as their compositions and needs change over time.

Another degrowth model is the apartment-house syndicate Mietshäuser Syndikat (Hurlin, 2018; Apartment Buildings Syndicate, 2023). Mietshäuser Syndikat is an umbrella association embracing, in mid-2023, some 200 autonomous self-organizing housing projects, each independently owned as a limited liability company (GmbH, in German). Recognizing that starting up these projects is often 'an economic high-wire act', new projects are advised and supported by established ones (Apartment Buildings Syndicate, 2023). The Syndikat's aim has been to support self-organized housing projects and their wider political acceptance as creating decent shelter for all. Members engage in urban planning and housing forums and debates in support of decent just housing.

A general meeting of the Syndikat decides (or not) to purchase an interest in each specific house as a GmbH. Among key conditions, the household must be self-organizing; the association has a right to purchase any property rather then it re-entering the market; a solidary contribution is made with the promise of free sharing of knowledge and practical support of like projects. Each housing project initially benefits from, and then pays back, such support from purchase through to paying off loans, to housing repair and operations, all with a view to eco-sustainability and affordability. The association benefits from diverse projects existing in various stages. General meetings allow for sharing information, mutual support, workshops and general intercourse between members. The approach to all relations, processes and communication is 'open-minded, non-hierarchical, and respectful', with due diligence paid to conflict resolution (Apartment Buildings Syndicate, 2023).

These three examples of degrowth housing illustrate transparently political and collective DIO approaches, models that support post-carbon inclusion through their practical attention to affordability and access, diversity, sharing and commoning.

Transition 2: Realizing narratives of post-carbon inclusive housing

Post-carbon inclusive housing can progress significantly through increased engagement with critical social theory (Kemeny, 1992). It is not going to emanate from ramping up the 'eco-housing' market through business as usual means, however superficially exciting is the promise. Equally, social and inclusive housing narratives can benefit from a more embedded engagement with critical socio-structural studies of decarbonization.

Following Weber (2016), out-of-date discourses and narratives are critical in allowing financialization to flourish, intensifying housing as a commodity, and diminishing it as a health-giving shelter, and as an affective place of emotional and ontological security. In the modern, low carbon house or suburb, the focus is on the wallet rather than the hearth. This diminishment matters; it reduces opportunities to connect with inclusion and post-carbon through ideas of justice, rights and meaning. As Mike Berry (2023: 221) puts it: 'The house appears as a commodity, a material artefact supporting multiple potential use values, produced at arms-length by strangers for strangers. The social link between people, producers and consumers is broken and hidden (fetishized in Marx's words) in the commodity form.' Thus, *unhoming* is a central feature of commoditized property (Nethercote, 2022).

The dominant model to provide new social housing involves displacement of residents, with long-standing community-oriented ties to place, from older units in renewal projects. Rebuilt developments allow for land price speculation. Significant elements of policy purportedly advancing housing inclusion seek to extend this financialized space further through homeownership via shared equity schemes, homebuyer grants and discounts on capital costs. Reasserting utility and home as central tenets of housing favour in-situ retrofit, ageing in place, retaining community and connection, and minimizing the traumatic impacts that financialized models impose. For post-carbon housing to be inclusive it must be protected from land price speculation. The influence of underlying narratives (Table 6.1) means that demonstrably scalable models cannot avoid land price speculation and green gentrification. Yet degrowth models offer ways forward that can be replicated across cultures.

Promising paths towards post-carbon inclusive housing policy start with:

- resolutely removing land and property from the market;
- guaranteeing affective dimensions of home; and
- demonstrating and propagating narratives of post-carbon inclusive housing that minimize the ravaging effects of financialization.

Places to start include cooperative and intentional degrowth housing. Many challenges lie in this path, including providing resources to navigate planning and regulatory processes that cater to speculative developers. However, the stakes are high. Places that fail to scale up new models that reflect post-carbon inclusion are increasingly prone to carbon conflicts, social conflicts and economic collapse through spiralling energy and living costs. Taking the primacy of detachment from financialization (growth) within a degrowth imaginary, Savini (2023) explores struggles in securing and maintaining autonomy in collective, affordable and decommodified housing, through a case study of the Nieuwe Meent housing commoning project in Amsterdam. Other research seeks aggregate datasets through which to measure housing degrowth, being 'a reduction of the total resources going into housing production and use, without an increase in inequality or a loss of wellbeing' (Tunstall, 2023, after Kallis et al, 2018).

Without these paths, housing – however decarbonized it might be – is doomed to a role as a fetishized, objectified means for dispossession through gentrification, accumulation and competition, creating an increasingly oppositional underclass with nothing to gain from decarbonization. The key challenge lies in shifting the Overton window that delineates the fiscally shaped institution of homeownership at the core of western society. The prospect of decommodification means turning the unthinkable radical into mainstream – a prerequisite to addressing the centrality of land, affect, inclusion and utility within the inequality/wellbeing rubric. There is a role here for practical stories of how decommoditized housing and home imaginaries can take up a replenished role as conduits for inclusion and post-carbon action. Sharing goods, services, facilities and space provides conduits to drawing down consumption, spreading ingenuity, new social meanings and practices of reciprocity. Homemaking, in contrast to property speculation, is a socially co-dependent process. It allows for narratives where housing becomes a site of production as well as consumption, where place matters, rather than 'location, location, location'.

References

Aalbers, M.B. (2017) 'The variegated financialization of housing', *International Journal of Urban and Regional Research*, 41(4): 542–54.

Abidoye, R., Ayub, B. and Ullah, F. (2022) 'Systematic literature review to identify the critical success factors of the build-to-rent housing model', *Buildings*, 12(2): 171. DOI: 10.3390/buildings12020171

Apartment Buildings Syndicate (2023) *Mietshäuser Syndikat* [English version]. Available from: https://www.syndikat.org/en/ [Accessed 26 May 2023].

Baker, E., Moore, T., Daniel, L., Caines, R., Padilla, H. and Lester, L. (2023) 'Sustainable social housing retrofit? Circular economy and tenant trade-offs', *AHURI Final Report, 397*, 4 May. Available from: https://www.ahuri.edu.au/research/final-reports/397 [Accessed 26 May 2023].

Ball, M. (1981) 'The development of capitalism in housing provision', *International Journal of Urban and Regional Research*, 5(2): 145–77.

Beer, A., Kearins, B. and Pieters, H. (2007) 'Housing affordability and planning in Australia: the challenge of policy under neo-liberalism', *Housing Studies*, 22(1): 11–24.

Berry, M. (2023) 'Concluding comments: the limits to capital', in Berry, M., *A Theory of Housing Provision under Capitalism: Marx, Engels, and Marxisms*, Cham: Palgrave Macmillan, pp 221–8.

Bierre, S. and Howden-Chapman, P. (2020) 'Telling stories: the role of narratives in rental housing policy change in New Zealand', *Housing Studies*, 35(1): 29–49.

Bioregional (2023) 'BedZED – the UK's first major sustainable community', *Bioregional*. Available from: https://www.bioregional.com/projects-and-services/case-studies/bedzed-the-uks-first-large-scale-eco-village [Accessed 18 May 2023].

Blunden, H. (2016) 'Discourses around negative gearing of investment properties in Australia', *Housing Studies*, 31(3): 340–57.

Bouzarovski, S., Frankowski, J. and Tirado Herrero, S. (2018) 'Low-carbon gentrification: when climate change encounters residential displacement', *International Journal of Urban and Regional Research*, 42(5): 845–63.

Brill, F. and Durrant, D. (2021) 'The emergence of a Build to Rent model: the role of narratives and discourses', *Environment and Planning A: Economy and Space*, 53(5): 1140–57.

Byrne, M. and Norris, M. (2019) 'Housing market financialization, neoliberalism and everyday retrenchment of social housing', *Environment and Planning A: Economy and Space*, 54(1): 182–98.

Chatterton, P. (2013) 'Towards an agenda for post-carbon cities: lessons from Lilac, the UK's first ecological, affordable cohousing community', *International Journal of Urban and Regional Research*, 37(5): 1654–74.

Chatterton, P. (2015) *Low Impact Living: A Field Guide to Ecological Affordable Community Building*, London: Routledge.

Clapham, D. (2017) 'Housing theory, housing research and housing policy', *Housing, Theory and Society*, 35(2): 163–77.

Cook, N. and Ruming, K. (2021) 'The financialisation of housing and the rise of the investor-activist', *Urban Studies*, 58(10): 2023–39.

Cooper, A.E., Hubbard, P. and Lees, L. (2020) 'Sold out? The Right-to-Buy, gentrification and working-class displacements in London', *The Sociological Review*, 68(6): 1354–69.

Crawford, J. and Flint, J. (2015) 'Rational fictions and imaginary systems: cynical ideology and the problem figuration and practise of public housing', *Housing Studies*, 30(5): 792–807.

Davoudi, S. (2022) 'Foreword: post-growth and the ontology of "not yet"', in Savini, F., Ferreira, A. and von Schönfeld, K.C. (eds), *Post-Growth Planning: Cities Beyond the Market Economy*, New York and Abingdon: Routledge, pp xvii–xx.

Dunster, B. (2013) 'BedZED community near London', in Voss, K., Musall, E. and O'Donovan, J.R. (eds), *Net Zero Energy Buildings: International Projects of Carbon Neutrality in Buildings*, Munich: Institut für Internationale Architektur-Dokumentation, pp 103–7.

Foye, C. (2022) 'Framing the housing crisis: how think-tanks frame politics and science to advance policy agendas', *Geoforum*, 34: 71–81.

Gabriel, M., Jacobs, K., Arthurson, K., Burke, T. and Yates, J. (2005) *Conceptualising and Measuring the Housing Affordability Problem: National Research Venture 3 – Housing Affordability for Lower Income Australians*, Research Paper No. 1, Melbourne: Australian Housing and Urban Research Institute.

Goulding, R., Leaver, A. and Silver, J. (2023) 'From homes to assets: transcalar territorial networks and the financialization of build to rent in Greater Manchester', *Environment and Planning A: Economy and Space*. DOI: 10.1177/0308518X221138104

Grisdale, S. (2021) 'Displacement by disruption: short-term rentals and the political economy of "belonging anywhere" in Toronto', *Urban Geography*, 42(5): 654–80.

Guironnet, A., Attuyer, K. and Halbert, L. (2016) 'Building cities on financial assets: the financialisation of property markets and its implications for city governments in the Paris city-region', *Urban Studies*, 53(7): 1442–64.

Gurran, N. and Ruming, K. (2016) 'Less planning, more development? Housing and urban reform discourses in Australia', *Journal of Economic Policy Reform*, 19(3): 262–80.

Hamiduddin, I. and Gallent, N. (2015) 'Self-build communities: the rationale and experiences of group-build (Baugruppen) housing development in Germany', *Housing Studies*, 31(4): 365–83.

Herman, D. (2009) *Basic Elements of Narrative*, Singapore: Wiley-Blackwell

Heslop, J. and Ormerod, E. (2019) 'The politics of crisis: deconstructing the dominant narratives of the housing crisis', *Antipode*, 52(1): 145–63.

Hodson, M., Burrai, E. and Barlow, C. (2016) 'Remaking the material fabric of the city: "alternative" low carbon spaces of transformation or continuity?', *Environmental Innovation and Societal Transitions*, 18: 128–46.

Horne, R.E. (2018) *Housing Sustainability in Low Carbon Cities*, London: Routledge.

Hurlin, L. (2018) 'Mietshäuser Syndikat: collective ownership, the "housing question" and degrowth', in Nelson, A. and Schneider, F. (eds) *Housing for Degrowth: Principles Models Challenges and Opportunities*, Abingdon: Routledge, pp 233–43.

Kadi, J., Vollmer, L. and Stein, S. (2021) 'Post-neoliberal housing policy? Disentangling recent reforms in New York, Berlin and Vienna', *European Urban and Regional Studies*, 28(4): 353–74.

Kallis, G., Kostakis, V., Lange, S., Muraca, B., Paulson, S. and Schmelzer, M. (2018) 'Research on degrowth', *Annual Review of Environment and Resources*, 43: 291–316.

Kemeny, J. (1992) *Housing and Social Theory*, London: Routledge

Knuth, S. (2019) 'Cities and planetary repair: the problem with climate retrofitting', *Environment and Planning A: Economy and Space*, 51(2): 487–504.

Maalsen, S. (2023) '"We're the cheap smart home": the actually existing smart home as rented and shared', *Social & Cultural Geography*, 24(8): 1383–402. DOI: 10.1080/14649365.2022.2065693

Maller, C., Horne, R. and Dalton, T. (2012) 'Green renovations: intersections of daily routines, housing aspirations and narratives of environmental sustainability', *Housing, Theory and Society*, 29(3): 255–75.

Mata, E., Korpal, A.K., Cheng, S.H., Jiménez Navarro, J.P., Filippidou, F., Reyna, J.L. and Wang, R. (2020) 'A map of roadmaps for zero and low energy and carbon buildings worldwide', *Environmental Research Letters*, 15: 113003.

Nelson, A. and Chatterton, P. (2022) 'Dwelling beyond growth: negotiating the state, mutualism and common', in Savini, F., Ferreira, A. and von Schönfeld, K.C. (eds), *Post-Growth Planning: Cities Beyond the Market Economy*, New York and Abingdon: Routledge, pp 49–62.

Nethercote, M. (2020) 'Build-to-Rent and the financialization of rental housing: future research directions', *Housing Studies*, 35(5): 839–74.

Nethercote, M. (2022) 'Racialized geographies of home: property, unhoming and other possible futures', *Progress in Human Geography*, 46(4): 935–59.

Nethercote, M. (2023) 'The techno-politics of rental housing financialization: real estate service companies and technocratic expertise in Australia's Build to Rent market', *Economic Geography*, 99(2): 191–219.

Nussbaum, F. (2015) 'Public inaction and private stasis: urban redevelopment's failure in Philadelphia', *Annales de Geographie*, 706(6): 603–26.

O'Callaghan, C. and McGuirk, P. (2021) 'Situating financialisation in the geographies of neoliberal housing restructuring: reflections from Ireland and Australia', *Environment and Planning A: Economy and Space*, 53(4): 809–27.

Oktay, D. (2022) 'Promoting energy-efficient neighbourhoods: learning from BedZED', in Sayigh, A. (ed), *Sustainable Energy Development and Innovation: Selected Papers from the World Renewable Energy Congress (WREC) 2020*, Berlin: Springer International Publishing, pp 841–7.

Pawson, I. (2018) 'Reframing Australia's housing affordability problem: the politics and economics of negative gearing', *Journal of Australian Political Economy*, 81: 121–43.

Savini, F. (2023) 'Maintaining autonomy: urban degrowth and the commoning of housing', *Urban Studies*, 60(7): 1231–48.

Selzer, S. and Lanzendorf, M. (2019) 'On the road to sustainable urban and transport development in the automobile society? Traced narratives of car-reduced neighborhoods', *Sustainability*, 11(16): 4375.

Sharam, A. (2020) 'Deliberative development: Australia's Baugruppen movement and the challenge of greater social inclusion', *Housing Studies*, 35(1): 107–22.

Tang, H., Hu, Q.G., Xu, Y.Y. and Yang, Y.H. (2011) 'Reuse of reclaimed materials in construction – from the process analysis of BedZED', *Applied Mechanics and Materials*, 99–100: 433–9.

Troy, L. (2017) 'The politics of urban renewal in Sydney's residential apartment market', *Urban Studies*, 55(6): 1329–45.

Tunstall, R. (2023) 'An empirical test of measures of housing degrowth: learning from the limited experience of England and Wales, 1981–2011', *Urban Studies*, 60(7): 1285–303.

Vance, J.E. (1971) 'Land assignment in the precapitalist, capitalist, and postcapitalist city', *Economic Geography*, 47(2): 101–20

Wainwright, T. and Demirel, P. (2023) 'Multiple logics in financialisation? Moving to carbon sustainability in build-to-rent development', *Environment and Planning A: Economy and Space*, 55(1): 22–45.

Weber, R. (2016) 'Performing property cycles', *Journal of Cultural Economy*, 9(6): 587–603.

Wetzstein, S. (2017) 'The global urban housing affordability crisis', *Urban Studies*, 54(14): 3159–77.

Wijburg, G., Aalbers, M.B. and Heeg, S. (2018) 'The financialisation of rental housing 2.0: releasing housing into the privatised mainstream of capital accumulation', *Antipode* 50(4): 1098–119.

Williams, J. (2017) 'Lost in translation: translating low carbon experiments into new spatial contexts viewed through the mobile-transitions lens', *Journal of Cleaner Production*, 169: 191–203.

7

Still Breathing Unequally? Air Pollution and Post-Carbon Transition

Gordon Walker, Douglas Booker and Paul J. Young

Introduction

Much that contributes to the making of urban air pollution also adds to the continued accumulation of carbon emissions in the global atmosphere. Urban areas are concentrated spaces of fossil fuel burning, this combustion varying in its intensity, purpose and make-up, but always contributing in some degree to both the damaging local effects of polluted urban air and the damaging consequences of accelerated global climate change. For this primary reason, there are clear and realizable synergies in acting across the domains of air quality governance and carbon governance simultaneously. Accordingly, sustainability transition and net zero discourses routinely enrol both local pollution and the global climate emergency in making claims about the co-benefits of urban action and in laying out strategies and programmes of action for city stakeholders (IPCC, 2022). For example, a recent report for the C40 cities network, focusing on acting on air pollution and climate together, asserts that: 'By integrating air quality and climate action planning processes, cities and other local jurisdictions can identify climate strategies with air quality benefits, air quality strategies with climate benefits and strategies that have both climate and air quality benefits' (Naidoo et al, 2021: 6).

Such claims are laudable but raise questions about the distribution of benefits that are to be realized. Inequalities and injustice already exist in both domains, with climate justice pointing to the radically uneven distribution of carbon emissions in relation to climate impacts (Schlosberg and Collins, 2014) and the environmental justice agenda highlighting the far from equal distribution of polluted urban air and its impact on breathing bodies (Walker, 2012; Chen et al, 2015). It remains, therefore, an open question whether in transitioning towards a post-carbon condition, such patterns of inequality will remain or diminish and whether the apparent co-benefits of acting on carbon and urban air pollutants together will be shared in ways that are inclusive of all parts of urban society or skewed towards only some. In this chapter we consider various dimensions of this question, focusing specifically on how urban air, and those breathing it in, may fare as transitions unfold. While there are other directions of interrelation, with, for example, the dynamics of urban air pollutants having consequences for the chemistry of climate change processes in the atmosphere (Shindell and Smith, 2019), we concentrate here on how inequalities in urban air pollution and vulnerabilities to its harmful effects may play out.

We begin by outlining what has been revealed about inequalities in urban air pollution, their depth, prevalence and processes of (re)production, drawing on environmental justice and related literatures. The ways in which systems of mobility, spatial ordering of land uses, unevenness in routines of movement and encasement, and pre-existing inequalities in health generate unequal patterns of burden and harm are emphasized. We then consider the sets of co-benefits for urban air pollution that might be realized through a range of actions to cut urban carbon emissions, including transport emissions, domestic and industrial fossil fuel combustion, and deforestation through tree-burning. Here both direct co-benefits related to reducing co-pollutant emissions and indirect co-benefits, such as moving towards forms of active mobility, are considered. How the potential future dynamics of inequality might work out in relation to these co-benefits is the focus of the final section of the chapter, considering a set of reasons why trajectories of improvement in air quality may not address existing patterns of inequality and environmental injustice. We conclude by identifying ways forward that may better build inclusion into synergies between decarbonization and air quality improvement.

Inequality, injustice and urban air

Attention first began to be given to the social distribution of air pollution emissions and poor air quality as part of the development of the environmental justice agenda, first in the United States (US) and then in other countries around the world (Walker, 2012; Holifield et al, 2018). Where data on emissions from industrial processes, or from monitoring stations measuring air quality, was routinely collected and publicly available, there was an opportunity to analyse the distribution of air pollution in relation to underlying socio-demographic patterns, following a geographical logic (Walker, 2009). The question of whether air pollution was equally shared across the census geography of different population groups soon began to be answered in quite clear terms – typically, air pollution problems were concentrated in places where already disadvantaged or marginalized populations live, for example, near to industrial sites, waste incinerators or busy roads. The nature of that disadvantage or marginalization – related variously to poverty, deprivation, race, ethnicity, migrant status, housing tenure – depends on context, as well as on the scale at which the analysis is undertaken (from within a region or city, to within a country) and the specific type of pollutant being examined (Deguen and Zmirou-Navier, 2010; Chen et al, 2015; Fecht et al, 2015; Miao et al, 2015). Not all studies have found a consistent pattern of air pollution following wider contours of social inequality and there are always methodological dependencies that can shape what is analytically revealed (Buzzelli, 2007). For example, ozone as a pollutant tends to be a worse problem in rural rather than urban areas, meaning that it is not generally associated with urban poverty (Bell et al, 2014), and studies in England and Wales have found that wealthy populations in cities can live in neighbourhoods with the highest average pollution levels, but not with the most frequent breaching of air quality standards (Mitchell and Dorling, 2003; Walker et al, 2003).

Such particular findings do not challenge the general pattern of association between poor air quality and disadvantage but do stress the need to see patterns of inequality in context, and crucially also take account of who is most vulnerable to breathing in polluted air (Walker et al, 2018). A pattern of higher pollution levels in urban wealthy neighbourhoods does not necessarily mean that they are most at harm, given that they typically have the resources to not always be 'at home' and to regularly escape the city air, including through forms of indoor encasement (Graham, 2015), and have generally better health and access to healthcare. Studies have accordingly centred on the 'triple jeopardy' (Briggs et al, 2008) that can serve to focus patterns of harm on deprived populations. In addition to being most at risk, they can experience differential susceptibility, in which for the same level of pollution, more disadvantaged groups can be more vulnerable to air pollution exposure. This is because poor health status, adverse health behaviours, multiple environmental exposures (including occupational) and psychosocial stress are more prevalent in disadvantaged groups and may act in addition to, or in synergy with, pollution exposure. Age differentials can also play into enhanced vulnerability in association with other variables, with young children and older people known to be more susceptible to poor air quality (Jephcote and Chen, 2012; Rodriguez-Villamizar et al, 2016).

Being cognizant of such complexities, estimates of the number of deaths arising from (unequal) exposure to air pollution have been made at different scales. Globally it has been estimated that three million premature deaths are caused by ambient air pollution, with the majority of these concentrated in the cities and urban areas of low and middle income countries (WHO, 2016). Across Africa, it has been estimated that outdoor air pollution was responsible for 394,000 premature deaths in 2019, with these increasing year-on-year as deaths from indoor air pollution have been in decline (Fisher et al, 2021). In the United Kingdom (UK) around 40,000 premature deaths per year have been estimated to be attributable to exposure to outdoor air pollution (Royal College of Physicians, 2016).

Where patterns of geographical association have been found between deprived and/or racial minority populations, various explanations have been put forward for why these exist. These include historical processes in which the development of industry and road systems have been related to the distribution of property values and the market-based 'sorting out' of who lives where (Liu, 2001), through to the overt racism of segregation and demarcating certain neighbourhoods as for 'Whites only' in, for example, the US and South Africa (Lopez, 2002; McDonald, 2002) and the fundamental structural reasons for poverty (Lipfert, 2004). In a study focused on the association between air pollution and history of 'red-lining' in the US, Lane et al quite strikingly conclude that:

> Present-day disparities in U.S. urban pollution levels reflect a legacy of structural racism in federal policy-making and resulting investment flows and land use decisions apparent in maps drawn more than 80 years ago. NO_2 and $PM_{2.5}$ are considered 'short-lived' pollutants ... yet the systems that created these disparities span more than a human lifetime. (Lane et al, 2022: 348)

Also implicated are differentials in political influence to resist polluting developments and, in the Global South, the prevalence of informal settlements on marginal land that offer little protection against the ingress of polluted air, combined with patterns of living and working 'on the street' (Véron, 2006). While the injustice of such situations may sometimes be self-evident and incontestable, particularly where there are large gaps between who is responsible for air pollution and who suffers its consequences, a range of considerations can be brought into determining (in)justice claims (Walker, 2012). These include challenges to the adequacy of apparently 'safe' air quality thresholds and limitations in the data through which polluted air is typically known. In a recent work, we have also brought into view the spatio-temporal complexity of 'breathing in the city' (Walker et al, 2022), opening up how the relationship between exposure, vulnerability and harm relates to the interrelated rhythms of urban environments and urban life that are not well captured by static and sparsely located monitoring stations. In relation to what this implies for environmental justice we argue that:

> Unequal patternings ... are not manifest within a static landscape of spatial relations, as conventionally understood in environmental justice and related assessments, but rather are made and remade through interactions and intersections between rhythms and the structuring effects of rhythmic repetition, such that certain spaces and certain lives recurrently become more subject to, and dominated by, the consequences of pollution than others. (Walker et al, 2022: 573)

It is clear, therefore, that polluted air and its breathing in are not equally experienced and that multiple considerations play into both why this is the case and the harmful consequences that follow. History is important in understanding both the dynamics of pollution problems and the generation and sustaining of patterns of inequality, but it is to future trajectories of post-carbon transition and urban air that we now turn.

Co-benefits of transition for urban air

That we should expect major co-benefits between the stripping out of emissions of carbon from urban energy systems and improvements in local urban air quality, stems primarily from their common origin. Take actions towards a post-carbon future, and through not burning petrol, diesel, gas, oil, coal or other carbon-based fuels, both carbon dioxide (CO_2) and other key pollutants that circulate and accumulate in urban areas will be cut out at their source. There is, therefore, a vast theoretical potential to radically reduce the harm done by urban air pollution through rapid and concerted climate action. Many studies have documented this close relationship (Gao et al, 2018; Karlsson et al, 2020). For example, at a global scale, Vandyck et al (2018) estimate that, if countries met the Paris Agreement contributions to mitigating carbon emissions, between 71,000 and 99,000 premature deaths from air pollution would be avoided annually in 2030, with a more ambitious pathway avoiding 178,000–346,000 premature deaths in 2030, and from 700,000 up to 1.5 million deaths in 2050. Yang and Teng (2018) model the outcomes of China committing to peak its carbon emissions by 2030 through following a strategy of simultaneously prioritizing air quality improvements, finding that emissions of key pollutants will be reduced by between 78 and 83 per cent compared to 2010 levels. A study across 74 metropolitan areas around the world, including 30 megacities, estimated that 408,270 avoidable deaths per year can be saved due to the air quality improvements that derive from a move to 100 per cent renewable energy (Jacobson et al, 2020). Most such studies remain at an aggregate level, demonstrating significant co-benefits for emission reduction and air quality, but without considering questions of distribution in any detail.

Such estimates of what can be achieved for air quality by cutting fossil fuel use are dependent on which particular carbon reduction strategies are chosen in order to build models and future scenarios. The route taken also matters more broadly for the types of further co-benefits for air quality and health that might be achievable. Four such co-benefits feature in the literature.

First, limiting the concentration of CO_2 in the atmosphere is not just about cutting fossil fuel use but also addressing large-scale deforestation. In some settings this has co-benefits for air quality because of the extent to which deforestation involves forest burning, thereby releasing CO_2 and destroying a carbon sink, but also generating particulate pollutants that can circulate, linger and accumulate locally and regionally, including within urban environments. For example, a study focused on the Amazon and the reduction in deforestation fires achieved over the period 2001–2012, estimated that surface particulate concentrations had been reduced by 30 per cent, contributing in turn to avoiding 400–1,700 premature deaths annually in the region (Reddington et al, 2015). Unsurprisingly, a study focused on the subsequent increase in deforestation fires since 2012 found a marked increase in attributable deaths by 2019 (Butt et al, 2021). In Indonesia peat fires associated with deforestation and consequent land degradation have led to a surge of 'fire-hazes' over recent decades, again releasing CO_2 but also high levels of particulate pollutants (Marlier et al, 2021). Palangkaraya, the capital of central Kalimantan, has recurrently recorded strikingly high pollution levels as a consequence. One recent study has estimated that reducing the area burned in large fires in 2015 through peatland restoration, would have reduced particulate emissions by 24 per cent, preventing 12,000 premature mortalities (Kiely et al, 2021).

Second, many have stressed the co-benefits of shifting mobility in urban settings to active forms of walking and cycling. In replacing hydrocarbon-powered movement, walking and cycling eliminate carbon and associated air pollutants, but also bring a range of other health and wellbeing outcomes associated with exercising regularly and using bodily energies rather than technological ones (see also Chapter 4). As just one example, a study of the potential health co-benefits of reducing carbon emissions in the transport sector in the city of Geneva (Thierno et al, 2016), found that by far most health improvement was achievable through prioritizing walking and sustainable transport modes, through the combined effects of both having better air to breathe and health improvement through exercise.

Third, transition policies that involve greening urban areas to various ends, including to sequester carbon, to make cities more walkable and 'liveable', and/or to moderate overheating (see Chapter 9), can bring co-benefits in health terms. Urban vegetation can 'scavenge' air pollutants before they reach sensitive lungs (Donovan et al, 2005; Maher et al, 2022), with effectiveness depending on the species and form of vegetation involved (Figure 7.1).

Figure 7.1: Cedar trees planted along a school fence to monitor their impact on reducing air pollutants in the school playground

Source: Professor Barbara Maher (reproduced with permission)

Co-benefits for improving air quality and health are derivable from a range of urban greening actions, including establishing greenways (a strip or corridor of green space), planting street trees and introducing or expanding areas of urban forest.

Fourth, there can be additional co-benefits from strategies to reduce and eventually eliminate fossil fuel use in domestic settings that extend beyond just cutting carbon and improving outdoor and indoor air quality. If significant improvements to building fabric and energy efficiency are implemented (as widely advocated), pervasive problems of energy poverty can be acted on, generating associated wellbeing benefits for health and the range of other harmful consequences of living in energy poverty, as literature on energy justice has long emphasized (Boardman, 1991; Bickerstaff et al, 2013). However, as with other co-benefits, much depends on how low carbon transition is taken forward, and the degree to which inequality, justice and inclusion figure as important considerations. It is to these matters that we now turn.

Urban air, vulnerability and inequality during transition

At a fundamental level, cutting emissions of air pollution at their source by reducing and eventually eliminating fossil fuel burning is closely aligned with outcomes for which environmental justice activists have long been calling (Pulido, 1994; Heiman, 1996). Eliminating the problem at source, rather than inadequately patching it up or distributing it around a little more fairly, has been a recurrent and important objective. At face value therefore the synergies between post-carbon and stopping the production of air pollutants appear to fit well with a concern for environmental justice. However, there are a set of considerations and cautions to be worked through which, to some degree, counter this general assertion.

First, past experience has shown that where and when air quality improvements are achieved the benefits are not necessarily felt by those most in need. In principle the most disadvantaged should benefit most from overall air quality improvements, for example, by eliminating breaches of standards in the most polluted areas, but evidence does not always point in that direction. For example, in a study of trends in air quality between 2001 and 2011 in Great Britain, Mitchell et al (2015) found a clear social gradient in patterns of decline and improvement. Where air quality had improved (associated largely with falling concentrations of NO_2) it had done so most quickly in the *least* deprived areas. Where it had worsened (associated with rising concentrations of PM_{10}) it had done so most quickly and substantially in the *most* deprived areas. While over this time period the overall health burden from air pollution might have improved, they conclude that this improvement was regressively distributed and little was achieved for addressing patterns of health inequality. This suggests, at least, that simple associations between reducing air pollution and reducing inequality should not be presumed.

Second, at a global scale, most action to eliminate carbon from energy systems is likely to take place in the Global North. That is where both the moral responsibility to act is situated, including in relation to historic emissions (see Chapter 5), and where the resources and capacity to move to differently configured sustainable energy systems also largely resides. It is not expected, for example, that the electrification of vehicle fleets will be seen first in African or Latin American cities, despite discourses arguing for 'leapfrogging' the polluting 'western model'. Millions of used cars every year are already being exported to low- and middle-income countries, taking their air pollution and CO_2 with them. The shift to an electrified vehicle fleet could reinforce and strengthen this parasitic relationship, particularly as significant growth in vehicle ownership is expected in countries which are importing used vehicles. While a study focused on Mexico estimated that imports of used cars from the US have actually improved local air quality by displacing older and more polluting vehicles in the Mexican car fleet (Chen et al, 2019), such differentials are unlikely to be sustained once the shift to electric vehicles (EVs) takes place. Moreover, such uneven outcomes are likely not only in transport systems, but also in the local pollution problems associated with power production. While many more wealthy countries are seeking to rapidly move towards non-fossil fuel energy sources, countries such as India are expected to continue their reliance on traditional coal-fired power generation. While there are techno-optimist ambitions to moderate the carbon emissions from coal burning in India by fitting carbon capture technologies (Kumar Shukla et al, 2020), this does not mean that other pollution emissions with local health impacts will simultaneously be addressed.

It is inevitable, therefore, that it will be in the cities of the Global North that air quality will improve as carbon emissions fall towards zero, potentially rapidly so. As a consequence, poor air quality and deaths and burdens on health will become yet more concentrated in the cities of the Global South, 'left behind' and still reliant on old fossil fuel technologies. Measures of inequality will become accentuated, rather than diminish. For deforestation, the air quality benefits that might be realized from reducing forest burning *will* be concentrated in affected regions of the Global South, but clearly are very dependent on the success with which deforestation is tackled. Recent experience is not encouraging, particularly in the Brazilian context, even though a change of government has reinvigorated anti-deforestation policy.

Third, various forms of 'redistribution' at other spatial scales might also figure during transition processes. In the US, environmental justice activists protested strongly that emission trading mechanisms enacted in the 1990s to successfully address acidity pollution problems at an aggregate level (Solomon and Lee, 2000; Corburn, 2001) were having distributional consequences that incentivized and concentrated emissions from power plants in poor and racial minority communities. Depending on the mechanisms used to promote carbon emissions reductions, such uneven outcomes could readily be seen elsewhere. Similarly, while the electrification of vehicle fleets might reduce pollution on city streets, if the electricity they are drawing on is still being generated from polluting power stations, the effect is to concentrate remaining pollution problems in the host communities in which these power stations are sited.

Fourth, becoming post-carbon does not necessarily eliminate all significant sources of air pollution affecting urban areas. For the transition to EVs, this is a particular concern. Despite often being touted as 'zero-emission' vehicles, they are still a significant source of air pollution through 'non-exhaust emissions' – emissions originating not from the tailpipe, but from brakes, tyres, road wear and the resuspension of road dust (Thorpe and Harrison, 2008). Indeed, it has been suggested that the heavier weight of EVs increase emissions of these forms of particulate matter and the associated health burdens (Timmers and Achten, 2016). Recent research indicates the multiple ways in which particulate emissions in an ultrafine form enter into human bodies. With the potential to inflict multiple forms of harm (Maher et al,

2020; Schraufnagel, 2020), these forms of pollution are likely to become of increasing concern, with health impacts concentrated, as they already are, in disadvantaged communities.

Fifth, while such concerns emphasize the need to more radically act to shift urban mobility away from the car and towards active forms of travel, even if this shift is realized, inequalities may persist. As discussed in Chapter 4, processes of green gentrification, driven ostensibly by sustainability and environmental concerns, have become part of regeneration and property development strategies selling green, walkable and liveable neighbourhoods to wealthy households. Lower income residents are displaced, with few of the health co-benefits of neighbourhood-level transition policies heading in their direction. Even if gentrification and displacement are not involved, interventions can still have uneven outcomes. A UK example, if a contested one, is low-traffic neighbourhoods (LTNs) that seek to reduce the amount of local motor vehicle traffic and promote active forms of mobility. It has been claimed, first, that LTNs are primarily being implemented in areas that are already wealthy and, second, that there is a 'zero-sum game', whereby the polluting traffic removed from LTNs is simply being redistributed to nearby major roads where those in lower socio-economic groups live. Early evidence from LTN implementation in London suggests that it has been broadly equitable in terms of the distribution of emissions at a city level. However, results are more mixed at the district level, with Aldred et al (2021: 9) commenting that 'while LTNs may have strong potential to improve equity of access to high-quality active travel infrastructure ... this will not automatically happen everywhere'.

Finally, the costs associated with shifts to zero carbon and clean technologies are important in terms of within-country distributional effects, as well as at a global scale. As noted earlier, technologies to promote low carbon home heating and insulation have a key role in transition processes, with potential co-benefits as outcomes, including for the fuel poor. However, these benefits may be unequally felt due to an uneven ability to pay, as there are often initial costs that consumers need to make to access long-term savings. Put simply, in the long run it is expensive to be poor. While these upfront costs are forecast to fall, much rests on the effectiveness of targeting support schemes to ensure that an 'energy underclass' (Walker and Cass, 2007), living with cold homes, expensive bills *and* polluted air, does not emerge and persist in the shadow of apparently successful transition processes at an aggregate level.

Conclusion

The uneven implications of transition towards a post-carbon future for urban air and the breathing of its inhabitants are many, varied and involved. Questions of distribution can be examined at different scales (international, intranational, intra-city), data can be interpreted in different ways, and there are major gaps in monitoring of air quality, particularly in the Global South – all of which can fundamentally obstruct seeing the intensity and differentiation of how poor air quality is currently experienced. Much variability and uncertainty also opens up when considering how different types of low carbon strategies, measures and actions might be implemented, and what this then means in terms of the direct and indirect benefits for urban air quality and health.

In this chapter we have identified the potential that exists for realizing co-benefits between low carbon and air quality, but also some of the reasons why trajectories of change may well not address patterns of air quality inequality that already exist at different scales. If we did get to the nirvana of a fully post-carbon condition across the globe, with fossil fuels eliminated from energy systems of all forms (assuming other new forms of pollution were avoided), there would undoubtedly be a radical improvement in urban air quality. It is also in theory possible that this could benefit the breathing of the disadvantaged as much as other parts of the population. However, in practice, the timescales and pace of change will not be even and transitions will not happen in ways that are somehow independent of existing structures of inequality and injustice. The spectre is raised of sustained enclaves, both globally and locally, within which continued fossil fuel use, poverty and marginalization remain unchecked, and the 'triple jeopardy' of impacts of air pollution on health remain unaddressed.

Our analysis guards against simplistic assumptions about carbon mitigation co-benefits and has made clear the importance of asserting the right to breathe clean air on a fully inclusive basis for all (Boyd, 2019). Inclusion also relates to how decision making is enacted. As noted earlier, environmental justice activists have long called for eliminating pollution at source, but also envisage this being realized through the radical democratization of decision making (Lake, 1996), aiming towards a 'productive justice' in which pollution is in 'not in anyone's backyard' (Faber, 2008: 252). Participatory inclusion has become an increasingly important principle in the doing of air quality research and monitoring, including within citizen science projects, and is central to our recent call for a critical air quality science (Booker et al, 2023). From the particularities of how air quality knowledge is generated, through to the global negotiations over how resources are secured for nations in the Global South so that they can fully engage with low carbon transition, ensuring that the voices of those most disadvantaged and most often excluded from participation are heard and have real influence is paramount.

References

Aldred, R., Verlinghieri, E., Sharkey, M., Itova, I. and Goodman, A. (2021) 'Equity in new active travel infrastructure: a spatial analysis of London's new Low Traffic Neighbourhoods', *Journal of Transport Geography*, 96: 103194.

Bell, M.L., Zanobetti, A. and Dominici, F. (2014) 'Who is more affected by ozone pollution? A systematic review and meta-analysis', *American Journal of Epidemiology*, 180(1): 15–28.

Bickerstaff, K., Walker, G. and Bulkeley, H. (eds) (2013) *Energy Justice in a Changing Climate*, London: Zed.

Boardman, B. (1991) *From Cold Homes to Affordable Warmth*, London: Belhaven Press.

Booker, D., Walker, G., Young, P.J. and Porroche-Escudero, A. (2023) 'A critical air quality science perspective on citizen science in action', *Local Environment*, 28(1): 31–46.

Boyd, D.R. (2019) 'The human right to breathe clean air', *Annals of Global Health*, 85(1): 146.

Briggs, D., Abellan, J.J. and Fecht, D. (2008) 'Environmental inequity in England: small area associations between socio-economic status and environmental pollution', *Social Science and Medicine*, 67(10): 1612–29.

Butt, E.W., Conibear, L., Knote, C. and Spracklen, D.V. (2021) 'Large air quality and public health impacts due to Amazonian deforestation fires in 2019', *GeoHealth*, 5(7): e2021GH000429.

Buzzelli, M. (2007) 'Bourdieu does environmental justice? Probing the linkages between population health and air pollution epidemiology', *Health and Place*, 13(1): 3–13.

Chen, D., Buzzelli, M. and Aronson, K.J. (2015) 'Environmental equity research: review with focus on outdoor air pollution research methods and analytic tools AU – Miao, Qun', *Archives of Environmental & Occupational Health*, 70(1): 47–55.

Chen, L., Garcia-Medina, B.C. and Wan, R. (2019) 'Trade liberalization, consumption shifting and pollution: evidence from Mexico's used vehicle imports', *Review of International Economics*, 27(5): 1591–608.

Corburn, J. (2001) 'Emissions trading and environmental justice: distributive fairness and the USA's Acid Rain Programme', *Environmental Conservation*, 28(4): 323–32.

Deguen, S.V. and Zmirou-Navier, D. (2010) 'Social inequalities resulting from health risks related to ambient air quality: a European review', *European Journal of Public Health*, 20(1): 27–35.

Donovan, R.G., Stewart, H.E., Owen, S.M., Mackenzie, A.R. and Hewitt, C.N. (2005) 'Development and application of an urban tree air quality score for photochemical pollution episodes using the Birmingham, United Kingdom, area as a case study', *Environmental Science & Technology*, 39: 6730–38.

Faber, D. (2008) *Capitalizing on Environmental Injustice: The Polluter-Industrial Complex in the Age of Globalization*, Lanham: Rowman & Littlefield.

Fecht, D., Fischer, P., Fortunato, L., Hoek, G., De Hoogh, K., Marra, M. et al (2015) 'Associations between air pollution and socioeconomic characteristics, ethnicity and age profile of neighbourhoods in England and the Netherlands', *Environmental Pollution*, 198: 201–10.

Fisher, S., Bellinger, D.C., Cropper, M.L., Kumar, P., Binagwaho, A., Koudenoukpo, J.B. et al (2021) 'Air pollution and development in Africa: impacts on health, the economy, and human capital', *The Lancet Planetary Health*, 5(10): e681–8.

Gao, J., Hou, H., Zhai, Y., Woodward, A., Vardoulakis, S., Kovats, S. et al (2018) 'Greenhouse gas emissions reduction in different economic sectors: mitigation measures, health co-benefits, knowledge gaps, and policy implications', *Environmental Pollution*, 240: 683–98.

Graham, S. (2015) 'Life support: the political ecology of urban air', *City*, 19(2–3): 192–215.

Heiman, M.K. (1996) 'Race, waste, and class: new perspectives on environmental justice', *Antipode*, 28(2): 111–21.

Holifield, R., Chakraborty, J. and Walker, G.P. (eds) (2018) *Routledge Handbook of Environmental Justice*, Abingdon: Routledge.

IPCC (2022) *Climate Change 2022: Mitigation of Climate Change. Contribution of Working Group III to the Sixth Assessment Report of the Intergovernmental Panel on Climate Change*, Cambridge: Cambridge University Press.

Jacobson, M.Z., von Krauland, A-K., Burton, Z.F.M., Coughlin, S.J., Jaeggli, C., Nelli, D. et al (2020) 'Transitioning all energy in 74 metropolitan areas, including 30 megacities, to 100% clean and renewable wind, water, and sunlight (WWS)', *Energies*, 13(18): 4934.

Jephcote, C. and Chen, H. (2012) 'Environmental injustices of children's exposure to air pollution from road-transport within the model British multicultural city of Leicester: 2000–09', *Science of the Total Environment*, 414: 140–51.

Karlsson, M., Alfredsson, E. and Westling, N. (2020) 'Climate policy co-benefits: a review', *Climate Policy*, 20(3): 292–316.

Kiely, L., Spracklen, D.V., Arnold, S.R., Papargyropoulou, E., Conibear, L., Wiedinmyer, C. et al (2021) 'Assessing costs of Indonesian fires and the benefits of restoring peatland', *Nature Communications*, 12: 7044.

Kumar Shukla, A., Ahmad, Z., Sharma, M., Dwivedi, G., Nath Verma, T., Jain, S. et al (2020) 'Advances of carbon capture and storage in coal-based power generating units in an Indian context', *Energies*, 13(16): 4124.

Lake, R.W. (1996) 'Volunteers, NIMBYs, and environmental justice: dilemmas of democratic practice', *Antipode*, 28(2): 160–74.

Lane, H.M., Morello-Frosch, R., Marshall, J.D. and Apte, J.S. (2022) 'Historical redlining is associated with present-day air pollution disparities in U.S. cities', *Environmental Science & Technology Letters*, 9(4): 345–50.

Lipfert, F.W. (2004) 'Air pollution and poverty: does the sword cut both ways?', *Journal of Epidemiology and Community Health*, 58(1): 2–3.

Liu, F. (2001) *Environmental Justice Analysis: Theories, Methods and Practice*, Boca Raton: Lewis Publishers.

Lopez, R. (2002) 'Segregation and black/white differences in exposure to air toxics in 1990', *Environmental Health Perspectives*, 110(2): 289–95.

Maher, B.A., González-Maciel, A., Reynoso-Robles, R., Torres-Jardón, R. and Calderón-Garcidueñas, L. (2020) 'Iron-rich air pollution nanoparticles: an unrecognised environmental risk factor for myocardial mitochondrial dysfunction and cardiac oxidative stress', *Environmental Research*, 188: 109816.

Maher, B.A., Gonet, T., Karloukovski, V.V., Wang, H. and Bannan, T.J. (2022) 'Protecting playgrounds: local-scale reduction of airborne particulate matter concentrations through particulate deposition on roadside "tredges" (green infrastructure)', *Scientific Reports*, 12(1): 14236.

Marlier, M.E., Madrigano, J., Huttinger, A. and Burger, N.E. (2021) *Indonesian Fires and Haze: Measuring the Health Consequences of Smoke Exposure*, Santa Monica: RAND Corporation.

McDonald, D.A. (2002) *Environmental Justice in South Africa*, Cape Town: University of Cape Town Press.

Miao, Q., Chen, D., Buzzelli, M. and Aronson, K.J. (2015) 'Environmental equity research: review with focus on outdoor air pollution research methods and analytic tools', *Archives of Environmental and Occupational Health*, 70(1): 47–55.

Mitchell, G. and Dorling, D. (2003) 'An environmental justice analysis of British air quality', *Environment and Planning A*, 35(5): 909–29.

Mitchell, G., Norman, P. and Mullin, K. (2015) 'Who benefits from environmental policy? An environmental justice analysis of air quality change in Britain, 2001–2011', *Environmental Research Letters*, 10: 105009.

Naidoo, S., Kleiman, G., Chafe, Z. and Kheirbek, I. (2021) *Clean Air Healthy Planet: A Framework for Integrating Air Quality Management and Climate Action Planning*, C40 Cities. Available from: https://www.c40knowledgehub.org [Accessed 10 January 2023].

Pulido, L. (1994) 'Restructuring and the contraction and expansion of environmental rights in the United States', *Environment and Planning A*, 26(6): 915–36.

Reddington, C.L., Butt, E.W., Ridley, D.A., Artaxo, P., Morgan, W.T., Coe, H. et al (2015) 'Air quality and human health improvements from reductions in deforestation-related fire in Brazil', *Nature Geoscience*, 8: 768–71.

Rodriguez-Villamizar, L.A., Berney, C., Villa-Roel, C., Ospina, M.B., Osornio-Vargas, A. and Rowe, B.H. (2016) 'The role of socioeconomic position as an effect-modifier of the association between outdoor air pollution and children's asthma exacerbations: an equity-focused systematic review', *Reviews on Environmental Health*, 31(3): 297–309.

Royal College of Physicians (2016) *Every Breath We Take: The Lifelong Impact of Air Pollution. Report of a Working Party*, London: Royal College of Physicians.

Schlosberg, D. and Collins, L.B. (2014) 'From environmental to climate justice: climate change and the discourse of environmental justice', *WIREs Climate Change*, 5(3): 359–74.

Schraufnagel, D.E. (2020) 'The health effects of ultrafine particles', *Experimental & Molecular Medicine*, 52: 311–17.

Shindell, D. and Smith, C.J. (2019) 'Climate and air-quality benefits of a realistic phase-out of fossil fuels', *Nature*, 573: 408–11.

Solomon, B.D. and Lee, R. (2000) 'Emissions trading systems and environmental justice', *Environment*, 42(8): 32–45.

Thierno, D., Nicola, C. and Jean, S. (2016) 'Co-bénéfices pour la santé des politiques urbaines relatives au changement climatique à l'échelon local: l'exemple de Genève' [Co-benefits for health of urban policies relating to climate change at the local level: the example of Geneva], *Environnement, Risques & Santé*, 15: 332–40.

Thorpe, A. and Harrison, R.M. (2008) 'Sources and properties of non-exhaust particulate matter from road traffic: a review', *Science of The Total Environment*, 400(1–3): 270–82.

Timmers, V.R.J.H. and Achten, P.A.J. (2016) 'Non-exhaust PM emissions from electric vehicles', *Atmospheric Environment*, 134: 10–17.

Vandyck, T., Keramidas, K., Kitous, A., Spadaro, J.V., Van Dingenen, R., Holland, M. et al (2018) 'Air quality co-benefits for human health and agriculture counterbalance costs to meet Paris Agreement pledges', *Nature Communications*, 9: 4939.

Véron, R. (2006) 'Remaking urban environments: the political ecology of air pollution in Delhi', *Environment and Planning A*, 38(11): 2093–109.

Walker, G. (2009) 'Beyond proximity: exploring the multiple spatialities of environmental justice', *Antipode*, 41(4): 614–36.

Walker, G. (2012) *Environmental Justice: Concepts, Evidence and Politics*, Abingdon: Routledge.

Walker, G. and Cass, N. (2007) 'Carbon reduction, "the public" and renewable energy: engaging with socio-technical configurations', *Area*, 39(4): 458–69.

Walker, G., Mitchell, G., Fairburn, J. and Smith, G. (2003) *Environmental Quality and Social Deprivation. Phase II: National Analysis of Flood Hazard, IPC Industries and Air Quality*, R&D Project Record E2-067/1/PR1, Bristol: The Environment Agency.

Walker, G., Mitchell, G. and Pearce, J. (2018) 'Pollution and inequality', in Dalton, A. (ed), *Annual Report of the Chief Medical Officer 2017, Health Impacts of All Pollution – What Do We Know?*, London: Department of Health and Social Care, pp 100–16.

Walker, G., Booker, D. and Young, P. (2022) 'Breathing in the polyrhythmic city: a spatiotemporal, rhythmanalytic account of urban air pollution and its inequalities', *Environment and Planning C*, 40(3): 572–91.

WHO (2016) *Ambient Air Pollution: A Global Assessment of Exposure and Burden of Disease*, Geneva: World Health Organization.

Yang, X. and Teng, F. (2018) 'Air quality benefit of China's mitigation target to peak its emission by 2030', *Climate Policy*, 18(1): 99–110.

8

Beyond Circular Economies: Rethinking Relations of Waste

Ralph Horne and Bhavna Middha

Domestic waste – the stock in trade of local governments across the westernized world – is in crisis. Ocean soups of plastic have provided increasingly visceral signs of major problems with modern systems of production and consumption, leading to increasing calls for action towards 'zero waste'. In late 2017, China banned international imports of waste, of recycled and recyclable post-consumer materials, followed by other countries such as Malaysia, Vietnam, Thailand and India. The bans brought a collapse in the global price of waste plastics, spiking rates of incineration and landfilling (OECD, 2018), further limiting the economic feasibility of market-based collection, sorting and recycling of plastic waste in western countries (Nielsen et al, 2020).

Rather than moving beyond market-based logics, much of the pro-circular economy (CE) debate accepts them, and promises a technically comprehensive solution to waste in a carbon-constrained world. The concept of 'waste' itself is seemingly to be dispensed with, as CE calls instead for all unused or rejected materials to become valuable feedstocks for upcycled goods. This, despite rules of entropy and dispersion pointing to the reality that less than 20 per cent of materials can actually be recycled, upcycled, and so on, and most either downcycle, deplete, disperse or 'end' in landfill (Valero and Valero, 2019). While superficially attractive, the CE idea faces a raft of problems that extend well beyond the technical and the monetary.

This chapter charts the problematic imaginary of the CE idea in terms of domestic waste. In so doing, we make five key points. First, that the CE focus on technology and behaviour change reflects a 'responsibilization' that pays insufficient attention to distributional impacts, inclusion and, indeed, to the role of social life in general. Second, we highlight the case of domestic (kerbside) recycling and show how, without a relational underpinning that accounts for social life, current approaches are set to exacerbate already existing inequalities, and are unlikely to truly advance sustainability. Third, we centre socio-material entanglements in domestic waste as a means to approach inclusion. Fourth, we advance social practices, and the capabilities approach, as positioning foundations for a future domestic discard regime. Finally, we present three ideas for thinking about relational-informed local waste governance, setting out examples that counter an assumption at the heart of CE – that recycling should be the primary focus of effort and action. We argue that not only is this the wrong path towards minimizing waste but also assumes the waste burden should rest upon households.

Circular economy governance and 'responsibilization'

The CE concept, and movement, is a call to action largely composed of recycled ideas. Origins include industrial ecology (Andersen, 2007) advocating the facilitation of material symbiosis between diverse companies and industrial processes (Gibbs and Deutz, 2007) that mobilize and exchange resources within their own domain and sites (Hobson and Lynch, 2016). The techno-economic orientation of CE leaves out much important detail of waste in society and allows current systems of consumption and production to continue, with the proviso of more attention to recycling. Indeed, in avoiding political and material realities (Corvellec et al, 2020) and reassuring policy makers about successful circular futures, a disingenuous picture about the crisis of waste is produced (Hobson, 2016; Bauwens et al, 2020). Moreover, as Zink and Geyer argue, there is 'no a priori reason to assume a closed loop is superior' (2017: 594).

Drawing on ideas about internalizing externalities, steeped in the ecological modernization paradigm, CE perpetuates New Public Management orthodoxy by advocating for resource taxes and landfill charges that penalize the most vulnerable in society. It places blame and responsibility upon hapless consumers and households via a 'behaviour change' orientation, and associated moral condemnation of waste and the circuits that characterize it (Gregson et al, 2015; Horne et al, 2016).

This responsibilization, in which CE is complicit, positions consumers as users who will become a part of a transformation imaginary. No concrete ways are offered to make the transformation happen, beyond what Shove (2010) calls the 'ABC model' where the consumer/user is a rational being pursuing activities with preferences and choices. This focus means that those producing and marketing consumption are indirectly excused; similarly, the waste produced by industries, agriculture and construction activities is spared the intensity of focus that is placed on households (Gregson and Crang, 2010). Take the example of 'wishcycling' (the contamination of recyclables with 'non recyclables'). Altman (2021) contends that this supposed poor behaviour by households is better seen as a production failure, requiring a shift of focus onto manufacturers rather than on households as resisters of recycling.

CE debates so far focus largely on developing new technologies and businesses so that materials are kept in circulation. This misses the central role of entanglements of daily lives with waste services and materials, and the implications of change. Some CE mechanisms such as product service systems assume that current material-based practices are exchangeable with services. Design solutions that *design* out waste also receive attention. However, leaving the 'social' out of design and consumption interventions ignores how 'we both make and are made (as social entities) by our material worlds' (Hobson, 2020: 108), and how practices can change only when social, material and cultural configurations align. Also underplayed are the exclusionary implications, as some people are not able to participate 'to accomplish those social practices (many of which involve mobility and co-presence) required for effective social participation' (Shove, 2002: 2).

Confronting the waste crisis through domestic waste

Confronting the waste crisis through efforts towards recycling domestic (kerbside) waste is an 'end of pipe' approach that not only diverts attention away from the mode of production, but also can be readily positioned as an economically beneficial activity. In other words, waste becomes a market commodity and, primarily, a means to expand the market-industrial complex. A more meaningful focus would be on mandating recycled content in place of virgin materials, as this would at least hold out the possibility of linking waste with overall consumption.

Despite questions about the limited impact of recycling on pollution, it continues to be the primary instrument in CE and waste management discourses (MacBride, 2013). The push for recycling means creating demand for material, which necessarily undermines eco-design, dematerialization, prevention, durability, longevity, serviceability and reuse. Moreover, making municipal recycling a stabilizing infrastructure cements this discourse and supports CE in valorizing waste. Hobson (2021) shows how recycling, as a techno-economic solution, does not replace primary or virgin material product but, rather, adds to production. More specifically, the limited climate benefits of global recycling of pulp and paper have been well documented (van Ewijk et al, 2021).

The diversion of attention that a focus on kerbside recycling provides is significant. In a case study of Swedish and Austrian policy, Johansson and Corvellec (2018) found disproportionate policy focus on domestic waste generation rather than on consumption, or on industrial, mining or dangerous waste types. Where the private sector is left to innovate in recycling, perverse outcomes, such as increased consumption, are likely. For example, being rewarded with store vouchers for recycling supports more consumption rather than simply curbing waste (Johansson and Corvellec, 2018). Even reuse involves resource consumption in repair, and recirculation. Thus, the European Waste Framework Directive classifying reuse as prevention is contentious (Gharfalkar et al, 2015).

Beyond recycling, CE tends to either advocate bans, or landfill diversion to 'renewable' energy from waste (local power and/or heat production from burning refuse). Bans – such as plastic bag bans – have had varied results around the world (Chida, 2011) and have 'worked' (in a material sense) only in limited circumstances, due to the local political, social and cultural contexts in play. Meanwhile, cities such as Melbourne, with no history of municipal waste-to-energy systems, but with a pressing landfill space crisis, are fair game for would-be providers of 'renewable' energy technologies that also reduce the landfill burden. Waste incineration has been criticized and opposed the world over for its polluting impact (Rushton, 2003; Davies, 2005); for the rebound effect, in which it is okay to 'waste' as discards are ultimately being converted to useable energy (Figge and Thorpe, 2019); and for social inequality issues, such as choosing an incineration plant site where people have the least power to oppose its construction (Johnson, 2013). Ironically, countries that were front runners in waste-to-energy infrastructure, such as Sweden, are trying to detach from incineration but experience lock-in to such systems (Johansson and Corvellec, 2018). Due to the initial investment costs not having been recovered thus far, there is a need to provide feedstock in the form of post-consumer combustible waste to keep the plants running – a logic that runs counter to that of waste minimization.

Thus, in reflecting ideas of competitive, private, individualistic, profit-seeking practice, CE tends to avoid the real challenge of downscaling, degrowth and rethinking production. In so doing, it largely preserves incumbents and advocates expanding the market-industrial complex by creating new markets (and demand) for waste, hence fuelling rather than confronting consumption. CE coexists with a passive state, dominance of self-regulation and the promise of technology. Instead of reducing virgin material production, the process of marketizing waste is likely to have the opposite effect, while also distracting attention from addressing the actual source of the waste crisis (Savini, 2019).

Beyond the techno-economic focus, design solutions that 'design' out waste have long received attention in line with the idea 'that over 80% of all product-related environmental impacts are determined during the design phase of a product' (EU Science Hub, 2016). However, the prevalence of self-regulation of the market operates against emergence of meaningful regulatory mechanisms to address waste at source. Fundamentally, by downplaying the social entanglements of daily lives with waste services and materials, there is an intellectual chasm created that cannot be bridged. Social theorists argue as one that there are no exclusively technical solutions to waste problems, and that every designed object has shared meanings and competencies as part of the practices of which technology is a part.

Indeed, social, moral and ethical issues generally are missing from CE discourses (Murray et al, 2017; Pla-Julián and Guevara, 2019). This brings us to questions of inclusionary dimensions of waste management, starting with social disengagement and disconnection from services, as well as economic exclusion (Saunders et al, 2008). As discussed in the following section, a central lacuna in the CE concept is the unevenness of society – inclusion and social equality, including intra-generational equity, diversity factors, financial equality, capabilities and social opportunity. This blind spot is also shared by major environmental groups; for example, Greenpeace's annual guide to 'greener' electronics rates Apple a top performer (Cook and Jardim, 2017) despite the exclusionary ramifications of the way global market systems are harnessed by the tech giant. Thus, before the discourse of CE becomes ubiquitous and normalized, the perverse outcomes that may occur due to social externalities and oversimplification of environmental consequences need critical reflection (Corvellec et al, 2022).

Social and inclusionary dimensions of waste

Waste carries with it emotions, affects and vulnerabilities – as highlighted in an increasingly diverse literature. Liboiron and Lepawsky (2022) adopt the term 'discard studies' – coined by Nagle (2013) – to focus on the politics and power of wasting, which involves how some materials, practices, regions and people are valued or devalued, becoming dominant or disposable. For example, eco-ableism in the zero-waste movement has been invoked in the context of policies where scholars question the definition of essential versus non-essential products and services, irrespective of different definitions of essential and non-essential for persons with disabilities (Bretz, 2020).

Hawkins (2013) draws attention to disposability and transience, pointing out that when we describe something as 'disposable' we are really describing it as rubbish, pointing to the fact that it was made to be wasted – not reused. Disposable goods are the ultimate expression of planned obsolescence; their imminent future as rubbish is tangible before we buy or use them. The design of materials as designated waste and the ways in which they are embedded in daily lives to make them indispensable or ubiquitous is also an important part of sustainable consumption and waste scholarship (Shove, 2003; Evans, 2011). More importantly, the embeddedness, obduracy and ongoing transition from the use of such materials begs questions about who or what gets affected inequitably when detachment from such materials or services, as the case might be, is operationalized through policy, market instruments or normative discourses (Hawkins, 2021).

Income is not the only indicator of exclusionary processes that encompass social isolation, stigma, and lack of capacity and opportunity to voice one's own narrative (Mann, 2020). Consumption is often

> deeply contentious for, and within, families and thus family consumption, especially consumption by vulnerable or dependent family members, has become a critical site of social contest, regulation and debate. This spotlight means that for families, the daily struggles about good and appropriate consumption are newly visible and ever more complicated. (Lindsay and Maher, 2013: 2)

Behavioural and technological change comprise the default mechanisms that governments turn to in addressing rising problems of plastic waste reduction and management (Lane and Watson, 2012). Many consumers and householders are being urged to organize their own material and social necessities, putting the onus on their uptake for the success of such policies and strategies (Hobson, 2021). A general observation is that plastic bags support marginal, vulnerable communities (Horne et al, 2022) who are dependent on cheap, ubiquitous packaging materials to make ends meet. Hence, measures such as bans tend to fall unevenly upon those least able to find alternatives or afford alternatives.

Drinking straw substitutes may inconvenience and even hurt disabled people. Replacing plastic bags with paper bags may inconvenience older people, and are cumbersome for people who mainly walk and use public transport for mobility. In a few cases, the obvious negative impacts on particular groups of such measures have led to temporary exclusions to single-use plastic bans based on health or medical reasons in an attempt to prevent certain groups being disadvantaged (Government of Western Australia, 2021; Government of Victoria, 2023). However, well-meaning reprieves do nothing to address the waste crisis itself, and generally cause confusion about who is to do what and focus on low hanging fruit rather than systemic, social practices or long-term change. Jurisdictions such as Western Australia are cognizant of the implications for inequalities and thus organizing action and advisory groups for waste policies (Government of Western Australia, 2021). However, there is no evidence base to draw on. In the end, consumer focused initiatives relegate responsibility to individuals and even suggest, for example, that people with disabilities 'bring their own single-use plastic items when they are out and about, once the ban begins' (Queensland Government, 2021).

While such exemptions point to awareness around the inequity, support measures like these are ad hoc, siloed and just-in-time measures, neglecting how entangled plastics and other potentially banned products are in everyday living. Hawkins and Race (2011) explain the challenge of detaching from plastic waste bottles in countries like Thailand, where infrastructure is not developed to make water universally potable, as such normalizing plastic bottle use as the dominant clean way of storing and accessing water. They argue for targeting *practices* of drinking water from bottles rather than simply the *material* of the bottle.

In sum, policy ideas to date have largely ignored how deeply entangled our lives are with the products and materials that are targeted for change, through the services and functions they provide, and the inequities any change might produce (Hobson et al, 2021; Horne et al, 2022). The 'waste burden' thus falls on householders and consumers, especially those on low incomes and women who (still) shoulder domestic burdens (Lindsay and Maher, 2013; Farbotko, 2018). Waste governance (Gregson and Forman, 2021), discard studies (Liboiron and Lepawsky, 2022) and sustainability transitions literature (Hobson et al, 2021) emphasize the need for inclusive and active participation, and public acceptance of policies and regulations for them to succeed. Otherwise, sustainability policies become a marker of social and economic distinction for consumers, in the process excluding, for example, lower socio-economic groups (Bryant et al, 2008). Additionally, technologically deterministic models have borne solutions that only focus on the material (such as single-use plastic bans) and have been unsuccessful in the long term in many places around the world (Chida, 2011; Borg et al, 2022). Some bans have led to different and perverse outcomes to those intended, such as where substituted products were as harmful (Wagner, 2020).

Thus, how we as a society deal with waste raises moral and ethical questions along the way (Idies, 2020; Kruger, 2020). Included in this are ideas of co-production of actions on waste. As described earlier, households have been made the focus of responsibility to curb household waste, yet they are rarely engaged in policy and action design. Instead, waste is currently conceived as an end-of-pipe issue and households as one of the main offenders (Evans, 2011). Strategies conventionally suggested involve changes in consumer attitudes and behaviours and provide them with choices to change (Shove, 2010). The alternative technological changes, such as biodegradable packaging, also, ultimately, puts the onus on consumers and retailers, either at the point of sale or at the point of disposal. Prohibitive costs, availability of sorting infrastructure and general availability issues are some of the ways that the use of such materials is challenged (Chida, 2011). Moreover, biodegradable or compostable substitutes may have overall negative impacts. Home and industrial composters have varied functionality and capacity to process compostable products, along with food and garden waste, and biodegradable products not as easily biodegraded as advertised (Goel et al, 2021).

In many cases, reuse systems clash with local informal arrangements, leading to increased landfill activity and volumes. For example, in Australia, the practice of leaving unwanted items and materials on the kerbside ('hard rubbish') is associated with gleaning, so people graze others' castoffs, allowing the expression of positive values associated with not-wasting, caring for others and social responsibility (Lewis et al, 2010). However, many municipal councils have sought to make gleaning illegal to protect the haul of professional resource recovery contractors. A socially based approach that engages with reuse and caring practices might promote new routes for resource recovery beyond the formal recycling and landfill economy. Recognizing social dimensions of waste opens up possibilities for circulating and reusing materials in practices of prosumption, closing the loop on supply and demand of waste (Savini, 2019).

Spatial distributions of waste inclusion are also associated with waste infrastructure configurations. Kruger (2020) shows how waste pickup routes in urban areas can be associated with clean and dirty neighbourhoods. On closer inspection this bureaucratic scheduling of waste collection ends up excluding areas inhabited by lower socio-economic cohorts. According to Kruger, such social and environmental injustices are common in the American waste regime. In the case of Campania, Italy, technical and rapid solutions were imposed, taking advantage of the shock of piling garbage due to the unavailability of any disposal route (Armiero and D'Alisa, 2012). The emergency solution of waste incinerators using renewable energy allowed private corporations to accumulate profits externalizing the costs to society and local citizens through taxes and pollution.

The combination of interconnected social structures that impact and oppress individuals and groups spanning, for example, race, gender, sexuality, ability or class, ensures that any market-based solution that does not account for differentials in social structures will lead to aggravating exclusionary outcomes. For example, banning single-use plastics (without other measures) can be expected to impose disproportionate burdens on already vulnerable people. Yet, health impacts of plastics in use may also be exacerbated in protected and vulnerable groups and individuals (Trasande et al, 2022).

Given the entanglements revealed here, policy interventions that target consumer behaviours and place responsibility with 'end users' can only be expected to have marginal, if any, positive impact on domestic waste. Thus, research is required that better describes the relationships of people and waste to navigate routes to post-carbon waste that might yield more inclusive outcomes.

Foundations of an inclusionary domestic discard regime

This section turns to concepts and mechanisms that might underpin more inclusionary domestic discard regimes, including opportunities that a relational and structural approach brings. As Bulkeley and Askins (2009: 259) argue, 'in order to move waste management towards sustainability, there is a need both to engage with the institutional and infrastructural dimensions of the systems of provision within which waste management occurs, and to take seriously the everyday contexts within which making waste is practiced'. For example, even in cases where recycling is one of 'the answers', priority should be given to addressing exclusionary and regressive impacts of resource taxes and bans (such as on plastic bags, waste or landfill).

Relational approaches are a necessary basis for engaging with inclusion since they provide ways of understanding the complex actual lived experiences of domestic waste beyond normative explanations of choice and behaviour. This highlights a central challenge facing attempts at innovative governance that accommodate relational perspectives; they immediately face incumbent market-based logics and existing siloed governmentalities.

Theories of practice are one such relational perspective in which consumption is considered part of, or a moment within, a practice such as eating, parenting or caring. In terms of the consumer, this means that routinized, embodied and unreflective aspects of consumption are emphasized (Warde, 2005). What matters then is the dynamics of practices, and elements and relationships with other practices and materials. For CE discourses, transformation becomes about social practices and its dynamics rather than an individual's ABC model of decision making.

Practices are a site for considering change, as they are both dynamic and obdurate, with crises of change prompting practices to change even as they are held together by daily reproduction of tasks. At the same time, social life is constituted by multiple practices that overlap in the form of bundles that have various characteristics, such as temporalities, spatialities, materialities, and so on. For example, eating practices are closely related to food waste and disposal practices, along with family and cultural practices. These bundles can be collaborative or competitive, resulting in various outcomes (Shove et al, 2012).

Linking social justice and socio-environmental equities and social practices with Sen's (1993: 30) capability and 'functionings' approach reveals useful insights into environmental justice and sustainability (see Chapter 9). Capabilities relate to the abilities to perform or enact practices – for example, being able to draw on materials, competences and meanings (Walker, 2013). Unevenly distributed abilities and limited capabilities may prevent a person from being recruited to a practice, or from accomplishing a practice in a successful way. So inequality becomes about recruitment to, and performance of, practices and, analytically speaking, variations in the performance of practice are reflections of differences in capability (Halkier and Holm, 2021). Thus, a social practices capability framework provides the basis 'for making normative judgements about where and how practices reproduce significant inequalities and diminish or fail to support well-being'

(Walker, 2013: 193). The framework innovatively distracts attention from individual focused capabilities towards societal change that supports such capabilities and embeds social justice as central to social practice analyses (Willand et al, 2021).

Opening up ideas for relational-informed local waste governance

Accepting that social change cannot be directed offers an opening for ideas of relational-informed local waste governance. In the search for better places to start than further marketizing recycling, Wishart and Bebbington (2020) consider the promise of zero waste governance. They focus on the Scottish government's Zero Waste Scotland policy, noting innovations that include the setting up of a specialized delivery body to manage the policy, a reuse labelling scheme and a local volunteer programme. They highlight and acknowledge the role and importance of networks and boundary organizations in sustainable waste management and the potential dominance of measurable targets in zero waste, such as developing broader and pluralistic zero waste indicators (Clay et al, 2007; Zaman, 2014).

Terrain is created that provides possibilities for new socio-material bundles of practices that might reduce waste and lead to minimizing, reusing or redeploying used materials without fuelling consumption. Structural and regulatory interventions might include stopping exporting wastes from their point of production or regulating producers to repair and recover broken, unwanted or unused commodities. Through a range of social, material and experimental action research interventions, new constellations of meanings, social and regulatory rules, and material relations emerge that offer promising routes to post-carbon inclusion in domestic discard regimes. They can inform new coalitions of post-carbon inclusion. By this, we mean the not-to-be-underestimated processes of establishing new discourses, language, meaning, practices and institutions, as indicated across the three ideas to which this chapter now turns.

Governance bundles

The explosion of interest in CE is prompting new institutions, but they are invariably, first, premised on production–consumption binaries; second, imbued with methodological individualism and responsibilization; third, technologically determinist; and, fourth, lacking a relational underpinning that allows for inclusion. It follows that we propose mechanisms for building coalitions that, instead, deliberately seek to subvert these constraints, enabled by intermediary functions to share knowledge, connect and mediate across experiments, regions, neighbourhoods and initiatives.

The concept of 'environmentality' (Agrawal, 2005) is useful here, revealing power and identity by examining relationships between humans and waste, and top-down and bottom-up measures (Barnhart, nd; Gordon and Foucault, 1980). Kębłowski et al (2020) show that while the CE narrative in Brussels serves the capitalistic needs of the food industry, it is heterogeneously constituted bottom-up activism that challenges mainstream business and industrial practices. Building knowledge, discourses and participatory action research as advocated by Foth and Brynskov (2016) provides a mechanism for knowledge building and coproduction. Anastasiu (2019) goes further, advocating systematic processes for learning across multiple cases.

Everyday waste routines

The centrality of practices and places within domestic discard regimes points to the importance of everyday waste routines in organizing future waste infrastructures, shaping and being shaped by waste management practices of councils and governments. The number and kind of bins will shape designs of houses, as will the futures of packaging stewardship and extended producer responsibility. How much space is needed, and how will it be configured, to accommodate sorting and storage of multiple discard streams? How do, or could, multiple households collectively plan and do things? (Chappells and Shove, 1999; du Toit and Wagner, 2020; Horne et al, 2022).

More bins, in different places and in different ways means engaging with the attempts of various stakeholders to figure out how waste can be sorted, collected and disposed of (Waitt et al, 2012). Everyday waste routines are not homogeneous, nor can they be detached from the rest of the everyday. The careful mapping of diverse lived experience is an essential precursor to planning for inclusion.

Giving the example of Bitterballen where an unsustainable material, veal, is replaced by mushrooms, in a systemic way, Hobson (2020) illustrates a small loop that makes overt links between seemingly small and mundane aspects of consumption and the principles of CE. The Bitterballen manufacturing site runs in a loop that connects production and consumption and links energy, nutrients and waste. According to Hobson (2020), the importance given to context, complex socio-technical relations and broader social patterns, evident in this example, may positively shape how we become part of a broad transformative agenda opposed to individualistic mechanisms.

Infrastructures and affective bundles

Notwithstanding the dangers of promoting recycling for unintended consumption, reimagining waste collection services as neighbourhood infrastructures, when goods and materials are (re)circulated close to sites of consumption, opens possibilities for value creation at the neighbourhood level (Bulkeley and Gregson, 2009). This not only reduces travel and courier logistics, it also potentially allows for relationships of care, community capacity and communitarian processes to become established as an antidote to marketized waste logics. A shift from 'waste as commodity' to 'waste as vector for care and community' prompts connection to degrowth and its instinctive inclusive and just environmental orientation. In opposing accumulation and de-commoning of resources, and favouring local human resources (Hickel, 2021), a degrowth imaginary has been proposed as possibly the only way that CE could achieve its stated aims (Lambert, 2020).

Conclusion

In focusing on markets, technology and behaviours, the CE concept points away from the core problems of waste and climate crises, towards arrangements where future domestic waste costs are disproportionally borne by those least able to participate or comply. This in turn exacerbates inequalities and alienation, risking the whole CE project. However triumphantly optimistic, CE advocacy cannot meaningfully make inroads into eliminating waste or advancing inclusion without attention to the structures and relations of waste. Such broadening of the CE agenda involves thinking beyond recycling or buying sustainable products. As Liboiron and Lepawsky (2022: 6) put it, troubling the 'assumptions, premises and mythologies of waste' in this way may divert attention towards materialities and systems that may have been missed during casual observation.

Instead of imagining whirling circular materialities, the expectations of the CE can only be made possible when 'life histories and chances are interwoven with material cultures and practices' (Hobson, 2021: 173). Practices and capabilities provide useful ways into this agenda. This is not to say that a relational-informed waste governance regime provides an overnight solution to the problem. Going beyond responsibilization and building a socially inclusive approach demands recalibration of everyday lives. This behoves us all to be open to the wide range of practical, inclusive, just, CE options, both radical and conventional, and to be critically engaged in their prospects and progress.

References

Agrawal, A. (2005) *Technologies of Government and the Making of Subjects*, London: Duke University Press.

Altman, R. (2021) 'On wishcycling', *Discard Studies*, 15 February. Available from: https://discardstudies.com/2021/02/15/on-wishcycling/ [Accessed 1 June 2023].

Anastasiu, I. (2019) 'Unpacking the smart city through the lens of the right to the city: a taxonomy as a way forward in participatory city-making', in de Lange, M. and de Waal, M. (eds) *The Hackable City*, Singapore: Springer, pp 239–60.

Andersen, M.S. (2007) 'An introductory note on the environmental economics of the circular economy', *Sustainability Science*, 2(1): 133–40.

Armiero, M. and D'Alisa, G. (2012) 'Rights of resistance: the garbage struggles for environmental justice in Campania, Italy', *Capitalism Nature Socialism*, 23(4): 52–68.

Barnhart, S. (nd) 'Environmentality', *Discard Studies Compendium*. Available from: https://discardstudies.com/discard-studies-compendium/#Wasteflows [Accessed 1 June 2023].

Bauwens, T., Hekkert, M. and Kirchherr, J. (2020) 'Circular futures: what will they look like?', *Ecological Economics*, 175: 106703.

Borg, K., Lennox, A., Kaufman, S., Tull, F., Prime, R., Rogers, L. et al (2022) 'Curbing plastic consumption: a review of single-use plastic behaviour change interventions', *Journal of Cleaner Production*, 344: 131077.

Bretz, T.H. (2020) 'Discussing harm without harming: disability and environmental justice', *Environmental Ethics*, 42(2): 169–87.

Bryant, R., Goodman, M.K. and Redclift, M. (2008) 'Spaces of intention as exclusionary practice: exploring ethical limits to "alternative" sustainable consumption'. Available from: https://api.semanticscholar.org/CorpusID:198903172?utm_source=wikipedia [Accessed 1 June 2023].

Bulkeley, H. and Askins, K. (2009) 'Waste interfaces: biodegradable waste, municipal policy and everyday practice', *The Geographical Journal*, 175(4): 251–60.

Bulkeley, H. and Gregson, N. (2009) 'Crossing the threshold: municipal waste policy and household waste generation', *Environment and Planning A*, 41(4): 929–45.

Chappells, H. and Shove, E. (1999) 'The dustbin: a study of domestic waste, household practices and utility services', *International Planning Studies*, 4(2): 267–80.

Chida, M. (2011) 'Sustainability in retail: the failed debate around plastic shopping bags', *Fashion Practice*, 3(2): 175–96.

Clay, S., Gibson, D. and Ward, J. (2007) 'Sustainability Victoria: influencing resource use, towards zero waste and sustainable production and consumption', *Journal of Cleaner Production*, 15(8–9): 782–6.

Cook, G. and Jardim, E. (2017) 'Guide to greener electronics 2017', *Greenpeace Reports*, 17 October. Available from: https://www.greenpeace.org/usa/reports/greener-electronics-2017/ [Accessed 1 June 2023].

Corvellec, H., Böhm, S., Stowell, A. and Valenzuela, F. (2020) 'Introduction to the special issue on the contested realities of the circular economy', *Culture and Organization*, 26(2): 97–102.

Corvellec, H., Stowell, A.F. and Johansson, N. (2022) 'Critiques of the circular economy', *Journal of Industrial Ecology*, 26(2): 421–32.

Davies, A.R. (2005) 'Incineration politics and the geographies of waste governance: a burning issue for Ireland?', *Environment and Planning C: Government and Policy*, 23(3): 375–97.

du Toit, J. and Wagner, C. (2020) 'The effect of housing type on householders' self-reported participation in recycling', *Smart and Sustainable Built Environment*, 9(4): 395–412.

EU Science Hub (2016) 'Sustainable product policy', *EU Science Hub*. Available from: https://joint-research-centre.ec.europa.eu/scientific-activities-z/sustainable-product-policy_en [Accessed 1 June 2023].

Evans, D. (2011) 'Beyond the throwaway society: ordinary domestic practice and a sociological approach to household food waste', *Sociology*, 46(1): 41–56.

Farbotko, C. (2018) *Domestic Environmental Labour: An Ecofeminist Perspective on Making Homes Greener*, Abingdon: Routledge.

Figge, F. and Thorpe, A.S. (2019) 'The symbiotic rebound effect in the circular economy', *Ecological Economics*, 163: 61–9.

Foth, M. and Brynskov, M. (2016) 'Participatory action research for civic engagement', in Gordon, E. and Mihailidis, P. (eds), *Civic Media: Technology, Design, Practice*, Cambridge, MA: MIT Press, pp 563–80.

Gharfalkar, M., Court, R., Campbell, C., Ali, Z. and Hillier, G. (2015) 'Analysis of waste hierarchy in the European waste directive 2008/98/EC', *Waste Management*, 39: 305–13.

Gibbs, D. and Deutz, P. (2007) 'Reflections on implementing industrial ecology through eco-industrial park development', *Journal of Cleaner Production*, 15(17): 1683–95.

Goel, V., Luthra, P., Kapur, G.S. and Ramakumar, S.S.V. (2021) 'Biodegradable/bio-plastics: myths and realities', *Journal of Polymers and the Environment*, 29(10): 3079–104.

Gordon, C. and Foucault, M. (1980) *Power/Knowledge: Selected Interviews and Other Writings, 1972–1977*, New York: Pantheon Books.

Government of Victoria (2023) 'Building Victoria's circular economy', *Victorian Government*, 23 May. Available from: https://www.vic.gov.au/building-victorias-circular-economy [Accessed 1 June 2023].

Government of Western Australia (2021) 'Single-use plastic working group – terms of reference', *Government of Western Australia*. Available from: https://www.wa.gov.au/system/files/2022-04/Singe-use-plastic-working-group-terms-of-reference.pdf [Accessed 1 June 2023].

Gregson, N. and Crang, M. (2010) 'Materiality and waste: inorganic vitality in a networked world', *Environment & Planning A*, 42(5): 1026–32.

Gregson, N. and Forman, P.J. (2021) 'England's municipal waste regime: challenges and prospects', *The Geographical Journal*, 187(3): 214–26.

Gregson, N., Crang, M., Fuller, S. and Holmes, H. (2015) 'Interrogating the circular economy: the moral economy of resource recovery in the EU', *Economy and Society*, 44(2): 218–43.

Halkier, B. and Holm, L. (2021) 'Linking socioeconomic disadvantage to healthiness of food practices: can a practice-theoretical perspective sharpen everyday life analysis?', *Sociology of Health & Illness*, 43(3): 750–63.

Hawkins, G. (2013) 'Made to be wasted: PET and topologies of disposability', in Gabrys, J., Hawkins, G. and Michael, M. (eds), *Accumulation*, London: Routledge, pp 63–81.

Hawkins, G. (2021) 'Detaching from plastic packaging: reconfiguring material responsibilities', *Consumption Markets & Culture*, 24(4): 405–18.

Hawkins, G. and Race, K. (2011) 'Bottled water practices: reconfiguring drinking in Bangkok households', in Lane, R. and Gorman-Murray, A. (eds), *Material Geographies of Household Sustainability*, London: Ashgate, pp 113–24.

Hickel, J. (2021) 'What does degrowth mean? A few points of clarification', *Globalizations*, 18(7): 1105–11.

Hobson, K. (2016) 'Closing the loop or squaring the circle? Locating generative spaces for the circular economy', *Progress in Human Geography*, 40(1): 88–104.

Hobson, K. (2020) '"Small stories of closing loops": social circularity and the everyday circular economy', *Climatic Change*, 163(1): 99–116.

Hobson, K. (2021) 'The limits of the loops: critical environmental politics and the Circular Economy', *Environmental Politics*, 30(1–2): 161–79.

Hobson, K. and Lynch, N. (2016) 'Diversifying and de-growing the circular economy: radical social transformation in a resource-scarce world', *Futures*, 82: 15–25.

Hobson, K., Holmes, H., Welch, D., Wheeler, K. and Wieser, H. (2021) 'Consumption work in the circular economy: a research agenda', *Journal of Cleaner Production*, 321: 128969.

Horne, R., Strengers, Y. and Strempel, A. (2016) 'Policing and polluting: the role of practices in contemporary urban environmental pollution governance', *Environmental Science & Policy*, 66: 112–18.

Horne, R., Dorignon, L. and Middha, B. (2022) 'High-rise plastic: socio-material entanglements in apartments', *The Geographical Journal*, 188(4): 571–84.

Idies, Y. (2020) 'The landfill paradox: reflections on the temporalities of waste', in Allon, F., Barcan, R. and Eddison-Cogan, K. (eds) *The Temporalities of Waste*, London: Routledge, pp 136–47.

Johansson, N. and Corvellec, H. (2018) 'Waste policies gone soft: an analysis of European and Swedish waste prevention plans', *Waste Management*, 77: 322–32.

Johnson, T. (2013) 'The politics of waste incineration in Beijing: the limits of a top-down approach?', *Journal of Environmental Policy & Planning*, 15(1): 109–28.

Kębłowski, W., Lambert, D. and Bassens, D. (2020) 'Circular economy and the city: an urban political economy agenda', *Culture and Organization*, 26(2): 142–58.

Kruger, R.M. (2020) 'Biopolitical temporalities of waste and the municipal collection schedule in the United States', in Allon, F., Barcan, R. and Eddison-Cogan, K. (eds), *The Temporalities of Waste: Out of Sight Out of Time*, London: Routledge, pp 61–74.

Lambert, D. (2020) 'Recycling old ideals? A utopian reading of "circular" food imaginaries', in Nelson, A. and Edwards, F. (eds), *Food for Degrowth*, Abingdon: Routledge, pp 159–72.

Lane, R. and Watson, M. (2012) 'Stewardship of things: the radical potential of product stewardship for re-framing responsibilities and relationships to products and materials', *Geoforum*, 43(6): 1254–65.

Lewis, H., Verghese, K. and Fitzpatrick, L. (2010) 'Evaluating the sustainability impacts of packaging: the plastic carry bag dilemma', *Packaging Technology and Science: An International Journal*, 23(3): 145–60.

Liboiron, M. and Lepawsky, J. (2022) *Discard Studies: Wasting, Systems, and Power*, Cambridge, MA: MIT Press.

Lindsay, J. and Maher, J. (2013) *Consuming Families: Buying, Making, Producing Family Life in the 21st Century*, New York: Routledge.

MacBride, S. (2013) *Recycling Reconsidered: The Present Failure and Future Promise of Environmental Action in the United States*, Cambridge, MA: MIT Press.

Mann, A. (2020) 'Are you local? Digital inclusion in participatory foodscapes', in Lupton, D. and Feldman, Z. (eds), *Digital Food Cultures*, Abingdon: Routledge, pp 147–61.

Murray, A., Skene, K. and Haynes, K. (2017) 'The circular economy: an interdisciplinary exploration of the concept and application in a global context', *Journal of Business Ethics*, 140(3): 369–80.

Nagle, R. (2013) *Picking Up: On The Streets and Behind the Trucks with the Sanitation Workers of New York City*, New York: Macmillan.

Nielsen, T.D., Hasselbalch, J., Holmberg, K. and Stripple, J. (2020) 'Politics and the plastic crisis: a review throughout the plastic life cycle', *Wiley Interdisciplinary Reviews: Energy & Environment*, 9(1): e360.

OECD (2018) *Improving Plastics Management: Trends, Policy, Responses, and the Role of International Co-operation and Trade*, Paris: OECD Publishing.

Pla-Julián, I. and Guevara, S. (2019) 'Is circular economy the key to transitioning towards sustainable development? Challenges from the perspective of care ethics', *Futures*, 105: 67–77.

Queensland Government (2021) 'Single-use plastic items ban: information for people with disability or healthcare needs'. Available from: https://www.qld.gov.au/environment/circular-economy-waste-reduction/reduction/plastic-pollution/single-use-plastic-products-ban/healthcare-needs [Accessed 19 January 2024].

Rushton, L. (2003) 'Health hazards and waste management', *British Medical Bulletin*, 68(1): 183–97.

Saunders, P., Naidoo, Y. and Griffiths, M. (2008) 'Towards new indicators of disadvantage: deprivation and social exclusion in Australia', *Australian Journal of Social Issues*, 43(2): 175–94.

Savini, F. (2019) 'The economy that runs on waste: accumulation in the circular city', *Journal of Environmental Policy & Planning*, 21(6): 675–91.

Sen, A. (1993) 'Capability and wellbeing', in Nussbaum, M. and Sen, A. (eds), *The Quality of Life*, Oxford: Clarendon Press, pp 30–53.

Shove, E. (2002) 'Rushing around: coordination, mobility and inequality', draft paper for the Mobile Network meeting, October. Available from: https://www.lancaster.ac.uk/staff/shove/choreography/rushingaround.pdf [Accessed 1 June 2023].

Shove, E. (2003) 'Users, technologies and expectations of comfort, cleanliness and convenience', *Innovation: The European Journal of Social Science Research*, 16(2): 193–206.

Shove, E. (2010) 'Beyond the ABC: climate change policy and theories of social change', *Environment and Planning A*, 42(6): 1273–85.

Shove, E., Pantzar, M. and Watson, M. (2012) *The Dynamics of Social Practice: Everyday Life and How it Changes*, London: SAGE.

Trasande, L., Liu, B. and Bao, W. (2022) 'Phthalates and attributable mortality: a population-based longitudinal cohort study and cost analysis', *Environmental Pollution*, 292(Part A): 118021.

Valero, A. and Valero, A. (2019) 'Thermodynamic rarity and recyclability of raw materials in the energy transition: the need for an in-spiral economy', *Entropy*, 21(9): 873.

van Ewijk, S., Stegemann, J.A. and Ekins, P. (2021) 'Limited climate benefits of global recycling of pulp and paper', *Nature Sustainability*, 4(2): 180–7.

Wagner, T.P. (2020) 'Policy instruments to reduce consumption of expanded polystyrene food service ware in the USA', *Detritus*, 9: 11–26.

Waitt, G., Caputi, P., Gibson, C., Farbotko, C., Head, L., Gill, N. et al (2012) 'Sustainable household capability: which households are doing the work of environmental sustainability?', *Australian Geographer*, 43(1): 51–74.

Walker, G. (2013) 'Inequality, sustainability and capability: locating justice in social practice', in Shove, E. and Spurling, N. (eds), *Sustainable Practices: Social Theory and Climate Change*, London: Routledge, pp 181–96.

Warde, A. (2005) 'Consumption and theories of practice', *Journal of Consumer Culture*, 5(2): 131–53.

Willand, N., Middha, B. and Walker, G. (2021) 'Using the capability approach to evaluate energy vulnerability policies and initiatives in Victoria, Australia', *Local Environment*, 26(9): 1109–27.

Wishart, L.J. and Bebbington, J. (2020) 'Zero waste governance: a Scottish case study', *International Journal of Sustainable Development*, 23(1–2): 128–47.

Zaman, A.U. (2014) 'Measuring waste management performance using the "Zero Waste Index": the case of Adelaide, Australia', *Journal of Cleaner Production*, 66: 407–19.

Zink, T. and Geyer, R. (2017) 'Circular economy rebound', *Journal of Industrial Ecology*, 21(3): 593–602.

9

Cool Inclusion: Thermal Inequality in an Overheating Climate

Elspeth Oppermann, Gordon Walker and Jamie Cross

Introduction

Staying cool in urban environments happens at the intersection of two competing climate change dynamics and objectives. On the one hand, populations are encouraged to stay cool to ward off the threat of heat-related illnesses, morbidity and mortality in a rapidly warming climate marked by intensifying and increasingly frequent heat waves. As the recent Intergovernmental Panel on Climate Change (IPCC, 2022: 1518) assessment states, 'the frequency and intensity of hot extremes will continue to increase ... at global and continental scales and in nearly all inhabited regions with increasing global warming levels'. On the other hand, populations are asked to reduce cooling activities that require energy or water use, particularly during heat waves or peak-load periods (Maller and Strengers, 2011), and specifically to avoid energy intensive air conditioning, a major contributor to greenhouse gas emissions (Zhang et al, 2020) and the urban heat island effect (Takane et al, 2019). This cooling contestation – that pits a logic of climate adaptation against a logic of climate mitigation – is sometimes reduced by social scientists to a question of temporal and spatial scale. Within behavioural psychology, for example, a lack of information, cognitive dissonance and discounting have been routinely mobilized as explanations for high emissions behaviours (Stoknes, 2015; Whitmarsh et al, 2021). We would argue that this contestation is also, and crucially, a question of inequality and injustice, framed in social, energy and climatic terms.

Being able to stay cool enough to be safe, healthy, able to flourish and live a decent life, is unequally distributed. Whether there is cooling to 'give up' or cooling to 'attain' varies dramatically in degree and achievability globally. The availability of these two choices for people differs between populations in high-, low- and middle-income countries; it differs within national populations in terms of interwoven fractures of wealth, ethnicity, age and gender; and these inequities are materialized by differential patterns of access to cooling technologies and infrastructures, including those currently embedded in high carbon dependency.

Take air conditioning, for example. For low-income urban populations in South Asian or sub-Saharan African cities, having an air conditioner, or the reliable electricity to run it, can be inconceivable. In some contexts, the most basic infrastructures for cooling living environments and/or the body – such as clean water to drink and bathe, or electricity to power a fan – can be severely limited and constrained (Opperman et al, 2022). Even the emerging middle classes can struggle with access to these cool infrastructures (Pavanello et al, 2021). By contrast, for upper- and middle-income urban populations in Northern and Southern Europe, which is also largely temperate, and where water and electricity for other modes of cooling is reliable, air conditioning is readily available, if often considered a luxury good.

With the intensification of climate change, however, the locus of where air conditioning is most likely to be needed is shifting (Davis et al, 2021; Pavanello et al, 2021; Parkes et al, 2022). As temperatures rise, it is becoming apparent that the basic requirements for a healthy life in very hot locations may only be able to be met by intensive cooling. This may take the form of the 'emergency' provision of air-conditioned cool spaces or refuges outside the home for those who are very young, elderly or unwell (Voelkel et al, 2018). But when environmental conditions cross thresholds considered fatal to human life, the need for intensive cooling may extend to entire populations, not just those considered the most vulnerable (Raymond et al, 2020). Against this backdrop, the 'choice' between cooling (for adaptation) and not cooling (for mitigation) takes on very different characteristics. Rights-based approaches to cooling – exemplified by the United Nations commitment to 'Cooling for All' (Cooling for All Secretariat, nd) – do not address the often problematic material-energetic and social relations through which cooling works. Neither do they ask the fundamental question demanded by our transition to a future post-carbon world – *when is* cooling necessary, and for whom?

This chapter seeks to grapple with these issues and go beyond a needs-based assessment framework for cooling, by proposing an account of cooling as capability, drawing on the capability approach (CA) as a normative, accomplishment-based framework for determining what should be at the foundation of human welfare and wellbeing (Sen, 2009). In so doing, we engage with the question of 'what cooling *does*', that is, how it secures basic or bare life, and we suggest that attention to 'thermal violence' and 'thermal autonomy' (Starosielski, 2019) can account for the ways that power relationships have historically manipulated the capacity of differentiated human bodies to mediate heat. We make three core arguments.

First, and keeping in view the commitment to post-carbon inclusion that runs through this book, we argue that achieving 'cool inclusion' demands explicit attention to social justice. Rather than simply stripping carbon out of existing energy production systems in a blanket fashion or arguing for limiting the further diffusion of energy intensive services such as air conditioning, a just approach to cooling during processes of transition must proceed in such a way that remains simultaneously attentive to the unequal consequences and the ethical implications of what energy is used for (Walker et al, 2016).

Second, we argue that cool inclusion entails a fundamental recognition of the struggles and challenges involved in avoiding or coping with heat and limiting its harmful consequences. Using the CA, we re-examine accounts of vulnerability and exposure to heat in the health and adaptation literature and open these out as ethical and justice questions ripe for social and political intervention.

Third, we argue that a definition of cool inclusion should be premised on the thermal autonomy to secure what cooling is most needed for, from its fundamental life-saving capacity, to the enabling of a healthy, productive and flourishing life. While we acknowledge the contextuality and dynamism of what is considered 'essential', we propose that working through the framework of linkages and mediating processes within the CA can move us towards interventions for cool inclusion that take account of both inflexible characteristics (such as age) and the situated factors that tend to be excluded from a rights-based or universal access model. This approach then allows for an explicit conversation about moving towards post-carbon based on capability and need.

We begin with a discussion of different ways of understanding thermal comfort, the need for cooling, and the processes involved in producing inequalities in both vulnerability and exposure to heat. We then position keeping cool within the framework of the CA, before considering how this provides a structure for seeing how cool exclusion operates within low-income communities in the Global South. We conclude by suggesting how our CA reframes questions of cooling in moving towards a post-carbon world.

Heat: from comfort, to health, wellbeing and productivity

How cooling is framed and understood varies across the physical and social sciences. Within architecture and engineering, cooling is understood primarily as a question of thermal comfort in relationship to the use of domestic and office space (de Dear et al, 2020). Here thermal comfort is typically defined as the 'condition of the mind that expresses satisfaction with the thermal environment', with 22°C routinely assessed to be the point at which this happens (de Dear et al 2020: 1, quoting ASHRAE Standard 55, 2020). Within the social sciences, however, such a position has been widely debunked as based on limited physiological or cognitive evidence, driven by the air-conditioning industry, culturally specific and gendered, and leading to the unnecessary energy and carbon-intensive overcooling of buildings. Since the late 1990s, the most common replacement model has been adaptive thermal comfort (Nicol et al, 2012) which accounts for greater variation in local preferences and local experience (including seasonal acclimatization) and for the ability of inhabitants to actively modify their environment (for example, through opening windows or removing a layer of clothing). Theories of social practice have also been brought into interaction with adaptive thermal comfort, aligning with some of its core ideas, but critiquing a reliance on behavioural models of the actions that people take, and emphasizing the wider dynamics of how air conditioning comes to be considered normal and necessary (Shove and Chappells, 2008; Shove et al, 2014; Walker et al, 2014).

A related shift has been seen in the literature on thermal physiology, that moves from an understanding of thermal comfort as an abstract, universal characterization of an environment, to something that is actively co-produced by human activity. Here, thermal comfort is viewed as one of many indexes of perceived and measurable effects of thermal conditions, embedded in and shaped by socio-cultural and neurological accounts (Mazzone and Khosla, 2021), that includes effects that are exogenous to the body (such as those produced from exposure to a hot environment or external heat sources) as well as those that are endogenous to the body (such as the effects of exertion and the metabolic production of heat). These shifts have made human actions even more central to the account of what makes thermal conditions acceptable or not, while continuing to account for the human body's autonomic thermoregulation system that is constantly at work, managing, for example, sweat response and blood flow at the surface of the skin.

Placing human actions at the centre of a more complex account of cooling does not, however, suggest that we are infinitely capable. At every level of response to heat there are significant dependencies and limitations which play into vulnerabilities to harmful effects. Infants, young children, the elderly and anyone unwell have much less effective thermoregulation capacity. With decreased thermoregulatory capacity, the human body is made much more vulnerable to heat and thus more in need of other modes of cooling. Vulnerability also exists in relation to the behaviours that are available to people to cool down – physical impairment, cultural norms about clothing practices or the gendering of certain spaces can all reduce the ability of some or all inhabitants to respond adaptively to thermal conditions (as discussed later in the chapter).

A further consideration is the question of exposure to heat and its differentiation between people and the environments they inhabit. In building terms, for example, exposure might relate both to the weather conditions that a building is subjected to and the micro-climatic zones that emerge across cities as a result of varying urban morphology, including the presence or absence of greenspaces (Kabisch and van den Bosch, 2017). Such conditions are difficult to change and, from an individual's perspective, regarded as largely set in place. Exposure can also refer to more local and personal forms of exposure – such as working near a heat source (for example, cooking over a fire), or working outdoors and being exposed to both exogenous (the sun) and internally generated (metabolic) heat. As a result, heat exposure in practice can be quite dynamic and differentiated. There may be opportunities for exposure to be avoided or reduced, but the degree of exposure will also determine the degree of cooling needed to return the body to a state that can sustain health and wellbeing.

To summarize, adaptive responses to heat describe ways of reducing vulnerability, exposure and exertion in ways that can reduce the amount of cooling the body requires. Where vulnerability, exposure and exertion cannot be changed, cooling may need to be increased to enable the return to 'safe' or comfortable thermal conditions at the bodily level. These combined elements of thermal management are visualized in Figure 9.1 as a pyramid in relation to progressively hotter environmental conditions, also indicating where and to what extent energy (and potentially carbon) intensive forms of cooling are involved.

Being cool enough

There has been a shift of approach then, from the engineering of cooled static spaces at set temperature levels, to a more dynamic understanding of how human actions are implicated in how thermal environments are shaped and experienced. This does not mean, however, that a judgement of what is 'cool' or 'cool enough' is simply open to interpretation or preference. Deeply rooted in the understanding of vulnerability to heat, and what constitutes dangerous exposure, are knowledges about states of health, wellbeing, and physical and cognitive performance. From these perspectives, cooling is sufficient when the body is operating, at the very least, within a safe range, such that autonomic and behavioural responses are sufficient to be able to live healthily and sustainably. In the literature from physiology, definitions for this safe range include the body being able to rapidly return to a core temperature of around 37°C. In the medical and epidemiological literature, such a norm is implicit, but the bar is a little lower, set at recovering fast

Figure 9.1: The pyramid of thermal management processes and their relationship to energy

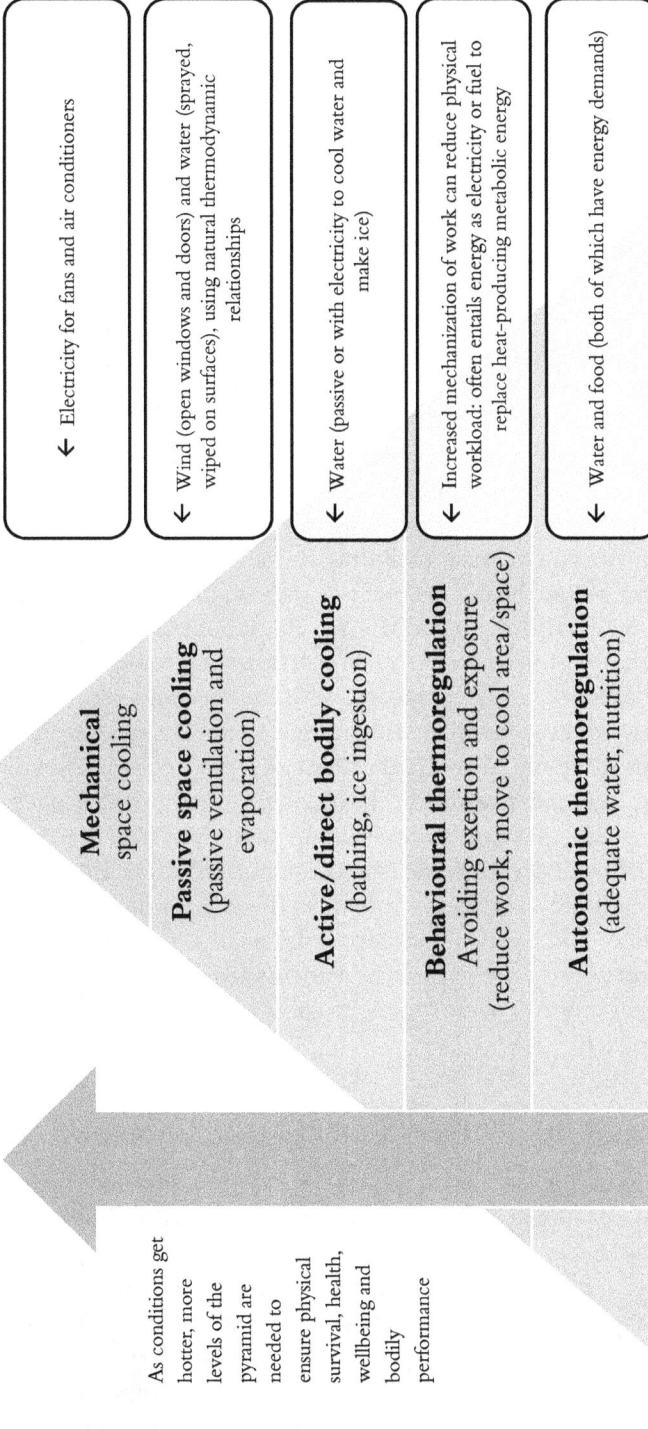

enough to avoid hospital presentations for heat-related illness, including heat exhaustion, and avoiding excess mortality and increased morbidity. Sufficient cooling then, with all these adaptive aspects discussed included, should at the very least result in the minimal definition of health – being alive, and no exacerbation of suffering from either a pre-existing or new heat-related disease or condition.

As should be apparent, this definition is a far cry from the concern with keeping domestic and office spaces comfortable that initially dominated how cooling was understood. However, we do not mean to claim that sustaining 'bare life' alone is an ethically sufficient threshold for cooling. In between these extremes, there remain significant concerns about mental health, wellbeing, performance and productivity (Rocque et al, 2020). Exposure to hot conditions, either acutely high for short periods, or moderately high but for long periods, can trigger declines in cognitive performance, affecting the ability to concentrate and perform at school or at work, and associated also with greater likelihood of being involved in accidents (Levi et al, 2018). A more extreme impact of heat exposure can be triggering irritability and violence, including domestic violence and the exacerbation of extant mental health problems (Liu et al, 2021). At a wider societal level, problematic impacts on educational attainment, household income security, economic performance, familial relationships, outbreaks of violence and public disorder are all associated with higher temperatures, driving calls to find ways to keep people cool enough to avoid such negative outcomes.

Far from being a luxury, therefore, keeping cool is essential for living a healthy, safe and secure life. Furthermore, rather than 'access to cooling' we have seen that the 'ability to cool' is the key issue. How that cooling is achieved depends on a range of overlapping and interacting mechanisms, from the autonomic to the behavioural, to the environmental and technological. Yet these mechanisms are not universally available or effective. The characteristics of individuals, and their various contexts, shape their access to, and ability to enact, sufficient cooling to manage their vulnerability to heat impacts.

Thermal inequalities and thermal violence

The discussion so far makes clear that we should expect there to be inequalities in the ability to keep sufficiently cool, but studies examining this have been limited in number and scope. Within the field of energy poverty research, long dominated in Global North contexts by concerns about affordable heating and the risks of being cold (Walker, 2022), questions of access to affordable air conditioning have now entered into view. In the United States, studies of who has air conditioning and who can afford to use it have brought into focus the ways that class and race intersect around cooling; contrasting the almost perpetually air-conditioned lives of wealthier populations in southern states (largely fossil-fuelled), with the unaffordability of air conditioning for poor and non-White communities (Mitchell and Chakraborty, 2014). These disparities are also manifested in the built environment. The ability or (in)ability to use mechanical cooling is compounded by the kind of buildings that people inhabit. Those unable to afford air conditioning are more likely to live in poorly constructed and maintained buildings that readily overheat, which are thus additionally and prohibitively expensive to keep cool. In a study focused on Eastern and Central Europe, Thomson et al (2019) identified the material, form and orientation of living accommodation as being all-important to the propensity to overheat, with low-income high-rise flats being particularly problematic.

Starosielski's (2019; 2021) account of thermal violence has, perhaps, gone furthest in examining the utilization and modulation of heating and cooling as a politics played out at the bodily level. This work compels us to acknowledge thermal violence as both the deliberate and incidental result of the space that bodies inhabit, and of the ways that bodily capacities are enrolled or restricted in feeling and responding to heat, which can be used violently to create pain or cause harm. In Starosielski's account, the thermal status of the subaltern and enslaved is effectively enrolled in the biopolitical and disciplinary exercise of power. Any agency or 'thermal autonomy' that individuals and groups have at their disposal can be removed or restricted in ways that cause pain, such as to produce particular behaviours. In this sense, the ability to cool is also a question about who controls the ability to cool, and the ends to which this control is used.

Living under conditions of thermal violence, the capacity to mobilize other cooling mechanisms to create acceptable thermal conditions becomes essential. In their European study, Thomson et al (2019) found that some households were able to make short-term adaptations that enabled degrees of coping with hot conditions, including behavioural and direct body-cooling as well as passive space and low-tech mechanical cooling, such as consuming cold drinks and food, moving to cooler locations, taking showers, adjusting ventilation and using fans. However, they observed 'striking unequal adaptive capacity, with many facing constraints on their ability to make alterations' (Thomson et al, 2019: 27), including factors such as housing tenure, the availability of cooler gardens or nearby greenspace, and the perceived safety of being outdoors or keeping windows open to cool dwellings overnight.

In previous work we have considered the behaviours of bodies and their engagement with spaces through a transdisciplinary account of thermal physiology, social practices and rhythmanalysis to identify cooling within a wider framework of socially and materially co-constructed management of thermal relations and energetic flows (Oppermann et al, 2020). Thinking along an energetic-material plane helps in understanding the relationship between the multiple mechanisms and processes of cooling and how they come together. It combines not just energy services, or resources that produce energy to run machines, but how these are deployed to respond to the multiple energies that traverse and are responsive to the urban and natural landscape – in heat-absorbing and re-radiating concrete, in the breeze from the ocean, in the kinetic and metabolic heat produced by the activity of moving bodies, or the (in)efficacy of evaporating sweat removing heat from the skin. At the individual and social level, we identify rhythms of thermal energy production, use and exchange as inherent to a nexus of practice that can be adaptive or maladaptive. At the level of the individual body, one critical point of distinction is the freedom and capability that individuals may, or may not, have to manage bodily heat accumulation, be it through resting, work rate or cooling and hydrating. While in principle these may be effective in managing bodily heat stress, such actions may not be readily realizable when they need to be, for example, in a work setting due to pressures for productivity and rules regulating worker behaviour.

In these approaches, there is a common concern with paying attention to thermal experience at the bodily level as what matters. While this is useful for *analysing* cooling, it has yet to be translated into an approach that asks what should be *done* to improve cooling. Cool inclusion is the right to be included – politically as well as materially – in the ability to keep cool and implies a commitment to including the needs of others. We move now to suggesting how the ability to cool, including at its political and ethical level, can be engaged with through the CA.

Keeping cool and justice through the capability approach

Since managing one's thermal status is essential to the basic needs of survival, keeping cool is ultimately an ethical question of justice, which needs be understood contextually. Considering the ability to manage thermal status and the context for doing so as not merely analytical questions about performances (as in social practice approaches) but as matters of justice, we consider here whether the CA might offer a useful framework for more expansive understandings of staying cool in transitioning to a post-carbon world.

The CA developed by Amartya Sen and Martha Nussbaum is a normative framework or perspective on human welfare and wellbeing that begins with the premise that 'what people can *do* and *be* is more important than what people have' (Sen, 2009: 18; emphasis in original). Within this framework, social justice is accomplishment-based, so it 'cannot be indifferent to the lives that people can actually live' (Sen, 2009: 18). What follows is that having the agency to choose whether things are done, or the freedom to shape how things are done, is politically essential to the achievement of basic human rights and human flourishing. Within the CA, basic or central elements of what constitutes a flourishing and a reasonable life, the things that people value, are termed 'functionings'. A person's capability to achieve these functionings is where the space for determining justice is located. The CA has been widely applied and developed since its initial formulation, including recently in work on energy poverty. Day et al (2016) propose it as a coherent and flexible way of conceptualizing how energy use matters to wellbeing. Others have extended this conceptualization and demonstrated its empirical application (Middlemiss et al, 2019; Bartiaux et al, 2021; Wang et al, 2021; Willand et al, 2021). This body of work provides a helpful starting point.

In their analysis, Day et al (2016) position valued outcomes that come from the use of energy in a domestic context – such as for washing clothes, preparing food, and keeping sufficiently warm or cool – not as central or basic capabilities, but as 'secondary capabilities'. Secondary capabilities are understood by Smith and Seward (2009: 229) as component parts of materializing one or more basic capabilities, having a 'concrete' and 'specific' quality and being 'at the heart of where most research and learning about capability resides'. As Day et al (2016: 259) state, 'we see an individual or household's ultimate concern as basic capabilities ... which require secondary capabilities, which sometimes require energy services'.

In Figure 9.2 we develop on the logic in a diagram in Day et al (2016: 262), to centre on 'keeping cool' as a secondary capability. To the right is a set of basic or central capabilities that being able to keep cool contributes to. 'Having a normal life expectancy' and 'being in good health' are at the centre, and most important, but 'being educated' and 'engaging in productive and valued activities' are included as examples of other central capabilities the achievement of which may be compromised. These examples draw from a proposed set of central capabilities and other similar formulations in Nussbaum (2003). There is extensive debate on the merits of different approaches to defining these (Kremakova, 2013; Robeyns, 2016). This is not intended as a definitive list, and these and other central capabilities may be seen as more or less relevant depending on context or how the relevant central capabilities themselves are defined.

Feeding into keeping cool are four forms of potential cooling 'services' that can be provided by electricity, water, shelter and vegetation. Although each has distinct roles, they also have significant interconnections. For example, electricity can be enabling of water provision and use where pumping is required, and the effectiveness of electricity-powered technologies within forms of shelter is strongly dependent on the building's efficiency and ventilation performance. Sitting behind each of these cooling services are forms of infrastructure for which various characteristics, including quality,

Figure 9.2: Keeping cool conceptualized within the capability approach

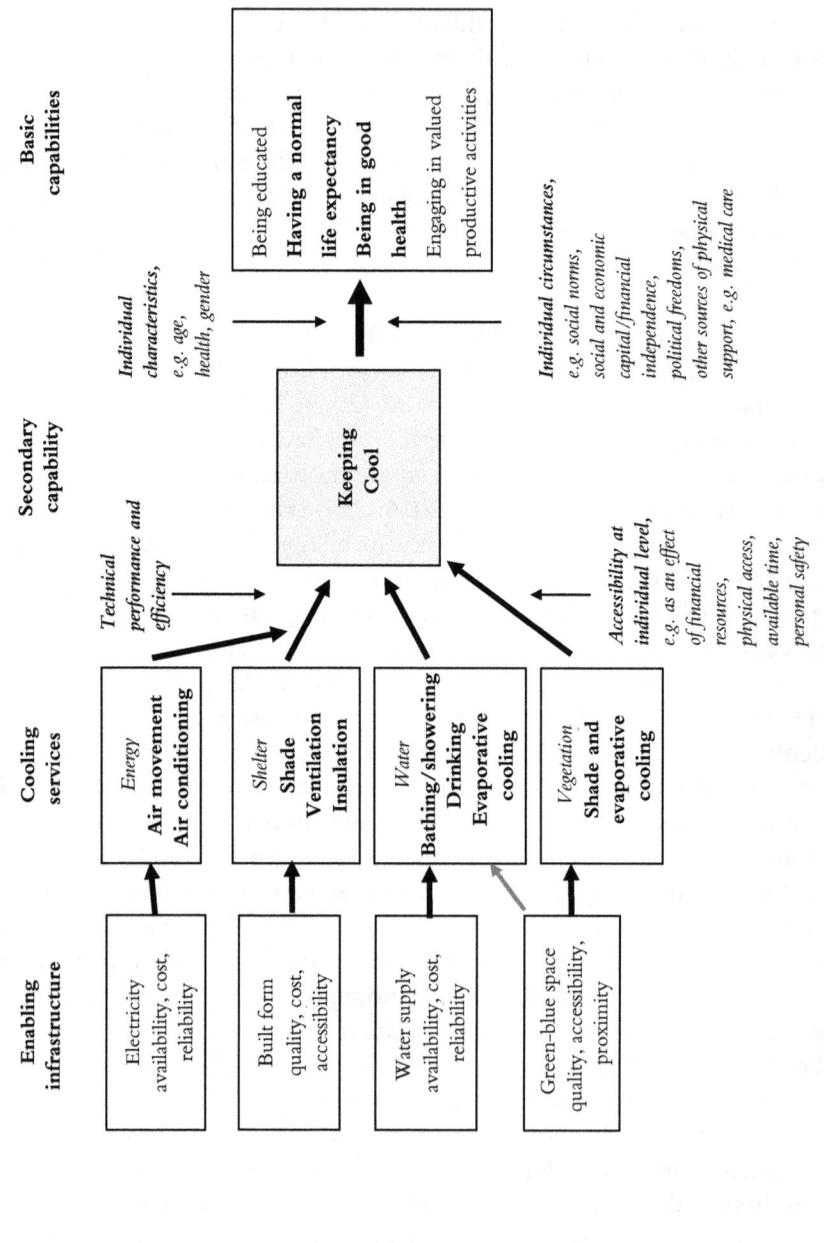

Source: Co-authors, following the logic in Figure 1 in Day et al (2016: 262)

reliability, accessibility and cost, are important in shaping whether or not each of the four cooling services are realizable.

In-between the horizontal steps in Figure 9.2 are vertical arrows indicating the types of mediating processes, or 'conversion factors' in the CA vocabulary, which can have consequences for whether keeping cool is in practice an achievable capability, and for how far this secondary capability matters for basic capabilities. This makes clear the contingency involved, relationships within the CA always being 'dynamic and context specific, rather than fixed' (Day et al, 2016: 260). As shown, these mediating processes include individual characteristics and circumstances (including economic and financial ones), environmental diversities, and the technical performance of technologies. Also important are variations in the social and political capacities of individuals or groups to arrange or modulate relationships to increase their ability to obtain cooling services. An example would be the ability of wealthier or economically significant parts of cities to pressure power companies to schedule power cuts elsewhere to protect their own continuity of supply, or to protect and control access to greenspace.

In forming this diagrammatic representation in Figure 9.2, the intention is *not* to provide a definitive account of how inequalities and injustice in relation to cooling are experienced or produced. Rather the intention is to provide a basic framework for understanding and analysis, which can be adapted to the context of its application. Cool inclusion, then, is the performance of thermal agency and the ability to cool, rather than a right or principle. In the next section, we illustrate how a thermal-agency-informed CA approach to cool inclusion can be applied to contemporary examples in low-income populations in the Global South.

Cool exclusion in the Global South

To date, questions about the ability to cool, and its functions for health, wellbeing and the broader means of a good life, have largely been focused on the Global North. In a systematic review of research literature on heatwave impacts on health, Campbell et al (2018) concluded that 'the global distribution of research into heatwaves and their impact on human health is not uniform and tends to cluster in regions with high levels of resources and income', finding, most remarkably, no studies *at all* focused on Africa.

There are multiple political, economic and research-infrastructure reasons for this, but there is also a widespread assumption that the typically 'hot' global tropics are well adapted to heat. Explanations of physiological acclimatization are routinely deployed to explain how bodies in hotter climates can tolerate higher temperatures, along with culturally embedded norms of dress, vernacular architecture, and ways of living that have been co-produced by the local climate and are assumed to be effective in providing for day-to-day cooling. However, there can be distinct colonial overtones to how acclimatization is assumed for non-White bodies, a privileged western perspective that sees living with heat in 'tropical climes' as normal and inherently unproblematic for those that are 'naturally evolved' to do so (Oppermann et al, 2017). Critical questions also have to be asked about the degree to which traditional practices for keeping cool have been sustained in the face of 'modernization' and urbanization processes (Mazzone, 2020) and, even where they have, whether they will be able to deal effectively with the ever-higher heat extremes under climate change. In a study focused on Southwest Asia, Pal and Eltahir (2016) conclude that future temperature extremes may likely exceed the threshold for the possibility of human habitability in a region that is expected to significantly expand its urban population centres.

To consider how the CA helps us examine cool inclusion in low-income urban communities in the Global South, we draw on the results of a survey – into cooling practices and thermal experience with 4,500 low-income residents in Jakarta, Hyderabad, Karachi and Douala – undertaken during the COVID-19 pandemic in 2020 (see Oppermann et al [2022] for a full methodological account and analysis). In terms of the 'enabling infrastructures' for cooling in Figure 9.2, there were notable absences. In Jakarta, for example, the city's water supply had never been able to expand fast enough to keep up with rapid urbanization and population growth, while in Douala, the extant network of water points was largely in disrepair. Many residents relied on water deliveries to supplement or replace their water access.

Being able to access water and electricity infrastructure provided key cooling services of water for bathing or energy for mechanical cooling. Electric fans were the most cited means of cooling across all the cities, yet key to their performance efficiency in providing the secondary capability of keeping cool was whether electricity supply was reliable or affordable, a situation made worse by the COVID-19 pandemic. Reliability and affordability issues meant that the majority of respondents in Karachi and Jakarta had less than 12 hours per day of access to electricity to run any devices, notably including fans.

Such conditions had real consequences for being able to keep cool, affecting people's functioning both physically and mentally. Across all four cities, reduced access to electricity correlated with a significant increase in the likelihood of thermal discomfort. Accounting for known characteristics that are likely to have shaped such a response, including age and any underlying health issues, this study also found gender to be a very strong indicator of the kinds of cooling with which individuals engaged. Women were far less likely use shaded areas outside their homes, for example, especially in Karachi, indicating a significant limitation to the kinds of thermal agency available to them. We surmise this is related to cultural norms regarding being accompanied when in public, familial duties in the home and, perhaps, more restrictive norms about dress when in public spaces that can contribute to heat stress.

Finally, the limitations to keeping cool were also seen to have knock-on effects on the basic capabilities of being in good health (combining with environmental and pandemic factors to increase the incidence of heat-related illness symptoms in some cities), but also having impacts on social relationships in the home. In all four cities, those who also reported increased thermal discomfort had more than twice as high odds of reporting an increase in physical conflict in the home, which certainly impacts on quality of life and, in the worst cases, endangers it fundamentally.

These examples point to a wide-ranging socio-spatially differentiated capability for cooling. Other issues not typically understood as significant for cooling must also be accounted for. These include limited healthcare and nutrition through the life course that leaves many of the urban poor with pre-existing chronic health conditions that disrupt bodily thermoregulation, and self-constructed housing that is often constrained by the availability and cost of materials, or made in a way that prioritizes security, but having thermal characteristics that render it more of a hazard than a help in managing heat stress at home.

Social and financial situations often constrain the possibilities for achieving bodily cooling and protective behaviour – men, women and children may be compelled to work in, as well as live in, hot conditions. Across all four cities, air conditioning was only available to just seven of the more than 4,500 people surveyed. In such a context it certainly was perceived as an unfeasible luxury. But, given widespread engagement in uncooled outdoor work (large numbers of respondents were engaged in informal street-sales or labour), in already hot and rapidly warming cities, this also begs the question of who actually most needs air conditioning. Indeed, once water and electricity are secured and the other mechanisms of cooling are enabled, it might well be that these measures are not enough in some overheating regions, and air conditioning does need to be available for all to ensure the essential functions of life as central capabilities.

Conclusion

Despite the critiques of the CA for minimizing power relations and political economy (Pogge, 2010), we suggest that it retains some utility in redefining where cool inclusion needs to happen. Rights-based inclusion focuses on enabling infrastructures and services and applies them universally regardless of how they actually contribute to cooling, and what purpose that cooling serves. Rather than determining cool inclusions based on standards of access to services and infrastructures, we argue that cool inclusion should be determined according to whose capability to keep cool is most restricted, whose bodies are falling furthest from a safe homeostatic range, and whose lives are being put most at risk in a more expansive sense (including safety, educational and income functions). Cool inclusion by this logic is the right to be included, both politically and materially, in the ability to keep cool – now, in transition, and in a post-carbon future.

On this basis, the CA allows us to work backwards along the framework of capabilities, conversion factors, services and enabling infrastructures in order to find the most effective and just responses that might be made. While this includes a range of responses that are not oriented towards air-conditioning-enabled cooling and the energy it requires, we cannot preclude the need to significantly expand energy consumption for cooling, particularly in the Global South, as heat extremes move into territory where keeping cool is not achievable by other means. As Davis et al (2021) have shown, the current trajectory is towards strong inequalities in the adoption of air-conditioning technologies, strikingly skewed towards high-income countries and high-income populations in poorer countries. Making air conditioning more widely available, they argue, would bring many benefits, including avoided mortality and increased productivity, education and human capital accumulation. However, such moves also have to demand the rapid expansion of affordable, low carbon energy infrastructures for energy-poor communities in the Global South, if more energy consumption for cooling is not simply to mean more carbon emissions. Taking forward strategies for cooling in a decarbonizing world must not assume blanket holding down of energy use, but rather engage in questions of justice in relation to populations routinely rendered invisible, illegal, impoverished and indentured, including in overarching transition discourses.

References

ASHRAE Standard 55 (2020) *ASHRAE Standard 55 – Thermal Environmental Conditions for Human Occupancy*, New York: American Society of Heating, Refrigerating and Air-Conditioning Engineers.

Bartiaux, F., Day, R. and Lahaye, W. (2021) 'Energy poverty as a restriction of multiple capabilities: a systemic approach for Belgium', *Journal of Human Development and Capabilities*, 22(2): 270–91.

Campbell, S., Remenyi, T.A., White, C.J. and Johnston, F.H. (2018) 'Heatwave and health impact research: a global review', *Health & Place*, 53: 210–18.

Cooling for All Secretariat (nd) *Cooling for All*. Available from: https://www.seforall.org/cooling-for-all/cooling-for-all-secretariat [Accessed 10 January 2023].

Davis, L., Gertler, P., Jarvis, S. and Wolfram, C. (2021) 'Air conditioning and global inequality', *Global Environmental Change*, 69: 102299.

Day, R., Walker, G. and Simcock, N. (2016) 'Conceptualising energy use and energy poverty using a capabilities framework', *Energy Policy*, 93: 255–64.

De Dear, R., Xiong, J., Kim, J. and Cao, B. (2020) 'A review of adaptive thermal comfort research since 1998', *Energy and Buildings*, 214: 109893.

IPCC (2022) *Climate Change 2021: The Physical Science Basis. Contribution of Working Group I to the Sixth Assessment Report of the Intergovernmental Panel on Climate Change*, Cambridge: Cambridge University Press.

Kabisch, N. and van den Bosch, M.A. (2017) 'Urban green spaces and the potential for health improvement and environmental justice in a changing climate', in Kabisch, N., Korn, H., Stadler, J. and Bonn, A. (eds), *Nature-Based Solutions to Climate Change Adaptation in Urban Areas*, Berlin and Heidelberg: Springer, pp 207–20.

Kremakova, M.I. (2013) 'Too soft for economics, too rigid for sociology, or just right? The productive ambiguities of Sen's Capability Approach', *Archives Europeennes De Sociologie*, 54(3): 393–419.

Levi, M., Kjellstrom, T. and Baldasseroni, A. (2018) 'Impact of climate change on occupational health and productivity: a systematic literature review focusing on workplace heat', *La Medicina del lavoro*, 109(3): 163–79.

Liu, J., Varghese, B.M., Hansen, A., Xiang, J., Zhang, Y., Dear, K. et al (2021) 'Is there an association between hot weather and poor mental health outcomes? A systematic review and meta-analysis', *Environment International*, 153: 106533.

Maller, C.J. and Strengers, Y. (2011) 'Housing, heat stress and health in a changing climate: promoting the adaptive capacity of vulnerable households, a suggested way forward', *Health Promotion International*, 26(4): 492–8.

Mazzone, A. (2020) 'Thermal comfort and cooling strategies in the Brazilian Amazon: an assessment of the concept of fuel poverty in tropical climates', *Energy Policy*, 139: 111256.

Mazzone, A. and Khosla, R. (2021) 'Socially constructed or physiologically informed? Placing humans at the core of understanding cooling needs', *Energy Research & Social Science*, 77: 102088.

Middlemiss, L., Ambrosio-Albala, P., Emmel, N., Gillard, R., Gilbertson, J., Hargreaves, T. et al (2019) 'Energy poverty and social relations: a capabilities approach', *Energy Research & Social Science*, 55: 227–35.

Mitchell, B.C. and Chakraborty, J. (2014) 'Urban heat and climate justice: a landscape of thermal inequity in Pinellas County, Florida', *Geographical Review*, 104(4): 459–80.

Nicol, F., Humphreys, M. and Roaf, S. (2012) *Adaptive Thermal Comfort: Principles and Practice*, Abingdon: Routledge.

Nussbaum, M.C. (2003) 'Capabilities as fundamental entitlements: Sen and global justice', *Feminist Economics*, 9(2–3): 33–59.

Oppermann, E., Brearley, M., Law, L., Smith, J.A., Clough, A. and Zander, K. (2017) 'Heat, health and humidity in Australia's monsoon tropics: a critical review of the problematisation of "heat" in a changing climate', *Wiley Interdisciplinary Reviews: Climate Change*, 8(4): e468.

Oppermann, E., Walker, G. and Brearely, M. (2020) 'Assembling a thermal rhythmanalysis: energetic flows, heat stress and polyrhythmic interactions in the context of climate change', *Geoforum*, 108: 275–85.

Oppermann, E., Friedrich, D., Abdullah, A., Amin, S., Amir, S., Anwar, N.H. et al (2022) *Extreme Heat and Covid-19: The Impact on the Urban Poor in Asia and Africa*, Edinburgh: Cool Infrastructures Project. Available from: DOI: 10.7488/era/2177 [Accessed 10 January 2023].

Pal, J.S. and Eltahir, E.A.B. (2016) 'Future temperature in southwest Asia projected to exceed a threshold for human adaptability', *Nature Climate Change*, 6: 197–200.

Parkes, B., Buzan, J.R. and Huber, M. (2022) 'Heat stress in Africa under high intensity climate change', *International Journal of Biometeorology*, 66(8): 1531–45.

Pavanello, F., De Cian, E., Davide, M., Mistry, M., Cruz, T., Bezerra, P. et al (2021) 'Air-conditioning and the adaptation cooling deficit in emerging economies', *Nature Communications*, 12(1): 6460.

Pogge, T. (2010) 'A critique on the capability approach', in Brighouse, H. and Robeyns, I. (eds), *Measuring Justice: Primary Goods and Capabilities*, Cambridge: Cambridge University Press, pp 17–60.

Raymond, C., Matthews, T. and Horton, R.M. (2020) 'The emergence of heat and humidity too severe for human tolerance', *Science Advances*, 6(19): eeaw1838.

Robeyns, I. (2016) 'Capabilitarianism', *Journal of Human Development and Capabilities*, 17(3): 397–414.

Rocque, R.J., Beaudoin C., Ndjaboue R., Cameron, L., Poirier-Bergeron, L., Poulin-Rheault, R.-A. et al (2020) 'Health effects of climate change: an overview of systematic reviews', *BMJ Open*, 11: e046333.

Sen, A. (2009) *The Idea of Justice*, London: Allen Lane.

Shove, E. and Chappells, H. (2008) 'Comfort in a lower carbon society', *Building Research and Information*, 4(4): 307–11.

Shove, E., Walker, G. and Brown, S. (2014) 'Transnational transitions: the diffusion and integration of mechanical cooling', *Urban Studies*, 51(7): 1504–17.

Smith, M.L. and Seward, C. (2009) 'The relational ontology of Amartya Sen's capability approach: incorporating social and individual causes', *Journal of Human Development and Capabilities*, 10(2): 213–35.

Starosielski, N. (2019) 'Thermal violence: heat rays, sweatboxes and the politics of exposure', *Culture Machine*, 17: 1–27.

Starosielski, N. (2021) 'Beyond the sun: embedded solarities and agricultural practice', *South Atlantic Quarterly*, 120(1): 13–24.

Stoknes, P.E. (2015) *What We Think About When We Try Not To Think About Global Warming: Toward a New Psychology of Climate Action*, Vermont: Chelsea Green Publishing.

Takane, Y., Kikegawa, Y., Hara, M. and Grimmond, C.S.B. (2019) 'Urban warming and future air-conditioning use in an Asian megacity: importance of positive feedback', *Climate and Atmospheric Science*, 2(1): 1–11.

Thomson, H., Simcock, N., Bouzarovski, S. and Petrova, S. (2019) 'Energy poverty and indoor cooling: an overlooked issue in Europe', *Energy and Buildings*, 196: 21–9.

Voelkel, J., Hellman, D., Sakuma, R. and Shandas, V. (2018) 'Assessing vulnerability to urban heat: a study of disproportionate heat exposure and access to refuge by socio-demographic status in Portland, Oregon', *International Journal of Environmental Research And Public Health*, 15(4): 15040640.

Walker, G. (2022) 'Whose energy use matters? Reflections on energy poverty and decolonisation', *People, Place and Policy*, 16(1): 6–12.

Walker, G., Shove, E. and Brown, S. (2014) 'How does air conditioning become "needed"? A case study of routes, rationales and dynamics', *Energy Research and Social Science*, 4: 1–9.

Walker, G., Simcock, N. and Day, R. (2016) 'Necessary energy uses and a minimum standard of living in the UK: energy justice or escalating expectations?', *Energy Research & Social Science*, 18: 129–38.

Wang, X.F., Day, R., Murrant, D., Marin, A.D., Botello, D.C., Gonzalez, F.L. et al (2021) 'A capabilities-led approach to assessing technological solutions for a rural community', *Energies*, 14(5): 14051398.

Whitmarsh, L., Poortinga, W. and Capstick, S. (2021) 'Behaviour change to address climate change', *Current Opinion in Psychology*, 42: 76–81.

Willand, N., Middha, B. and Walker, G. (2021) 'Using the capability approach to evaluate energy vulnerability policies and initiatives in Victoria, Australia', *Local Environment*, 26(9): 1109–27.

Zhang, N., Wang, H., Gallagher, J., Song, Q., Tam, V.W. and Duan, H. (2020) 'A dynamic analysis of the global warming potential associated with air conditioning at a city scale: an empirical study in Shenzhen, China', *Environmental Impact Assessment Review*, 81: 106354.

10

Pre-Figurative Hybrids for Post-Carbon Inclusion

Anitra Nelson

Degrowth developed as an idea in the latter decades of the 20th century but only emerged as a visibly active movement in the 21st century, initially in France, then Europe more generally. In the mid-2020s, degrowth has come of age. As outlined in Chapter 1, bodies such as the Intergovernmental Panel on Climate Change and the European Commission now refer to degrowth as a critical element in curbing carbon emissions and achieving ecological sustainability and stability. So, what is 'degrowth' (aka 'postgrowth')?

Degrowth targets *growth* economies as the main source of ecological unsustainability and socio-political inequalities. Following capitalists, capitalist states measure economic progress through a peculiarly quantitative, monetary, concept of growth. In contrast, degrowth advocates support a transformation to a world of 'sufficiency' based on ecological and social values applying principles of social justice, conviviality, solidarity, security and ecologically sustainable living for everyone.

Degrowth activists acknowledge and address ecological crises beyond increasing carbon emissions as well as inclusionary practices beyond simple affordability and familiar forms of democratic representation. Most degrowth activists aspire to global appreciations of inequities and unsustainabilities (Chapter 13) and, likewise, seek glocal solutions, as shown in this chapter. The degrowth movement favours autonomy alongside horizontal forms of direct democracy. Not surprisingly, the anti-systemic nature of degrowth and its scope demand actions that fall into the category of prefigurative politics.

This chapter focuses on three cases of 'prefigurative degrowth hybrids', starting with a brief discussion of such hybrids, followed by sketches of the cases, and discussion of the ethnographic approach. The chapter progresses case-by-case, identifying key characteristics of these experimental and aspirational degrowth efforts, and certain achievements and challenges in realizing principles of post-carbon inclusion in mundane living. It is concluded that such prefigurative degrowth hybrids have experimental and experiential values, and potential for 'scaling out', affirming their function within post-carbon transitions.

Degrowth and prefigurative hybrids

Clusters of integrated degrowth activities, 'degrowth formations', are appearing in major cities and in rural areas with aims to trial degrowth in practice, to demonstrate adaptable principles for new ways of living, organizing and provisioning, and to inspire actions elsewhere (Liegey and Nelson, 2020: 49–85). The three cases presented in this chapter have attracted and benefited from increasing scholarly work on degrowth, which as Fitzpatrick et al (2022: 2) indicate in their survey of *select* works, increased fivefold between 2014 and the end of 2020, to over 1,150 works. In the years since, this tendency has only heightened.

It is notable that the surveyed work was filtered according to those that 'focus on degrowth in the context of ecological sustainability and social equity' (Fitzpatrick et al, 2022: 3). Their analysis identifies ten foci of degrowth advocates – to minimize effort in paid work; to redistribute a broad range of resources universally; to fulfil all people's basic needs; to decentralize decision making; to encourage eco-collaborative housing; to engage in alternative (to mainstream monetary) exchanges; to 'prioritise small, highly self-sufficient communities'; to 'create a culture of sufficiency and self-limitation'; to re-localize economies; and to support and engage in commoning (Fitzpatrick et al, 2022: 5).

Certain activists – including activist scholars – apply degrowth principles in action by practising 'prefigurative politics' (Törnberg, 2021) in living laboratories (Bulkeley et al, 2019). Prefigurative politics embodies means and ends, attempting to embed imaginaries of preferred futures in the here-and-now both as a testing ground and as a demonstration site (Monticelli, 2021). As Törnberg (2021: 102) points out, 'experiences from transition studies strongly suggest that radical change does not happen by simply fighting the old, but through building the new ... actors advocating radical societal change must confront the old forms and simultaneously articulate concrete alternatives'. Occupations of squares in capital and other major cities during the early 2010s, from uprisings known as the Arab Spring to Occupy Wall Street in New York, and the ensuing global Occupy movement, not only called for democratic change and inclusion but also practised in situ real, substantive, democratic processes such as general assemblies. The prolongation of such occupations called for self-organization to meet the basic needs of occupiers and are examples of prefigurative politics.

Degrowth formations represent forms of prefigurative practices best referred to as 'prefigurative hybrids' (Leahy, 2021: 128–69). Self-organizing collectives are involved in multiple activities co-created and situated in the present but seeking to model, or at least point towards, equitable and sustainable ways of living in a degrowth future. The tensions of such hybrids centre on their anti-systemic activity, which is characteristic of prefigurative politics as it 'aims at transcending capitalism by tackling social reproduction, by embodying change, and by radically reshaping human needs, habits, and beliefs' and 'must be considered a pivotal concept for a progressive public philosophy for the 2020s' (Monticelli, 2021: 102).

The three cases I selected to examine here are radical in their international and deep approach to 'one planet living'. An example of the application of 'one planet living', guided by the Swiss Federal Institute of Technology (ETH Zürich) with its 2,000-watt society models and menus, is the postgrowth 'young housing cooperatives' movement in Zürich (Nelson and Chatterton, 2022). The UK Scientists for Global Responsibility 1.5°C Living Targets suggest that 'everyone in the world' needs to adopt a 'lifestyle carbon footprint' with an average annual total limit of 2.5 tonnes of CO_2 equivalent before 2030, then reduce further 'to give a relatively high chance of meeting the 1.5°C temperature goal' (Parkinson and Kallaugher, 2022). Targets defined by the latter include zero personal airflights; almost wholly plant-based diets; zero ownership and solely personal use of cars; an average of 33 m^2 home space per resident; and zero large and/or meat-eating pets – with suggestions as to personalizing targets around individual priorities and needs.

These targets, and the Scientists for Global Responsibility's list of target-free activities – such as socializing, making, and enjoying music and dance, cooking, gardening, home crafts, repairing, exercising, reading, writing and story-telling – are demonstratively degrowth. The transformation in livelihoods required to conform to such targets make obvious and significant the purposes of prefigurative hybrids experimenting with how we achieve them. The intentions of the cases presented is misconstrued if viewed as models for direct replication. These cases are more appropriately acknowledged, approached and assessed as *vehicles* for trialling post-carbon futures, as 'cultural laboratories' and 'protective spaces that fulfil both shielding, nurturing, and empowering functions' (Törnberg, 2021: 89–90).

Prefigurative degrowth hybrids demonstrably inspire reflection and activity both internally and externally through experimenting with practices of social inclusion and ecological sustainability. Beyond personal or individual household targets, such formations exist to prompt creative and constructive thinking, and action, on what collective and neighbourhood changes in socio-political relations are necessary in order to achieve aspirations such as post-carbon inclusion. Significantly, the approaches taken in the cases presented here are consistent with key literature addressing injustice, such as the ten core drivers identified by Kotsila et al (2022), and the findings of Hendrickson and Fernández Arrigiotia (2022) with respect to the intersectionality demonstrated in community-driven collaborative housing in the UK.

It is important to point out that degrowth activists and advocates are not narrowly focused on the carbon emissions of their activities. They seek to become knowledgeable about all types of ecologically and socially damaging practices in order to avoid or minimize such activities as much as possible. Global heating is viewed as a symptom of broad spread ecological degradation, in much the same way as a fever is a symptom of more generalized ill-health, so both source and symptom require treatment. Degrowth activists take an holistic perspective, and incorporate regeneration, resilience and healing into their transformational approaches.

It is just as important to point out that critics often misconstrue the role of prefigurative hybrids, many of which exist as research sites for activist-scholars. Indeed, Escobar (2022: xxvii) observes that 'pluriversal principles of struggle – when genuinely conceived from the perspective of radical interdependence, such as autonomy, territoriality, communality and care – cannot easily be accommodated within existing Left discourses'. This is the case with leftists who profess to support transformation but who remain closed to the possible necessity of totally deconstructing the market and the state. Critics – many profoundly privileged themselves – often point out that the composition of many prefigurative hybrids is skewed to those from well-off backgrounds. But, is this surprising, given that hybrids exist in a present that constantly minimizes options for those on low incomes? Why is this contextual characteristic blamed on the workings of such hybrids? Moreover, ameliorating effects include hybrid members consciously living modestly, and losing mainstream status through prefigurative activities. Monticelli (2022: 3) points out that prefigurative activities are neither intended to be 'the panacea to all of the problems in this world' nor are such bottom-up creations readily 'scaled up' for top-down application by states or markets. They are human scale, and 'follow non-linear, rhizomatic, network-like and place-based patterns of change diffusion' (Monticelli, 2022: 6).

Introduction to the cases and approach

In order to identify key experiences, challenges and achievements of inclusionary sustainability, an ethnographic approach has been taken. Primary sources are interviews with, and works on and by, founding members of three distinctive degrowth initiatives. Common to action research, a researching-with, participatory (Lazányi, 2022: 76–82) and convivial (Adloff, 2020) approach was taken. These cases were selected because they are well-established, well-known, represent key types, and the author has visited all three. Readers can look up their sites and read other analyses (see references and further reading at the end of this chapter). All include activist-scholars who critically and creatively reflect on their experimentation, some of whom were interviewed and others whose works are drawn on.

At the time of writing (2023), these three degrowth formations had existed for between five and 12 years. Konzeptwerk Neue Ökonomie (A Laboratory for New Economic Ideas) was established earliest, in Leipzig (Germany) in 2011. Cargonomia, in Budapest and its surrounds (Hungary), was seeded in the early 2010s to visibly, if informally, emerge with six co-founders (three non-Hungarian) in mid-2015. Haus des Wandels (House of Change or House for Transformation) started later, in mid-2018, in Heinersdorf (rural Brandenburg) within 20 km of the German border with Poland.

Cargonomia in brief

The degrowth formation Cargonomia embraces a suite of economic, social, research and educational activities centring on three small enterprises. One of the co-founders describes their mission as 'to contribute to sustainable transformation toward a socially and environmentally just future by questioning the dominant economic system through practical, educational and research activities' (Lazányi, 2022: 82). On 12 November 2021, Vincent Liegey and Logan Strenchock were interviewed together online. Consequently, all data on Cargonomia not otherwise referenced derives from this interview or is common knowledge. Moreover, I have relied heavily for critical assessments on the well-received doctoral dissertation of co-founder Orsolya Lazányi (2022). Orsolya conducted this action research on Cargonomia with other Cargonomia members and interns for a few years starting in 2017. The findings are collectively wrought as raw material, which Lazányi has skilfully marshalled and contextualized, especially in social and solidarity economy literature, to contribute to a tertiary level of analysis.

Cargonomia was born formally in mid-2015 with a shared public space for community activities, including the bike messenger service Kantaa bicycle cooperative. Moreover, Cargonomia integrated Cyclonomia (2013), a do-it-yourself bicycle social cooperative. A distribution point for weekly vegetable boxes to households from organic vegetable farm, Zsamboki Biokert, Cargonomia offers options of home delivery via bike or pickup from the community space. Over the years, Cargonomia has incorporated a range of other projects and programmes by way of working alliances and partnerships. This multi-scalar degrowth formation aims to embody principles of ecological sustainability, fair and direct trade, and cultural inclusion, in accessible open spaces for activities promoting solidarity, sustainable transitions, research, conviviality and degrowth.

Haus des Wandels *in brief*

The residential, cultural and community centre, Haus des Wandels, employs artistic and permaculture methods (similar to, if distinct from, agroecology), practices commoning, and seeks to optimize opportunities for social change in both its local community and rural post-socialist region. It is creating a self-organizing working, learning and living space out of a deserted and rundown agricultural training college set in an ordinary street in the middle of the town. Originally built in the 1950s, four co-founders bought the property in mid-2018. On 24 November 2021, I interviewed co-founder Andrea Vetter online. Consequently, all data on Haus des Wandels not otherwise referenced derives from this interview, or is common knowledge.

Haus des Wandels is located just 200 metres from a lake (Heinesdorfer See), and is around 8 km south-east of the small town Müncheberg. The interior of 3,000 m² comprises more than 60 rooms with a large hall and stage, complemented by outdoor areas of 1,700 m² and several buildings including an old distillery, big shacks, a wood workshop and garages. In addition to permanent and temporary living, a distinctive goal is to bridge rural and urban economies and cultures in creative ways, and to remain a self-managed commons for both permanent residents and temporary collaborators.

Konzeptwerk Neue Ökonomie *in brief*

Since its inception as an independent charitable association, Konzeptwerk Neue Ökonomie (A Laboratory for New Economic Ideas) has created forums for political discussions; facilitated information and skill sharing for degrowth; initiated organizational partnerships; educated, advocated for and promoted alternative economic practices; and encouraged engagement through talks by, and debates with, journalists, academics, activists and policy makers. Topics orient around enhancing direct and substantive democracy; social justice, as in social housing and fair treatment of migrants; climate change; energy poverty; and environmentally sound food security.

Moreover, Konzeptwerk Neue Ökonomie has promoted critical reflection and debate on degrowth activism and alternative economic practices by, for instance, hosting a 3,000-strong international degrowth conference in Leipzig in 2014. It has provided the impetus, effort and editors for a groundbreaking project and book, *Degrowth in Movement(s): Exploring Pathways for Transformation* (Burkhart et al, 2020). Finally, Konzeptwerk Neue Ökonomie stewarded the establishment of a multi-lingual online international degrowth hub (Degrowth.Info). As such, its operating principles involve outreach, inclusion, consciousness-raising and action around critical contemporary environmental challenges typified by actions for climate justice. On 25 November 2021, I interviewed co-founder Nina Treu online. Andrea Vetter also spoke (in the previously mentioned Haus des Wandels interview) about her active involvement in Konzeptwerk Neue Ökonomie. Consequently, all data on the organization not otherwise referenced derives from these interviews (mainly from Treu), or is common knowledge.

This introduction to all three cases indicates common aims of degrowth transformative approaches, which are characterized by intervening, and negotiating in, sophisticated and locally customized ways. Rather than scale up, as in capitalist growth cookie-cutter ways, disregarding critical social and ecological factors of diversity and inequity, degrowth advocates and activists iterate influentially 'scaling out' in a multiplicity of locally negotiated actions and responses, for instance via human scale 'fractals' (McCaffrey and Boucher, 2022), and through rippling impacts in networks. The procedural strength of degrowth activities derives from attending to matters of inequity and inclusion as necessarily slow, care-full and intensive efforts of human solidarity (Dengler and Lang, 2022).

Cargonomia

In mid-2013, Adrien Havas, Vincent Liegey (later a Cargonomia co-founder) and Levente Erös established Cyclonomia, initially making cargo bikes but now serving as a 'community bike kitchen'. Today, Cargonomia manages the bike sharing scheme while Cyclonomia shares knowledge and a service centre, offering access to bikes and trailers to citizens, community groups and some small enterprises via donations that support bike maintenance. Bikes, bike trailers and cargo bikes carry people, shopping and substitute for delivery trucks. These convivial user-friendly tools embody degrowth principles, modestly using our living planet and renewable energy, including direct human effort, and proved to be ideal transport during COVID-19 restrictions.

Cyclonomia embodies a participative approach to the ongoing use of cycles to prolong their life, supervising the proper use of equipment to repair bikes, and demonstrating degrowth principles of conviviality, cooperation, mutual support and sharing. Once a bike is beyond use, its parts are repaired and re-used in other cycles or for different, novel and creative, uses. Cargonomia and Cyclonomia have offered dozens of events to encourage and support people who fear using bikes, cargo bikes and trailers by offering them trials. Experiencing 'a slice of a completely different worldview' (Cyclonomia, 2013), such practices consciously aim to build autonomy, and individual and collective agency. Indeed, the common suffix in Cargonomia and Cyclonomia draws from the Latin *autonomia* (autonomy).

Sibling enterprises of Cargonomia give substance to its description as a 'logistics centre' (François and Gaillard, 2019: 22), self-organizing along principles of autonomy and participatory processes. Fresh organic vegetables grown at Zsámboki Biokert (their independently managed organic micro-farm [3.5 ha] in the town of Zsámbok, 50 km from Budapest in the Gödöllő-Budapest region) and by neighbouring partner farms are ferried to collection points in Budapest, including Cargonomia, each delivery node servicing, say, a couple of dozen households. Cargonomia supports the farm's work by co-organizing events, recruiting trainees hosted on the farm and co-organizing on-farm educational outreach programmes.

Members of the organic box ordering scheme eat seasonal food to become more in tune with nature and more conscious of farmers' challenges, which are substantial. The box ordering scheme has proved to be a reasonably affordable and convivial way of self-provisioning with fresh, high quality, nutritious, organic foods. In holistic ways, the box scheme enhances quality of life, characterizing the degrowth principle of 'frugal abundance', valuing, respecting and caring for people and planet. But it is a strain on farmers, administrators and outreach workers to realize their anti-systemic aims within a globalized capitalist food system. Strenchock (2021: esp 87) details tensions in terms of the extra time, effort and networking necessary to achieve ecological and convivial ideals, concluding that self-organized communal farming relies on commitment and interpersonal relationships meaning that they can be 'either very successful or very unsuccessful'.

Similarly, the ideals of re-localization and conviviality face practical and personal challenges. Living a prefigurative hybrid existence with an ironic sense of awareness, members sometimes eat foods out-of-season or from far away. Lazányi (2022: 128) quotes a member quipping, 'The pears from Argentina were delicious … we deal with our contradictions!' Moreover, there are obstacles with integrating those inexperienced at self-organizing, and in accommodating others with little time in their over-committed lives to pursue quality of life or ecological issues (Lazányi, 2022: 129–30). While members continue to try and work in decommodified and environmentally sustainable ways – acting in multiple relational directions with ecological integrity and social justice at the fore – impediments, compromises and tensions still arise. As such, Lazányi (2022: 86) refers to being challenged 'to move out from my comfort zone'.

Although autonomy is valued, and a community of practice action-learning approach consciously adopted, some informal, gender and educational-cum-class hierarchies arise, emphasizing their collective motto, 'challenge ourselves' (Lazányi, 2022: 88, 100). For instance, those unable to do other-gendered tasks have been encouraged – and sometimes very challenged – to learn new skills, as highly skilled people give way to learners to become more experienced. Walking the talk, self-organizing is 'accompanied by discussions, debates, questioning goals and assumptions which allow critical reflection' (Lazányi, 2022: 148).

In terms of scale, members sometimes feel that Cargonomia's orientation around small-is-beautiful relations, quality and environmental principles contradicts its mission to influence and make an impact (Lazányi, 2022: 125–6). But, ultimately, the collective values its small scale, without which self-organization would be unwieldy, and loyalty, learning-together and trust might well evaporate (Lazányi, 2022: 149). They access resources in kind through strong social relations and networking, spreading their principles, processes and practices to raise awareness and influence (Lazányi, 2022: 125, 134, 150–1). As an example of the impact of their regular outreach – nine cargo-bike oriented events, mainly in Budapest, held over a 14-month period in 2017–18 attracted over 900 participants, and generated much social and mainstream media (Lazányi, 2022: 119).

In summary, stepping back from its activities and achievements, the horizontal self-organizing Cargonomia self-consciously confronts challenges of working within a productivist market. It speaks of new social and ecological relations and values in a 'reciprocal economy', conscientiously minimizing monetary relations, and criteria for decision-making. Yet this is only feasible because members do other, even if sometimes complementary, wage-earning work (François and Gaillard, 2019: 22–3). As such, the hybrid nature of a necessarily 'plural economy' presents constant tensions. Similarly, frustrations with the everyday functions and social norms of a market economy are challenges only likely to be overcome with radical society-wide change (Nelson, 2022). Finally, although their work practices are radical, convivial and intertwined, Cargonomia founders lament that they do not gain the environmental economies and efficiencies of living together – the focus of other degrowth activists, including activist-scholars, who established Haus des Wandels.

Haus des Wandels

Haus des Wandels began mid-2018 when, as a registered association, four co-founders purchased a neglected public building on a rural property for the market price of the land (€80,000) using both private loans and savings. By the end of 2021, around ten people lived in and held the space, sharing it with collaborators temporarily staying there. In the few years since taking over responsibility – including the long COVID-19 period of restrictions – the community has worked hard at renovation and regeneration, reusing salvaged materials and planting free, unwanted fruit trees from a local store. They freely pass on such items too, a praxis that they feel aligns well with their surrounding post-socialist village cultures of solidarity. Their activities align with the sustainable practices and skills of financially poor but somewhat resilient local villagers who, when the German Democratic Republic ended, 'had very bad experiences during the last few decades when a lot of infrastructure was just shut down' and for whom 'the topic of social justice and inclusion is very important' (Vetter, in Meyerricks, 2021: np). Andrea, interviewed, referred to such villagers as 'total pros' at upcycling.

Haus des Wandels residents draw on practices of 'counter economies', such as caring economies, gift economies and solidarity economies. Following principles of 'convivial technologies' and 'society is culture', there is a strong emphasis both on integrating creativity and art into daily activities to enhance quality of life, and on arranging creative arts projects, residencies and exhibitions (Haus des Wandels, 2021: np). As Adloff (2020: 121) asserts, '[o]nly a post-utilitarian and post-capitalist society can make technical conviviality possible'.

The term 'convivial technologies' was coined by Haus des Wandels co-founder Andrea Vetter to define degrowth technologies. Vetter (2018) characterizes convivial technologies in a matrix of five dimensions (relatedness, accessibility, adaptability, bio-interaction and appropriateness) across four factors (materials, production, use and infrastructure). This matrix itself is a convivial tool for use by groups to interrogate and assess various technological options by applying degrowth principles and criteria. What makes convivial technologies distinctive is their beneficial (or at least neutral) effect on people's interrelations. Moreover, convivial technology enables optimal access for all to create, maintain, repair and use tools that are assessed in terms of ownership, use-rights, skills and knowledge. The tool's independence or dependence on sources of energy and materials, and its effect on living organisms, including soil, water and air, are interrogated. In short, the technology is assessed as fit-for-purpose in the current time and locality in terms of human and non-human factors.

Bobulescu and Fritscheova (2021: 2) identify intentional communities such as Haus des Wandels as nurturing contexts for their allied concept of 'convivial innovations', which refers to the practice of devising, inventing and adapting convivial technologies. Alongside pressuring for system change, decisions within Haus des Wandels are taken in a self-organized way to adjust to and experiment with using do-it-yourself, or do-it-ourselves, approaches. Residents use convivial social techniques with the aim of developing a semi-permeable, place-based community caring for their commons. Principles of inclusion and ecological sustainability are integrated into communication and organizational processes; intergenerational living and caring; property relations; and the design of, and access to, buildings, open spaces and services, such as renewable energy.

The inclusive convivial community

The community of residents in Haus des Wandels pays a great deal of attention to lowering inequities across various dimensions. As Aguayo-Krauthausen

(2017: 10) writes in the foreword to *CoHousing Inclusive*, '(s)elf-determined living is an important factor on the way to inclusion' and '(i)nclusion is not an aim, and not a task in the to-do-list which can later be marked as done, but rather a process of accepting and dealing with human diversity'.

There is no specific charge for staying and living at Haus des Wandels; the space is potentially accessible to all irrespective of monetary means. Yet the household requires thousands of euros per month to operate, so guests and residents are expected to contribute voluntarily, mindful of such expenses and of their own capacity. During the 2021/2022 winter, heating for 100–350 m^3 cost €60–200 per day (Haus des Wandels, 2021: np). Common spaces in Haus des Wandels, such as the two kitchens, are categorized as temporary autonomous zones, 'kept alive by the care of those that inhibit' them (Haus des Wandels, 2021: np). Its *Care Book* counsels 'it nurtures you, but in order for it to do so, it needs to be nurtured, too', and cautions that if 'care disappears the autonomous zone disappears, and all that's left is human trash' (Haus des Wandels, 2021: np). In short, residing temporarily or permanently at Haus des Wandels demands contributions in kind, sharing in mundane tasks.

Collective co-creation is a special art that needs to be inviting, safe and transparent. Haus des Wandels operates on a basis of radical, active and holistic caring for both people and planet. In its introductory *Care Book* (Haus des Wandels, 2021: np), it describes itself as a 'post-local village square', exercising anti-authoritarian ways of organizing and generating a 'connecting, accessible, resisting place'. As such, Haus des Wandels draws on a range of collaborative skills and conflict resolution approaches common to social change agents, and codified by practitioners such as Ochre (2013).

This 'heterotopia' is a feminist, autonomist household and collectively held commons developing 'embodied' trust (Haus des Wandels, 2021: np). In contrast to explicit mission statements and printed contracts, trust is developed in oral, visceral and experiential ways through human interaction. It is a space of co-created, negotiated and re-negotiated living. Conflicts, say those prompted by mansplaining, are pointed out and discussed. 'Be aware of your state of being, seek help and conversation if you're confused, sad, angry' advises the *Care Book* (Haus des Wandels, 2021: np): 'Everything you do and feel will affect the house and the people around you.' Haus des Wandels has found that print privileges literacy and mimics upper-middle-class protocol, alienating those more comfortable with, and oriented around, informal oral cultures – more inclusive of migrants, the disadvantaged, working classes, all genders, and younger and older people. This is especially important in a context within which migration is viewed as 'the basic source of (r)evolutionary development' (Haus des Wandels, 2021: np).

Participation in a network of anti-racist and rehumanizing local projects within the 'neighbourhood' of Oder-Spree (a district of around 2,250 km^2

in eastern Brandenburg, with 180,000 residents) shows commitment to the locale (Haus des Wandels, 2021: np). When Russia invaded Ukraine, on 24 February 2022, refugees accumulated in Poland and sought wide-ranging support to enter Germany. In solidarity, Haus des Wandels contributed, illustrating 'utopian hospitality' and 'post localism' (Haus des Wandels, 2021: np). Utopian hospitality is a caring and holistic approach facilitating the transformation of social dynamics and establishment of counter economies, developing trust internally and through networks and the local environs. In a complementary way, 'post localism' (akin to degrowth's 'open localization') is the community intentionally and caringly relating with other localities and communities through people, communication channels and acts of solidarity (Haus des Wandels, 2021: np). Hendrickson and Fernández Arrigoitia (2022) confirm the appropriateness and effectiveness of such opportunities for migrants more generally.

Food self-provisioning and localized food provisioning through community supported agriculture demonstrate fair and ecological approaches. Both involve ecologically sound practices, harvesting and eating, or otherwise using, the harvest. Haus des Wandels (2021: np) is a delivery collection point for a community supported agriculture scheme and a feminist farmers' collective. Space is available for events on non-commercial terms for locals and other activities deemed deserving, for example, neighbouring villagers who use some of the ground floor as a village library, pottery space and sewing workshop. Villagers work as volunteers in these spaces while the regional government recompenses Haus des Wandels for associated running costs.

Resident artists, volunteers, friends and collaborating groups hosted by Haus des Wandels have a scout team to orient them and, when necessary, to mediate. Deconstructing hierarchy for self-organization requires sharing a range of practical skills and knowledge in everyday living and working. Housework is approached as care for the house and its residents; all are 'expected to nurture, clean, maintain or beautify the space in collective use for one hour per day' (Haus des Wandels, 2021: np). Sharing vehicles means relating with people and the vehicle, in terms of sharing time schedules, vehicle space and doing pickups for others. Jobs are not occupied by particular people as in permanent positions but, rather, particular roles are fulfilled by and frequently swapped by a range of people (Haus des Wandels, 2021: np).

In short, Haus des Wandels is a commons under the *collective care* of residents. Such a caring economy is oriented around needs and their satisfaction changing over time. Food is shared with protocol around give-and-take, respecting other people's needs and those of Earth regarding source, type and amount of foods (Haus des Wandels, 2021: np). A huge 19th-century antique wooden cabinet (on permanent loan from the regional museum in Beeskow) houses a 'free box' to leave unwanted clothes for others' use.

Waste is sorted but minimizing use, repair and re-use are prioritized. Haus des Wandels aims for its energy use (mainly for heating) to become fossil fuel free as soon as possible, by increasing use of solar energy.

Residents are expected both to be mindful and responsible for their words and actions, and to continuously renegotiate their way of being through respectful listening, active expression and flexibly contributing to the common good. Beyond a core of committed permanent residents there is some turnover. Details of caring practices might alter but not principles, such as resisting hateful, belittling words and acts (Haus des Wandels, 2021: np). Solidarity and love stops with negative, timewasting behaviour. Guilt is disparaged and constructive responses encouraged. The *Care Book* cautions to observe and respect personal boundaries around giving and receiving support (Haus des Wandels, 2021: np). As in permaculture more generally, conflicts are composted and solutions grown. Intersectional, queer-friendly and feminist, transforming ways of living and working is a learning work-in-progress where communication is defined as 'the key to bliss'. The *Care Book* (Haus des Wandels, 2021: np) explains: '[W]e understand ourselves as participants of a radical, deep and necessary transformation of life forms, societies and economies. … Interconnected with people at other places in other times, rooted at this place in this time. We hope it's contagious.'

Konzeptwerk Neue Ökonomie

Like many radical 21st-century movements, the international degrowth movement is a multidimensional, horizontally organized, decentralized and open network without any headquarters but rather a suite of distinctive hubs of activity (including national, urban and academic ones), opportunistic convergences, and a plethora of passionate advocates and activists. The movement is especially concerned with discursive consciousness-raising and establishing practices and processes of a self-organizing democracy alongside appropriate alternative economies – matters central to Konzeptwerk Neue Ökonomie.

This 'Laboratory for New Economic Ideas' evolved when a couple of dozen activists – who knew one another through joint activities, including as students and organizing radical conferences – identified a gap: solid social and environmental organizations existed without a complementary strength in compatible *economic* practices. The inexperienced founders were determinedly anti-capitalist and degrowth-oriented, envisaging an organization quite different from an ordinary think tank. Konzeptwerk Neue Ökonomie aims to be a laboratory in form and substance. It has sought narratives for degrowth in practice; targeting youth across Germany with respect to consciousness-raising; engaging with self-organizing migrants on common struggles; and highlighting injustice, especially regarding precarious working conditions. It promotes the growth of a 'care economy' understood in the broadest sense.

Beyond Leipzig, Konzeptwerk Neue Ökonomie is active across Germany, especially its eastern regions. It developed and held the key international degrowth online institution 'Degrowth.Info' from 2018 through to 2021, afterwards supporting its devolution to an international collective. This site has material in English and German. 'Degrowth' and its French root '*décroissance*' translate to the German '*Postwachstum*' (literally 'postgrowth'), *Wachstumsrücknahme* and *Entwachstum* (meaning to grow out of, or spring from, an outgrowth). These terms raise fewer hackles than the controversial English word. One of the largest face-to-face degrowth conferences so far took place in Germany with the Berlin Conference Beyond Growth (May 2011) attracting 2,500 participants. The 4th International Degrowth Conference for Ecological Sustainability and Social Equity (Leipzig, September 2014), which included 500 events and 3,000 attendees, was organized by Konzeptwerk Neue Ökonomie and several partners.

Konzeptwerk Neue Ökonomie which, in September 2022, comprised a team of 22 workers and four freelancers, has been keen to walk its talk in its internal organization. Consequently, it uses open source software and second-hand digital equipment. It designs educational materials, especially for young adults, teachers and open access train-the-trainer courses. But it has encountered serious hurdles. Its space is rented, minimizing opportunities to renovate. Interviewees reported that writing grant applications within deadlines constrained work on other projects; that an internal hierarchy has existed between long-term and short-term workers and volunteers; and that even waged workers tend to subsidize their livelihoods with other paid work, which inevitably skews their demographics to the relatively privileged.

Konzeptwerk Neue Ökonomie has undergone a long and deep process to try to dissolve this privileged status, making practical virtuous alliances a core approach in its theory, practice and strategy. More people with diverse backgrounds, especially Black, Indigenous, and People of Colour and queers, have joined the group. Working with anti-racist, women's and migrant organizations on projects, from co-applying for funding, develops practical working relationships with less privileged others. Simultaneously, Konzeptwerk Neue Ökonomie has developed experience and skills in bringing more conventional groups together with radical ones, such as organizing discussion and practices around commoning and caring economies.

Konzeptwerk Neue Ökonomie has an holistic view of transformation. It sees a strong need for communities and neighbourhoods to reappropriate power at a collective level, transforming industry and governance. It advocates strong democratic participation in climate action within localizing economies, and promotes community discussion and decision making around topics such as re-orienting diets around plant-based food, and questioning whether urban living is more sustainable simply because of the density of their settlement while ignoring city-dwellers' holistic ecological footprint via consumption.

For years Konzeptwerk Neue Ökonomie has modelled, and encouraged discussions on, part-time work as a norm – to allow all parents to genuinely share personal and collective caring (including via public childcare) and household duties, to earn money doing paid work, and to enjoy recreational and creative activities – a measure that demands evening out wages so that those who are on low wages are not disadvantaged.

By 2022, it had advanced programmes dedicated to 'a 4-day week for everyone', and other practical social measures in a set of socio-ecological transformative steps to achieve climate justice and a climate-friendly society – car-free cities; improved public transport; progressive energy tariffs; decentralized energy production and distribution; more social housing, and housing for all; and climate debt reparations. Konzeptwerk Neue Ökonomie promotes withdrawing state support for large monopolistic firms in preference of expanding the number of small worker cooperatives. By proposing such measures, it promotes practical policy-oriented discussion, and movement towards post-carbon inclusion.

Transformation

In the most general terms, the collection to which this chapter belongs aims to show how successful efforts to address the climate emergency and heal the planet for future generations need to integrate ecological and social justice and inclusion. As such, 'five common lines of inquiry' listed in Chapter 1 centre on the constitution of 'post-carbon inclusion' in terms of characteristics such as socio-materialities, agency, barriers and narratives. This particular chapter has attempted to show the potential of, and challenges confronted by, grassroots degrowth approaches, namely within those clusters of integrated degrowth activities referred to as prefigurative degrowth formations. In concert, social geographer Helen Jarvis (2020: 109–10) locates the appeal and intrigue of degrowth for geographers in its 're-politicising humanistic debates concerning where and how we live with each other on the earth' and, in associated ways, adjusting the focus of geography towards 'the scale of living and the scale of civil society alliance and activism'.

Perceiving climate change as simply the tip of the iceberg of a vast range of practices breaching Earth's limits, grassroots action has several benefits. The prefigurative degrowth hybrids discussed in this chapter tend to engage younger (as well as older) generations in their operation and uptake. They address inclusion as a wicked problem by acknowledging and embracing it in intersectional ways across economic, spatial and social dimensions. They have the potential for multiple, numerous and rippling impacts on individuals and groups, due to their open, inventive, activist character. They are intimately practical, involving reflective scholars who generate academic discussion around their activities, and popular interest through international social media.

Yet hurdles to potential advance are equally clear. It takes substantial will, stamina and creativity to actively engage in these types of prefigurative hybrids. Addressing carbon emissions, especially in inclusionary ways, demands *transformation* of oneself and one's relations to alter the everyday practices of mundane living. That such grassroots activities require local adaptation makes every attempt unique to the communities and neighbourhoods concerned, who become enriched by a transformation in tune with both the local environs and their community as a newly formed entity and work-in-progress. Yet all are driven by the same principles and a similar suite of processes, making comparisons possible and analysis useful for ongoing learning, for scaling out, and for enhancing theories of transformation, specifically theories of change.

These types of transformative activities are intentionally anti-systemic, and attract derision from those more convinced in enacting state and market oriented reforms, which, such critics argue, can be achieved at scale and with speed. However, governments have been notoriously tardy, inefficient and ineffective with respect to addressing both global heating and inclusion. Yet, it is precisely at the local scale that governments have been most effective in climate action. Moreover, as stated in Chapter 1, 'efforts to rapidly decarbonize and address increasing, diverse and sometimes hidden inequalities are rarely matters that are addressed conjointly'. This is precisely why degrowth prefigurative formations, clusters of integrated degrowth activities, offer crucial insights into both processes for a decarbonizing transformation and directions for ways of living, organizing and provisioning in a post-carbon future.

As hybrids, degrowth prefigurative formations reveal the types of tensions and conundrums a post-carbon inclusion transition poses. As demonstration sites for transformation, they offer substantially market-free spaces for people to learn and share new ways forward. They inspire action elsewhere, action which will never be replicated by the very nature of open community-oriented localism. Yet all rely on identifying and addressing challenges of altering everyday practices following universal principles of inclusion, and seek to satisfy not just material, but emotional, social and political human needs. They rely, too, on grassroots motivation and solidarity. Grassroots action holds the greatest potential for rapidly enacting such change, and it is urgent change that is required right now. This leaves us questioning whether a prime role for the state is not to simply enable and facilitate such action?

In short, this chapter constitutes a call for prefigurative degrowth hybrids as vehicles for achieving post-carbon inclusion.

References

Adloff, F. (2020) 'Experimental conviviality: exploring convivial and sustainable practices', *Open Cultural Studies*, 4(1): 112–21.

Aguayo-Krauthausen, R. (2017) 'Self-determined living but alone at home?', in LaFond, M. and Tsvetkova, L. (eds), *CoHousing Inclusive: Self-Organized, Community-Led Housing for All*, Berlin: JOVIS Verlag, pp 10–11.

Bobulescu, R. and Fritscheova, A. (2021) 'Convivial innovation in sustainable communities: four cases in France', *Ecological Economics*, 181: 106932.

Bulkeley, H., Marvin, S., Palgan, Y.V., McCormick, K., Breitfuss-Loidl, M., Mai, L. et al (2019) 'Urban living laboratories: conducting the experimental city?', *European Urban and Regional Studies*, 26(4): 317–35.

Burkhart, C., Schmelzer, M. and True, N. (eds) (2020) *Degrowth in Movement(s): Exploring Pathways for Transformation*, Winchester and Washington: Zer0 Books.

Cyclonomia (2013) *Cyclonomia Budapest – English Subtitles*, Vimeo. Available from: https://vimeo.com/69600044 [Accessed 5 June 2023].

Dengler, C. and Lang, M. (2022) 'Commoning care: feminist degrowth visions for a socio-ecological transformation', *Feminist Economics*, 28(1): 1–28.

Escobar A. (2022) 'Foreword', in Monticelli, L. (ed), *The Future is Now: An Introduction to Prefigurative Politics*, Bristol: Bristol University Press, pp xxii–xxx.

Fitzpatrick N., Parrique T. and Cosme, I. (2022) 'Exploring degrowth policy proposals: a systematic mapping with thematic synthesis', *Journal of Cleaner Production*, 365(2): 132764.

François, P.-H. and Gaillard, C. (2019) *Rethinking the Role of the Engineer in a Degrowth Society*. End of studies internship report for École Centrale de Nantes, Nantes, France. Available from: https://cargonomia.hu/trainees-projects/ [Accessed 6 June 2023].

Haus des Wandels (2021) *HDW Care Book*, Heinersdorf: Haus des Wandels. Available from: https://hausdeswandels.org [Accessed 6 June 2023].

Hendrickson, C. and Fernández Arrigoitia, M. (2022) 'Community-led housing in the UK: learning from Black British and migrant histories', *Radical Housing Journal*, 4(2): 183–91.

Jarvis, H. (2020) 'Degrowth: a kind of pragmatic utopian thinking, re-politicising humanistic debates', in *Sozial- und Kulturgeographie; Postwachstumsgeographien*, Bielefeld: transcript.

Kotsila, P., Anguelovski, I., García-Lamarca, M. and Sekulova, F. (2022) *Injustice in Urban Sustainability: Ten Core Drivers*, London: Routledge.

Lazányi, O. (2022) 'An ecological economics inquiry into the social and solidarity economy', PhD Thesis, Corvinus University of Budapest, Budapest.

Leahy, T. (2021) *The Politics of Permaculture*, London: Pluto Press.

Liegey, V. and Nelson, A. (2020) *Exploring Degrowth: A Critical Guide*, London: Pluto Press.

McCaffrey, M.S. and Boucher, J.L. (2022) 'Pedagogy of agency and action, powers of 10, and fractal entanglement: radical means for rapid societal transformation toward survivability and justice', *Energy Research & Social Science*, 90: 102668.

Meyerricks, S. (2021) 'On degrowth and an economy of care', *Enough!*, 5 June. Available from: https://www.enough.scot/2021/06/05/on-degrowth-and-an-economy-of-care/ [Accessed 6 June 2023].

Monticelli, L. (2021) 'On the necessity of prefigurative politics', *Thesis 11*, 167(1): 99–118.

Monticelli, L. (2022) 'Introduction', in Monticelli, L. (ed), *The Future is Now: An Introduction to Prefigurative Politics*, Bristol: Bristol University Press, pp 1–12.

Nelson, A. (2022) *Beyond Money: A Postcapitalist Strategy*, London: Pluto Press.

Nelson, A. and Chatterton, P. (2022) 'Dwelling beyond growth: negotiating the state, mutualism and commons', in Savini, F., Ferreira, A. and von Schönfeld, K.C. (eds) *Post-Growth Planning: Cities Beyond the Market Economy*, New York and Abingdon: Routledge, pp 49–62.

Ochre, G. (2013) *Getting our Act Together: How to Harness the Power of Groups*, Thornbury: Groupwork Press.

Parkinson, S. and Kallaugher, L. (2022) '1.5°C living targets', *Scientists for Global Responsibility*. Available from: https://www.sgr.org.uk/projects/living-targets [Accessed 6 June 2023].

Strenchock, L. (2021) 'Germinating degrowth? On-farm adaptation and survival in Hungarian alternative food networks', in Nelson, A. and Edwards, F. (eds), *Food for Degrowth: Perspectives and Practices*, Abingdon: Routledge, pp 77–89.

Törnberg, A. (2021) 'Prefigurative politics and social change: a typology drawing on transition studies', *Distinktion: Journal of Social Theory*, 22(1): 83–107.

Vetter, A. (2018) 'The matrix of convivial technology: assessing technologies for degrowth,' *Journal of Cleaner Production*, 197(2): 1778–86.

Further reading: relevant sites
Cargonomia: https://cargonomia.hu/
Degrowth.Info: https://www.degrowth.info
Haus des Wandels: https://hausdeswandels.org
Konzeptwerk Neue Ökonomie – A Laboratory for New Economic Ideas: https://konzeptwerk-neue-oekonomie.org
Scientists for Global Responsibility: https://www.sgr.org.uk/
Zsámboki Biokert: https://www.zsambokibiokert.hu/

11

Uneven Consumption and the Work of Being a High Consumer

Aimee Ambrose, Alvaro Castano-Garcia, Anna Hawkins, Stephen Parkes, Beth Speake and Yael Arbell

Introduction

This chapter argues that, to achieve the carbon reductions necessary to secure our future and to achieve a more equitable distribution of the Earth's resources, research attention must focus on some of the most privileged among us (Castano-Garcia et al, 2021). It is recognized that debates around how to secure an inclusive post-carbon society must pay close attention to those who excessively consume resources in order to help halt environmental decline and secure a more equitable distribution of resources across society. This relies on some groups consuming less to enable others to increase their consumption to a level which enables healthy and socially included lives.

This chapter also explores why high and escalating consumption is problematic in the context of the climate crisis and equitable and inclusive solutions to it, and includes discussion about how high consumers might be conceptualized and defined. Furthermore, in attempting to advance a research agenda focused on high consumers, reflections are made on the challenges of conducting research which challenges the dominant economic paradigms and social conventions of the developed world.

We draw on a literature review and insights from stakeholder interviews with academics and practitioners within non-governmental organizations (NGOs) and academia, which highlight the need for a greater focus on high consuming households and some of the conceptual and ethical dilemmas this presents. The chapter proceeds to discuss how research with this elusive group might best be approached and how a novel application of institutional ethnography may help to explicate the 'work' of being wealthy. The conclusion reflects on how high consumers fit into debates around rapid decarbonization, spatial inequalities and just transition at this critical juncture in the climate crisis, and outlines the next steps for this vital field of inquiry.

High consumers: what is the problem?

High consumers of energy and resources in domestic settings make a disproportionately large contribution in terms of their greenhouse gas (GHG) emissions and resource use, with the richest 10 per cent of households being responsible for 49 per cent of carbon emissions globally (Kartha et al, 2020). This issue is firmly on the radar of the International Panel on Climate Change (IPCC, 2022: 505–6), which states that 'conspicuous consumption by the wealthy is the cause of a large proportion of emissions in all countries', and that 'vital dimensions of human well-being correlate with consumption, but only up to a threshold'. The concern here is with consumption beyond this threshold, beyond what might be considered 'sufficient' (Darby and Fawcett, 2019). Progress to date on emissions reduction has relied largely on decarbonizing the energy supply through changes to energy sources (such as the shift from gas to wind power in the United Kingdom [UK]) and heating technologies in the home (such as substitution of gas boilers for air source heat pumps), while progress on curbing high (and rapidly escalating) demand for energy, transport, food and consumer goods has been evaded.

The highest consumers also act as trend-setters or aspirational peers, thus driving high consumption more widely within society and normalizing practices such as carbon intensive transport choices and long haul holidays (Cohen et al, 2021). As such, efforts to confine global warming to 1.5°C will be unworkable unless the wealthy change their lifestyles (Gore, 2021) and we reign in rising consumption expectations.

The rich have caused climate change (Oswald et al, 2020) yet there have been limited attempts to define high consumption or what constitutes 'too much'. There also appears to be no political will to tackle what might be regarded as excess consumption and there is limited direct interest in the issue within research, with attention focused instead on low- or under-consumers and more abstract debates about sustainable consumption across society. Such debates often overlook the fact that low-income households are among the lowest emitters and should not form the target for consumption reduction initiatives.

This chapter is not concerned with households who, for example, due to their health, family structure, location or the energy performance of their home, are above average consumers. It is not concerned exclusively with the super-rich, but instead focuses on a broader group that are consuming resources beyond what is termed sufficiency, which refers to consumption beyond that required to meet our needs and some of our wants (Fawcett and Darby, 2019). More specifically, this chapter refers to those powering large homes filled with devices, owning multiple vehicles driven often and flying frequently (Weidmann et al, 2020), eating meat-rich diets, owning a wide range of consumer goods and acquiring new ones regularly (Pieper et al, 2020). The interest here is in those they influence in their roles as aspirational consumers, contributing to the reproduction of a world where individuals and states regard wealth and conspicuous consumption as markers of success.

The widening gulf between rich and poor, and levels of consumption that continue to escalate despite climate and ecological breakdown, leaves unanswered questions about whether high consuming households either do not realize the impact of their actions, think that these messages do not apply to them, do not judge their behaviour to be problematic and/or are hostages to compelling social and cultural pressures and influences that instil and perpetuate high consumption. The research on which this chapter is based asks why it is so hard to consume less, even when the evidence that we need to do so is so compelling.

High consumers: an academic and policy blind spot?

In 2010, the 10 per cent most affluent households emitted 34 per cent of global carbon dioxide emissions, while the 50 per cent of the global population in lower income brackets accounted for just 15 per cent (Hubacek et al, 2017). By 2015, the disparity stretched to 49 per cent against 7 per cent (Kartha et al, 2020), indicating that resource consumption is becoming increasingly polarized, with low-income households on an opposite trajectory to the affluent. A disparity of ecological footprints across wealth brackets is seen within, and between, nations and regions of the world, and within towns and cities. At all scales, the wealthy generate more negative environmental impacts than lower income groups (Lynch et al, 2019).

Despite the extent of these inequalities, our literature review on high consuming households found that they have received limited explicit attention in academic studies. There are, however, some exceptions from the fields of energy and transport studies, and from the degrowth literature, including the work of Fawcett and Darby (2019) and Chatterton et al (2019), who focus, respectively, on questions around excessive energy and transport consumption, and how much consumption is sufficient in the context of planetary limits (Druckman and Jackson, 2010; Gough, 2020; Hickel, 2020). Others have experimented with how sufficiency, or greater simplicity, might be achieved in practice (Cherrier et al, 2012; McGoran and Prothero, 2016). These contributions galvanized and informed the research, confirming that addressing excessive consumption is one of the most important factors in curbing GHG emissions and environmental destruction, and redressing increasingly unfair resource distribution.

While the academic community is waking up to the significance of high consumption, policy communities are yet to acknowledge the urgent need to understand and address extremes of consumption (Mundaca et al, 2019), beyond fleeting consideration of personal carbon budgets and carbon taxes (Schubert, 2019).

In pursuit of status and happiness?

The lack of policy focus on high consumption may stem from political reluctance to back policies apparently at loggerheads with dominant neoliberal economic paradigms supporting the rights of high earners to consume and pollute without limits. Efforts to curb consumption among high earners may also call into question widely accepted cultural beliefs that owning an increasing quantity or range of goods and services is a normal motivation, acceptable cultural desire and means of achieving happiness, conveying status, and personal and national success (Brown and Cameron, 2000). However, as alluded to by DiMuzio (2015), consumption can only be effective as a symbol of success and status if intra-class consumption remains uneven and lower socio-economic groups cannot join in. This approach to the pursuit and communication of status and fulfilment relies on keeping the majority of the world's population poor and exposes the world's poorest nations to the worst effects of climate change, a problem to which they have barely contributed (James et al, 2014).

Income is a reliable predictor of a household's consumption and environmental impacts (Büchs and Schnepf, 2013; Hubacek et al, 2017; Wiedenhofer et al, 2017). For example, it has been demonstrated (in the UK) that CO_2 emissions increase with income (Chatterton et al, 2019) and this trend resonates internationally (Hubacek et al, 2017). Domestic energy use, private transport and food are the main sources of an individual's environmental impact in developed countries (Peattie and Peattie, 2009) and high consumption at a household level usually appears at the same time across these different domains (Shackleton and Shackleton, 2006; Chatterton et al, 2016; Wiedenhofer et al, 2017).

Therefore, although there might be difficulties in terms of definition and identification, targeting higher consumers with consumption reduction measures should make a more significant contribution towards reducing emissions across multiple consumption domains than focusing on larger groups of lower consumers. Yet, more evidence is needed to understand what drives and perpetuates high consumption to ensure that these efforts are as effective and enduring in their impact as possible.

What drives and normalizes high consumption?

Beyond highlighting links to the expression of status and the pursuit of happiness among the wealthy (Brown and Cameron, 2000), the literature offers a range of perspectives on the drivers of high consumption. It has been linked to psychological weaknesses and certain personality traits that leave people predisposed to high consumption (Humphery, 2009; Håkansson, 2014). Others, such as Chatterton et al (2019), emphasize personal responsibility, and frame excessive consumption as the result of personal choices driven by ignorance (a lack of awareness of the consequences) or accident (not planned, unexpected, unintended), frivolity (not having any serious purpose or value) or decadence (luxurious self-indulgence). Rucker et al (2014) characterize the 'desire to acquire' as an attempt to compensate for feelings of feared or actual impotence. Giddens (1984) takes a less individualistic view, presenting consumption as a set of social practices, influenced by social norms primarily governed by the institutions and structures of society.

Charting a middle course, Dubuisson-Quellier (2022) asserts that the success or otherwise of the transition to a more sustainable way of life cannot rest on consumers alone, and points to a complex interaction between public policies, corporate business models and consumer practices underpinning what they term 'affluent consumption' as a legitimized and institutionalized norm. They combine a firm belief that high consumption is structurally constituted alongside recognition of personal choice, but arguably neglect the potential role that emotion and coercion might play in consumption choices (March and Olsen, 2013).

Despite these divergent ideas about what drives (high) consumption, the literature points to a complex web of personal, social, cultural and corporate influences. However, there is a degree of consensus that the pursuit of social status, and a desire to demonstrate it, forms a key driver of consumption habits (Bronner and de Hoog, 2018; Ramakrishnan et al, 2020).

Consequences of high consumption for high consumers

Beyond consideration of the drivers of high consumption and the environmental damage wrought, far less attention is paid to the implications of intense consumerism for high consumers themselves. For example, does high consumption represent a successful strategy, in practice, for conveying or asserting social status? Does it bring the lasting sense of happiness that marketeers may espouse? Or, is there great pressure and unhappiness associated with aspiring to ever-increasing consumption expectations, constantly benchmarking yourself against what others have and do, and to keeping up with the latest 'must have' items and experiences? Does adhering to a high consumption lifestyle necessitate long working hours or high-risk investment strategies to maintain and increase spending power? Does it mean that there is a long way to fall if income levels can no longer support our consumption expectations and we fall out of kilter with peers?

In relation to these questions, we are influenced by Kasser and Kanner (2004), who highlight the negative impacts of consumerism and materialism, including the prioritization of money and possessions over activities that promote and sustain happiness. Wide-ranging threats associated with consumerism for, among others, intimate relationships, child development and identity formation are identified.

Within our research, we conceptualize the potentially deleterious impacts of high consumption on the individual and the family and the labour involved in attaining and maintaining high consuming lifestyles, as potential opportunities to 'release' high consumers from increasing pressure. In essence, our hypothesis goes that these stresses, strains and fears of being unable (for financial and personal reasons rather than ecological reasons) to sustain high consumption represent intervention points, where high consumers may be receptive to change.

Academic and stakeholder perspectives on drivers and solutions

To better understand the state of the art, academics and practitioners (primarily within NGOs) who lead agendas around sustainable consumption and resource inequality in the UK and Europe, were interviewed. A series of ten semi-structured interviews explored what was already known about the ways in which problematic consumption was characterized in the working practices of participants, the extent to which their work engaged with high consumption, and their suggestions for how more sustainable and equitable consumption might be characterized and attained.

It was notable, and to some extent anticipated, that the work of most respondents focused on energy poverty or what might be termed 'under-consumption'. Indeed, many researchers in the field of sustainable consumption feel a moral imperative to focus on low consumers and how they might be supported to increase their consumption to levels required to achieve and maintain health and wellbeing (for example, if underheating the home or eating food with poor nutritional content) and economic inclusion (for example, having the means and possessions such as clothing and transport to access employment). This perspective fails to take account of the fact that, within the context of finite resources, the consumption of one social group or region of the world cannot always be increased without consumption reduction on the part of another.

Defining high consumption

There was broad consensus among participants that, reflecting the literature, high consumption is closely associated with high levels of personal wealth.

Yet, it was acknowledged that there are socio-structural factors that also lock people with modest incomes into patterns of higher consumption, such as transport infrastructure that prioritizes car ownership and poorly insulated homes which necessitate high energy consumption.

Participants were not able to offer any quantitative definitions of high or excess consumption and caution was expressed in relation to the use of average consumption data to identify high consumers, on the basis that this may involve problematizing those who, due to factors beyond their control, are above average consumers. In light of this, some participants felt that high consumption was defined by choosing high emission options when low emission options are accessible and available. Some normative examples of problematic high consumption that emerged from the interviews included frequent flying (this was set at more than five flights per year) and the ownership of large and second homes.

It was agreed that any definition of high consumption should consider differences between elite and more common forms of high consumption, for example, collective subscription to wasteful but not elitist practices (cultures of car driving) versus elite consumption that is less pervasive yet accounts for far greater emissions per person (such as frequent, long haul flying and exclusive use of multiple homes), with elite consumption viewed as more problematic.

Participants suggested that future research on high consumption needed to consider the appropriate measurements for different types of consumption, as the way that current consumption research quantifies and reports on consumption often fails to capture both the environmental impact of the activity (as in number of flights taken rather than the amount of carbon emissions generated) and what it achieves (as in units of energy consumed rather than warmth levels achieved). In this context, discussions about how much consumption is necessary to achieve and maintain a good, fulfilling life never reached a firm conclusion but a greater emphasis on outcomes achieved for health, wellbeing and social and economic inclusion was generally advocated over a simplistic focus on quantifying emissions. However, it was noted that a balance must be struck between what is required to maintain health and wellbeing and what is possible within planetary limits. Hirsch (2019) provides a good illustration of how what are regarded as minimum socially and culturally necessary consumption expectations, particularly in the Global North, may be out of kilter with planetary limits, finding that people in the UK see buying birthday presents, alcohol and eating out as minimum necessities (see Chapter 13).

In light of these dilemmas, interviewees suggested that definitions of a good life should not focus on subjective happiness measures but on universal needs, such as participation in society and maintaining good levels of physical and mental health, recognizing that while these needs are universal, the way to satisfy them is culturally specific. In this context, several interviewees referred to Max-Neef's (1982) Fundamental Human Needs theory, arguing that high consumption uses material satisfiers when social ones might more effective and sustainable.

Tackling high consumption

Four main approaches to tackling high consumption were identified by participants: tax, regulation, cultural change, and political change. Some of these approaches frame consumption as individual choice and others as sociostructurally determined, but all participants felt that consumption reduction should be a just process that reduces inequality, rather than relying on financial mechanisms that the wealthy could withstand and which may penalize lower income groups, such as higher fuel prices or taxes on certain foods.

It was acknowledged that higher taxation or new taxes are unlikely to deter high-income groups and challenge the status quo. Legal limits on consumption rather than regulation by price was seen as a more progressive and effective approach, albeit unlikely due to the radical shift in political ideology and social norms that regulated consumption would require, not to mention development of new legal frameworks. Similarly, the potential for cultural change was acknowledged as relying on a shift away from a free-market capitalist approach, recognizing that voluntary approaches from either producers or consumers would be unlikely to succeed at the scales required to reduce consumption in line with natural resource availability (Brown and Cameron, 2000).

While some participants saw education and awareness raising as important in the move towards more sustainable consumption, others were more sceptical about this approach and referenced research critiquing approaches based upon individualizing behavioural models, which neglect the normative and socio-cultural context in which consumption takes place (Giddens, 1984).

Difficult territory for the researcher

The academics and practitioners interviewed were evidently grappling with the many tensions and potential pitfalls that arise when attempting to identify and target groups that cause environmental harm. Research that seeks to understand the plight of vulnerable under-consumers and improve their circumstances is common and morally safe territory, but rarely do such studies seek to understand the counterpoint – by engaging with those benefiting from dominant, high consuming regimes – and are, therefore, incentivized to sustain and reproduce them (path dependency). There is a perception that to do so would be to blame not just big business and policy regimes but could also involve problematizing conventions and ways of life that are widely considered not only acceptable, but aspirational.

This is difficult territory for the researcher, philosophically and practically. It is difficult to know where to draw the line between acceptable, necessary and sufficient consumption required for health, wellbeing and social inclusion, and that which is problematic and threatens survival. But researchers must also be transparent – the very suggestion that someone is invited to participate in research because their way of life could be considered damaging risks alienating them and blurs the distinction between research and intervention.

We know who we need to speak to in order to build a more full and nuanced picture of the forces shaping rising levels of consumption which cause over-use of natural resources and set unsustainable expectations of consumption in wider society. It is abundantly clear that consumption rises with income, so it is the wealthy that we need to target, and those with sufficient incomes to follow or partially follow the standards and expectations they set. But we need to go deeper still to understand the normative conditions that reproduce inequality and the socio-structural and cultural forces that drive and lock in high consuming lifestyles. Framing high consumption in this way brings it into line with the conceptualization of consumption as driven by structures and norms and not just individuals making (deliberately) bad or immoral choices (Giddens, 1984).

A further reason why the study of high consumers is relatively underdeveloped may stem from the sense of hopelessness that arises when attempting to challenge the fundamental paradigms by which the world is either organized or aspires to be organized, that is, the pursuit of perpetual economic growth. We choose, therefore, to frame our research as a deep and probing investigation of why it is so difficult to consume less, thus avoiding alienating the people we need to speak to. This focus acknowledges the forces almost certainly at play that make high consumption, or a desire to participate in it, almost inevitable and not entirely a matter of choice.

The literature speculates, among other things, that overconsumption of resources may be driven by the pursuit of happiness and the need to tangibly convey social status (Brown and Cameron, 2000). It may offer a material alternative in the absence of socially derived satisfaction (Max-Neef, 1982). Or, it may result from adherence to the ideal life course mapped out by capitalism, which some will attain at the expense of others, and which Giddens (1984) contends infiltrates our discursive consciousness. Personality traits and emotion may also play a role, with some more susceptible to materiality than others (Humphery, 2009; Håkansson, 2014). All are merely hypotheses but point to useful lines of inquiry for empirical investigation.

Towards a better understanding of high consumers

We identify a clear disconnect within the current evidence base between evidence of the impact of high consumption lifestyles on the environment and a limited focus on high consumers within research and policy. In response to this, we have embarked upon a new research agenda dedicated to understanding why it is so hard to consume less: a question emerging as vital to limiting global warming to safe levels.

We conclude that deep qualitative exploration with high consuming households is urgently required and should form a priority within the field of sustainable consumption and allied fields. Institutional ethnography (IE) emerges as our favoured method for doing so because it is deployed when attempts to change or improve a working practice are unsuccessful, making it well suited to exploring escalating consumption in the context of the climate crisis and resource scarcity (Hawkins, 2023). Moreover, in contrast to the notion of consumption as a means of achieving personal happiness and satisfaction, IE reveals the maintenance of high consuming lifestyles as a form of work (Smith, 2005). Framing them as work will be important in developing a non-judgemental approach which avoids alienating participants.

Within IE, research informants are regarded as the experts in the routinized practices under observation, requiring researchers to confine themselves to explicating why these practices happen as they do, rather than suggesting how they need to change. IE employs ethnographic research tools, such as observation and interviews to explore working and social practices, to reveal the hidden power dynamics and socio-structural forces shaping them (Smith, 2005). It is particularly useful in situations where an established way of doing things is entrenched but poorly understood, and the status quo is unsustainable (Campbell and Gregor, 2008). The methodology has recently been adapted to explore opportunities for changing consumption practices by identifying potential intervention points where the status quo is less than satisfactory and opportunities to change course may be more appealing (Hawkins, 2023).

As a hypothesis, we suggest that high consuming lifestyles deliver important benefits – such as comfort, clean air, safety, convenience, luxury, health, choice, privacy and so on – but that maintaining and going beyond or extending these benefits creates pressures (financial, social and time related), and represents a form of work that some may crave to escape (whether concerned for the environment or not). We also anticipate finding that, after a certain point, high consumption yields diminishing returns for households, thus establishing the point at which the pursuit of high consumption becomes counterproductive for wellbeing.

Conclusion

Insights into factors fuelling high consumption are emerging from an increasing corpus of work on sufficiency and excess consumption across different domains of consumption (notably transport and energy), but there is no clear thesis or policy pathway. Deepening this programme of work is a priority for the pursuit of post-carbon inclusion, and is of at least equal importance to the study of low- or under-consumers. Questions regarding how we can prevent wealth going hand in hand with environmental destruction and how we might achieve more even distributions of consumption across spatial scales and social groups are paramount to unlocking post-carbon inclusion

Yet, however much we accept the rationale for greater research and policy focus on high consumers, this will be a challenging programme of research to execute, not least because it breaks with path dependency in the field of consumption research, where the focus is firmly on those deprived of adequate resources in a world where the gap between rich and poor is always widening. Moreover, as a research agenda, it also comes into conflict with dominant concepts of what social mobility and success look like and may, therefore, struggle to attract political and public support. We are prepared for self-reflection and uncomfortable encounters with the self, as we face the reality that we are just as much a part of the problem and display many of the same damaging and contradictory practices as we are likely to identify among participants.

This research is proceeding into deep qualitative exploration of the drivers, challenges and practical and emotional work of living beyond planetary limits. It will need to do so in a manner that avoids blame and judgement in order to achieve access to the lives of high consumers and incentivize their engagement. The focus will be on unpicking psychological, social, cultural and structural drivers of rising consumption. Such insights have the potential to inform progressive interventions that do not rely on fiscal measures that the wealthy can withstand and that fail to challenge the dominant ideologies and conceptualizations of success underlying ever greater consumption.

Key research questions will include why it is hard to consume less across the core domains of consumption (material and experiential), how much is perceived as necessary for a good life, and why resource intensive options are pursued when lower impact ones are available. In relation to the latter, which (ostensibly) lower impact choices appeal to high consumers (and why), will be explored. Another priority for exploration is the notion that concerns about climate breakdown may be fuelling compensatory consumption, which involves purchasing products that appear (but may not actually be) environmentally friendly (such as electric vehicles or organic food) in a bid to offset discomfort about carbon fuelled lifestyles, or to shore up a particular image or identity being sought (Kim and Rucker, 2012). A further hypothesis is that high consuming households may have limited understanding of what their most environmentally damaging activities are, and, for example, they may go to great lengths to source local, organic food but never consider the impact of their financial investments.

Ultimately, the hope is that deeper socio-structural and cultural understandings of high consumption will contribute towards post-carbon inclusion through evidence-based recommendations for carefully timed and formulated interventions. Such interventions would ideally enable reductions in consumption which are broadly acceptable to high consuming groups without compromising their health, wellbeing and social inclusion but also free up resources to enable greater access to these benefits among those currently not accessing sufficient resources.

References

Bronner, F. and de Hoog, R. (2018) 'Conspicuous consumption and the rising importance of experiential purchases', *International Journal of Market Research*, 60(1): 88–103.

Brown, P.M and Cameron, L.D. (2000) 'What can be done to reduce overconsumption?', *Ecological Economics*, 32(1): 27–41.

Büchs, M. and Schnepf, S.V. (2013) 'Who emits most? Associations between socio-economic factors and UK households' home energy, transport, indirect and total CO2 emissions', *Ecological Economics*, 90: 114–23.

Campbell, M.L. and Gregor, F.M. (2008) *Mapping Social Relations: A Primer in Doing Institutional Ethnography*, Toronto: University of Toronto Press.

Castano-Garcia, A., Ambrose, A., Hawkins, A. and Parkes, S. (2021) 'High consumption, an unsustainable habit that needs more attention', *Energy Research & Social Science*, 80: 102241.

Chatterton, T., Anable, J., Barnes, J. and Yeboah, G. (2016) 'Mapping household direct energy consumption in the United Kingdom to provide a new perspective on energy justice', *Energy Research and Social Science*, 18: 71–87.

Chatterton, T., Anable, J., Buchs, M., Lovelace, R., Lucas, K., Mullen, C. et al (2019) 'Excess? Exploring social, structural and behavioural drivers of energy demand in areas of high combined energy consumption or "how much energy is enough"?', in *Proceedings of the ECEEE [European Council for an Energy Efficient Economy] Summer Study on Energy Efficiency 2019*, Paper 6-019-19. Available from: https://www.eceee.org/library/conference_proceedings/eceee_Summer_Studies/ [Accessed 30 May 2023].

Cherrier, H., Szuba, M. and Özçağlar-Toulouse, N. (2012) 'Barriers to downward carbon emission: exploring sustainable consumption in the face of the glass floor', *Journal of Marketing Management*, 28(3–4): 397–419.

Cohen, S.A., Liu, H., Hanna, P., Hopkins, D., Higham, J. and Gössling, S. (2021) 'The rich kids of Instagram: luxury travel, transport modes, and desire', *Journal of Travel Research*, 61(7): 1479–94.

DiMuzio, T. (2015) 'The plutonomy of the 1%: dominant ownership and conspicuous consumption in the New Gilded Age', *Millennium: Journal of International Studies*, 43(2): 492–510.

Druckman, A. and Jackson, T. (2010) 'The bare necessities: how much household carbon do we really need?', *Ecological Economics*, 69(9): 1794–804.

Dubuisson-Quellier, S. (2022) 'How does affluent consumption come to consumers? A research agenda for exploring the foundations and lock-ins of affluent consumption', *Consumption and Society*, 1(1): 31–50.

Fawcett, T. and Darby, S. (2019) 'Energy sufficiency in policy and practice: the question of needs and wants', in *Proceedings of the ECEEE [European Council for an Energy Efficient Economy] Summer Study on Energy Efficiency 2019*, pp 361–70. Available from: https://www.eceee.org/library/conference_proceedings/eceee_Summer_Studies/ [Accessed 30 May 2023].

Giddens, A. (1984) *The Constitution of Society: Outline of the Theory of Structuration*, Berkeley and Los Angeles: University of California Press.

Gore, T. (2021) 'Carbon inequality in 2030: per capita consumption emissions and the 1.5°C goal', Joint agency briefing note (Institute for European Environmental Policy and Oxfam), Oxford: Oxfam GB and Oxfam International. Available from: https://policy-practice.oxfam.org/resources/carbon-inequality-in-2030-per-capita-consumption-emissions-and-the-15c-goal-621305/ [Accessed 30 May 2023].

Gough, I. (2020) 'Defining floors and ceilings: the contribution of human needs theory', *Sustainability: Science, Practice and Policy*, 16(1): 208–19.

Håkansson, A (2014) 'What is overconsumption? A step towards a common understanding', *International Journal of Consumer Studies*, 38(6): 692–700.

Hawkins, A. (2023) 'Mapping working practices as systems: an analytical model for visualising findings from an Institutional Ethnography', *Qualitative Research*.

Hickel, J. (2020) *Less Is More: How Degrowth Will Save the World*, London: Random House.

Hirsch, D. (2019) *A Minimum Income Standard for the United Kingdom in 2019*, final report, Joseph Rowntree Foundation. Available from: https://www.jrf.org.uk/report/minimum-income-standard-uk-2019 [Accessed 29 May 2023].

Hubacek, K., Baiocchi, G., Feng, K., Muñoz Castillo, R., Sun, L. and Xue, J. (2017) 'Global carbon inequality', *Energy, Ecology and Environment*, 2(6): 361–9.

Humphery, K. (2009) *Excess: Anti-Consumerism in the West*, Cambridge: Polity Press.

IPCC (2022) *Climate Change 2022: Impacts, Adaptation, and Vulnerability*, contribution of Working Group II to the Sixth Assessment Report of the Intergovernmental Panel on Climate Change, edited by Pörtner, H.-O., Roberts, D.C., Tignor, M., Poloczanska, E.S., Mintenbeck, K., Alegría, A. et al, Cambridge and New York: Cambridge University Press.

James, R., Otto, F., Parker, H., Boyd, E., Cornforth, R., Mitchell, D. et al (2014) 'Characterizing loss and damage from climate change', *Nature Climate Change*, 4(11): 938–9.

Kartha, S., Kemp-Benedict, E., Ghosh, E., Nazareth, A. and Gore, T. (2020) *The Carbon Inequality Era: An Assessment of the Global Distribution of Consumption Emissions Among Individuals from 1990 to 2015 and Beyond*, Oxfam & Stockholm Environment Institute. Available from: https://policy-practice.oxfam.org/resources/the-carbon-inequality-era-an-assessment-of-the-global-distribution-of-consumpti-621049/ [Accessed 30 May 2023].

Kasser, T. and Kanner, A.D. (eds) (2004) *Psychology and Consumer Culture: The Struggle for a Good Life in a Materialistic World*, Washington, DC: American Psychological Association.

Kim, S. and Rucker, D. (2012) 'Bracing for the psychological storm: proactive versus reactive compensatory consumption', *Journal of Consumer Research*, 39(4): 815–30.

Lynch, M.J., Long, M.A., Stretesky, P.B. and Barrett, K.L. (2019) 'Measuring the ecological impact of the wealthy: excessive consumption, ecological disorganization, green crime, and justice', *Social Currents*, 6(4): 377–95.

March, J.G. and Olsen, J.P. (2013) 'The logic of appropriateness', in Goodin, R. (ed), *The Oxford Handbook of Political Science*, Oxford: Oxford University Press, pp 478–97. Available from: https://www.oxfordhandbooks.com/view/10.1093/oxfordhb/9780199604456.001.0001/oxfordhb-9780199604456-e-024 [Accessed 29 May 2023].

Max-Neef, M. (1982) *From the Outside Looking In: Experiences in Barefoot Economics*, London: Bloomsbury.

McGouran, C. and Prothero, A. (2016) 'Enacted voluntary simplicity: exploring the consequences of requesting consumers to intentionally consume less', *European Journal of Marketing*, 50(1/2): 189–212.

Mundaca, L., Ürge-Vorsatz, D. and Wilson, C. (2019) 'Demand-side approaches for limiting global warming to 1.5°C', *Energy Efficiency*, 12(2): 343–62.

Oswald, Y., Owen, A. and Steinberger, J.K. (2020) 'Large inequality in international and intranational energy footprints between income groups and across consumption categories', *Nature Energy*, 5(3): 231–9.

Peattie, K. and Peattie, S. (2009) 'Social marketing: a pathway to consumption reduction?', *Journal of Business Research*, 62(2): 260–8.

Pieper, M., Michalke, A. and Gaugler, T. (2020) 'Calculation of external climate costs for food highlights inadequate pricing of animal products', *Nature Communications*, 11(1): 6117.

Ramakrishnan, A., Kalkuhl, M., Ahmad, S. and Creutzig, F. (2020) 'Keeping up with the Patels: conspicuous consumption drives the adoption of cars and appliances in India', *Energy Research & Social Science*, 70: 101742.

Rucker, D.D., Hu, M. and Galinsky, A.D. (2014) 'The experience versus the expectations of power: a recipe for altering the effects of power on behavior', *Journal of Consumer Research*, 41(2): 381–96.

Schubert, E. (2019) *Carbon Taxation: The French Experience 2014–2019*, presentation to Coalition of Finance Ministers for Climate Action Workshop on Carbon Taxation 3–4 October. Available from: https://www.financeministersforclimate.org/sites/cape/files/inline-files/Carbon%20Taxation%20in%20France.pdf [Accessed 29 May 2023].

Shackleton, C.M. and Shackleton, S.E. (2006) 'Household wealth status and natural resource use in the Kat River valley, South Africa', *Ecological Economics*, 57(2): 306–17.

Smith, D. (2005) *Institutional Ethnography: A Sociology for People*, Oxford: AltaMira Press.

Wiedenhofer, D., Guan, D., Liu, Z. Meng, J., Zhang, N. and Wei, Y.M. (2017) 'Unequal household carbon footprints in China', *Nature Climate Change*, 7(1): 75–80.

Wiedmann, T., Lenzen, M., Keyßer, L.T. and Steinberger, J.K. (2020) 'Scientists' warning on affluence', *Nature Communications*, 11(1): 3107.

12

Housing Retrofit for Post-Carbon Inclusion

Ralph Horne and Lisa de Kleyn

Housing retrofit for decarbonization (hereafter 'retrofit') occupies a central project in addressing the climate emergency, and this is made even more pressing by rising pressure on access to decent affordable housing. Contributing factors include conflict, trade wars, financialized housing systems, COVID-19 and complexities in retrofit services of provision. While commonplace ideas of fitting extra insulation and choosing efficient appliances may seem modest and achievable at first glance, in reality, housing retrofit involves a heady mix of affective experiences of home, in place-specific, socio-material assemblages reflecting different eras of norms and standards. Added to this are contemporary structural inequities in housing, and the dynamics and heterogeneity of households, homemaking, property condition, tenure, typology and histories of refurbishment.

While conventional approaches of cost–benefit analysis and energy paybacks may be useful tools to incentivize retrofit in some circumstances, they are insufficient. Moreover, as indicated in Chapter 6 on homeowner-dominated, market-based housing systems (such as Australia, the context for this chapter), financialization of housing driven by deregulation policy markedly complicates the important task of scaling-up retrofit to meet climate mitigation imperatives. Policies that incentivize land price speculation, and widening gaps between 'haves' and 'have nots', conflict with rights to the ontological security of access to sustainable housing and, subservient to profit maximization imperatives, demote ideas of community-wide retrofit for the planetary commons.

This chapter explores inclusive and decommodified approaches to post-carbon housing retrofit grounded in people's socio-material experiences of retrofit and their homes. Drawing upon a large four-year project involving over 100 interviews with householders in Australia, it aims to contribute to an agenda of housing retrofit for post-carbon inclusion. Ways of shifting industry practices are contrasted with local self-organized approaches to examine how to scale-up retrofit in heterogeneous socio-material conditions. Deliberative and radical experiments and prospects for how they might be mainstreamed are discussed. Ways of understanding and institution building necessary to integrate and centralize inclusion and decarbonization in practical policy approaches to retrofit housing for universal carbon-free energy-enabled futures are posited.

Policy context of homeowner-dominated housing retrofit

In an era where ecological modernization is a dominant paradigm, market and technological approaches to understanding housing retrofit tend to assume an overt role for households as primary actors. Implicit is the idea that retrofit is conscious, that all households have agency, capabilities and resources to make such decisions, and that the market is configured in order to allow provision. Environmental 'goods' are typically financialized through, for example, taxes or carbon markets, and incentives such as grant schemes, favouring those with the capabilities to benefit from these policy instruments. Moreover, there is a predominance of market-based approaches oriented towards addressing market failures (such as through information provision), developing the market for retrofit (say, by providing rebates), and supporting innovation, for instance, in providing support for research and development (Bobrova et al, 2021). Predominant government interventions remain hampered by policy reversals, a lack of socio-materially integrated approaches (Walker et al, 2015) and a lack of policy justice in retrofit (Sovacool and Dworkin, 2015; Day et al, 2016; Bouzarovski and Tirado Herrero, 2017).

In common with many other owner-occupier based housing contexts, Australia faces growing housing and energy injustice (Willand and Horne, 2018) and, within this, the phenomenon of hidden energy poverty and energy vulnerability. In retrofit injustice, multiple vulnerabilities often play a role. For example, a study of Australia's rental housing context found that material conditions of housing interrelate in complex ways with tenure, income, existing health issues and lack of support networks, contributing to conditions for energy hardship (Daniel et al, 2020). Such compound vulnerabilities have also been exacerbated by the COVID-19 pandemic and associated stay-at-home measures (Horne et al, 2021; Oswald et al, 2023). The role of social justice in the form of enabling opportunities and freedoms is an emerging topic. Melin et al (2021) have edited a special issue of the *Journal of Human Development and Capabilities* on energy justice and the capability approach. In particular, the application of ideas from Sen's (2005) capabilities approach – detailed in Chapter 9 – is relevant here. Willand et al (2021) use capabilities to draw links between the ability to heat a home adequately (a secondary capability) and being able to lead a healthy life (a primary capability).

In the current dominant policy trajectory, post-carbon housing will be primarily available to the financially equipped. We can see this emerging. In Australia, for example, a 'successful' domestic photovoltaic (PV) transition has seen some three million homes – over 25 per cent of households (Australian Government, 2021) – fitted with PV panels in the decade to 2022. Installations are subsidized via energy price increases driven by Renewable Energy Target obligations on liable entities (generally energy retailers). These energy price increases apply to all households. Those who are renters invariably cannot access this PV benefit. Those who purchase a PV system tend to be owner-occupiers in detached dwellings (or at least with their own rooftop) and those who also have the requisite knowledge, trust, time, matching cash, situation and outlook that enables them to voluntarily participate in the scheme.

In effect, low-income renters pay higher bills so that better-off owner occupiers can secure cheaper renewable power and the kudos of going green to boot. A significant minority, 20–25 per cent of households (Azpitarte et al, 2015), experience energy vulnerability and are least able to pay the increased bills that in effect transfer resources to the already better-off group. Thus, an attempt to generate post-carbon arrangements sees poor families paying for panels for rich ones. Prior evidence from the United Kingdom (UK) shows how the distribution of costs of similar schemes then increased energy prices, adversely affecting those already in energy poverty (Walker and Day, 2012). In such ways, retrofit might exacerbate already existing dynamics and cumulative vulnerabilities of housing affordability stress (Baker et al, 2015, Baker and Lester, 2017).

An often unquestioned and seemingly rarely mentioned market assumption is that private actors have an equal playing field on which to make decisions to maximize their utility, resulting in optimal social outcomes via the most efficient means, as in an analysis by Haughton (1999). In relation to housing, such assumptions include that people are likely to own their home, have the capabilities to make modifications and stay in their homes long enough to achieve the payback. There are a number of lived realities that contradict these assumptions, thereby rendering them a barrier to equitable retrofit for carbon reduction.

Around 30 per cent of Australians are renters (ABS, 2022) in a situation where housing is insecure, and they are reliant on landlords for dwelling modifications. In Australia, homeownership is a means of investment yet house 'turnover' and people moving based on changing life stages and associated needs mean that people often don't stay long enough to achieve a return on their investment based on the energy-focused cost–benefit equation. Low socio-economic groups and Culturally and Linguistically Diverse Groups experience a range of structural barriers in relation to retrofit, yet they are most likely to realize benefits that are externalities in the retrofit market, such as health benefits (Daly et al, 2018). The cost–benefit in relation to social housing has also been shown to be a flawed calculation for people experiencing a 'pre-bound effect', such that their energy use is so low due to limited capabilities and housing condition, that a cost–benefit cannot be achieved viably (Daly et al, 2018; Desvallées, 2022). Furthermore, homeowners and landlords have interests and objectives associated with property, wealth and security in a market-driven economy, which do not necessarily align with the affective interests of residents in relation to their home.

Clearly, alternatives to commodified retrofit and market-based policy responses are needed if we are to scale retrofit sufficiently to respond to the urgency of climate change, address both energy vulnerability and energy poverty, and support an adequate and affordable energy supply. In exploring such alternatives, a key ontological starting point accepts that housing retrofit involves diverse and dynamic relationships between people across supply, demand and governance, and that retrofit is part of the broader phenomenon of homemaking and home improvements.

Situating epistemologies of post-carbon retrofit

Scholarship on retrofit that might inform better post-carbon outcomes for housing access and services compared to market-technology-behaviour dominated policies includes:

- policy approaches focusing on social inequality including on social housing;
- political economy approaches that are responsive to the role of power and governance in retrofit;
- local engagement-based approaches, ranging from local authorities as key actors to more overt housing activist approaches that seek to establish retrofit as part of a broader degrowth movement involving innovative and grassroots action;
- social structural and practice-based approaches to understanding how and why households do or do not retrofit, and the role of industry practices and transitions including suppliers, intermediaries and specific technologies.

This is by no means an exhaustive list but situates our approach here. Studies of housing inequalities and energy vulnerabilities often raise power and agency in housing and energy access and, increasingly, the social structures that configure households' abilities to access, participate in, or benefit from, retrofit. For example, Daly et al (2018) articulate energy poverty and energy vulnerability for people in social housing in Australia, finding that people's low energy use invalidates cost–benefit models, and that low-income tenants are more likely to receive additional benefits that are not quantified, including benefits to their health. Research involving social housing providers in Greater Manchester, England (Cauvain et al, 2018: 948), indicates that the interaction between austerity measures, privatization of public housing and decarbonization governance co-opts social landlords into market-based retrofit and repositions a public-sector service 'into serving the forces of market environmentalism', with 'patchy' results in a diverse social housing sector.

Approaches that attend to social structures and focus on households and their relationships with retrofit providers offer a means to reveal more-than-market dimensions of housing retrofit for post-carbon inclusion. Bobrova et al (2021) examine retrofit through an innovation framework based on eight UK cases that achieved significant reductions as part of the SuperHomes network, to highlight the importance of information, capacity to realize low carbon goals and positive experiences, which reinforce the importance of the social context of a household in retrofits. Trust also extends beyond the functions of technologies and markets. De Wilde (2019) distinguishes three categories of trust in decision-making processes for homeowners, including interpersonal trust associated with social networks, impersonal trust based on information that is perceived as independent, and professional trust based on perceptions of supplier behaviour including capacities and ethics.

What this research termed 'local engagement-based approaches' incorporates a wide range of projects and approaches, the common factor being a central role for attempts to build proximal groups of households bound together by shared goals and common understandings of retrofit. Tingey et al (2021) research energy service models provided by local authorities, acknowledging the potential of local authorities to develop ambitious programmes, in part, deriving from their experience in retrofit of both social housing and their own corporate estate. The models involve different sectoral ownership, including public, private, public–private and third sector ownership of independent local organizations. Tingey et al (2021) find that, while the different models provided successes, there were limited services for homeowners and, while all models are part of scaling and accelerating energy efficiency, the models are constrained in market-based and policy environments. Putnam and Brown (2021) research community-led retrofit approaches and find that these approaches overcome barriers associated with retrofit and are able to engage households, develop the local supply chain, overcome economic barriers and address fuel poverty.

Degrowth approaches are more radical in that they envisage a future beyond capitalist modes of economic growth. In general, the intent is to avoid unplanned abrupt economic crises borne out of unsustainable expectations of capital accumulation (Jarvis, 2017) and, instead, begin a practice of equitable, just and localized transitions to housing that are sustainable and fit-for-purpose, rather than first and foremost a financial product. Housing for degrowth (Nelson and Schneider, 2018: 14) proposes 'reducing the total urban area; simplifying and redistributing access to housing; halting industrial urbanization; deurbanizing and renaturalizing areas; renovating dwellings to improve living conditions; sharing dwellings more; and developing low-level, low-impact, small-scale, decentralized, compact settlements'.

This points to a role for shifting community aspirations and expectations of consumption and housing towards ideas of ecological efficiency, sufficiency, frugality, sharing and ideas of fairness, including meeting 'needs' rather than 'wants'. Efficiency is not only about the building envelope, but also about building occupancy; empty buildings are clearly inefficient. Degrowth emphasizes retrofit as a means to avoid demolition, to extend building life, to house more people, and to do this through lower environmental burdens (Cuchi and Sweatman, 2011). Carrying capacity thus becomes more central to the frame of retrofit.

Following the socio-material turn, the approach here is founded on understandings of household dynamics and social structuring of material consumption. With origins in the entanglements of social and material agency, two particular genres that engage empirically with carbon, housing and households are material anthropology (Miller, 2012) and social practice theory (Shove, 2003; Hand et al, 2007). Accordingly, a growing literature has developed that informs our understanding of the complex social relations between Australian housing, households, home improvements, retrofit and the social structures at play (Blunt and Dowling, 2006; Allon, 2008; Gibson et al, 2011; Maller and Horne, 2011; Gabriel and Watson, 2013; Horne and Dalton, 2014).

Applying this approach highlights retrofit 'transitions' as systemic shifts in practice of retrofit. Informed by science and technology studies, urban sociology and political ecology, ideas of socio-technical transitions investigate contested and fraught processes of purposive material and social change. Hence, of particular importance here is the need to account for local/spatial and socio-material conditions (Coenen et al, 2012; Horne, 2017; Moore et al, 2017) among calls for governments to develop strategic and systematic retrofit (Hodson and Marvin, 2017).

Approaching the question of justice, the focus is on the idea of necessary human capabilities to achieve wellbeing, following the 'capability approach' developed by Sen (2005) – as explicated in Chapter 9 – and applied to housing by Day et al (2016). Detailed householder accounts are key in revealing structures, heterogeneity, affect, materials and power that have been underplayed in housing retrofit studies. Moreover, the capabilities approach is a useful way to articulate nuanced factors left aside by established approaches.

Voices from ordinary retrofit households

A large research team, including the co-authors, undertook the Housing Energy Efficiency Transitions project funded by the Australian Research Council in conjunction with government and non-government partners.[1] This qualitative research, with over 150 households and stakeholders across the states of Victoria and South Australia, investigated the lived experience of energy poverty and retrofit, with a focus on lower income households. In the context of understanding the lived experience of retrofit, we focus on 'ordinary' households, that is, the wonderfully rich diversity of households for whom retrofit is a part of life and embedded in ideas of home improvements, as distinct from the idea of retrofit as a specific, spectacular, eco-techno-centric and new imaginary. Interviews reported later in the chapter were undertaken in the second half of 2019, immediately prior to the COVID-19 pandemic outbreak. Questions explored the interviewee's dwelling, its use, their housing histories and aspirations, and experiences with retrofit. This ethnographic research provided insights into experiences with energy efficiency retrofit that are generally in the shadows of policy discourse, such as heterogeneity, social structures that produce disempowerment, affect and life stage, each being crucial to retrofit. All participants are anonymized and pseudonyms have been applied.

Thematic analysis of ordinary lower income household and supplier accounts of retrofit reveals diverse interests, values, connections, aspirations and concerns. As others have previously found in a range of situations and contexts, individual accounts often exceed material issues of economics, property and infrastructure, and values of efficiency and productivity (Graham and Barnett, 2017). Home dominates and encircles retrofit, rendering it affective, embodied and temporally bound up in aspirations, memories, possibilities, relationships and hopes. The lived experience of low-quality housing is an ongoing story of tolerating inadequate conditions – heat in summer, cold in winter – reflecting entrenched material inequity. Capabilities are critical in this context, such that they support coping strategies. Furthermore, and when these allow, inclusive, decommodified and radical approaches emerge shaped by (and in the process reshaping) relationships, identities and values.

Home as a heterogeneous socio-material and affective place

Heterogeneity is reflected in shifting life stages (variously); growing families; shrinking households; migration; changing relationships; accidents, ill-health and death; evolving neighbourhood characters; identities; pets; and relocating or changes in relation to work and study. These factors all influence change – whether such change was made under pressure, or from decisions about whether to stay, modify or move. Resistance to change can arise from more than simply lack of resources or know-how, and includes affective and emotional ties. People describe the "heart of the house" (Clara) where people gather, or ungather, and affective ties span time, as shown in this exchange between daughter (Vanessa) and mother (Clara):

Vanessa:	This house has got a lot of memories for all of us and it's not just a house, it's a home. As far as I'm concerned, it's still my home.
Clara:	I said the place was lived in from the front gate to the back fence.
Vanessa:	Every square inch of this house was lived in.
Interviewer:	Fantastic.
Clara:	Damn lot of love in it.

Many retrofit projects are entangled with lives on hold, waiting for envisaged future arrangements to unfold and/or for fortunes to change. There is, for some, hope for a stable imagined future; or, as in Miranda's case, the idea of providing for the next generation:

'This is "home sweet home". And it'd be too inconvenient to move anywhere. Yeah, just watch the kids get older now and just give them all the room. When they grow up they get married or whatever and that's it. The house is theirs. They can fill the house up for me.'

Despite outward appearances of similarity, inside homes are modified, configured, diverse in many ways – some delightfully cluttered, others stylishly but minimally furnished in individual styles, according to households' means and taste.

Emotions were not all positive, and were culturally and structurally mediated. There was a theme of 'putting up with' low quality housing and appliances. One participant (Ellen) described their previous cooling system, which they had for 15 years: "We had to put up with the other one, it was so noisy and loud [and] it wouldn't do anything." The dwelling was intolerable during summer heat and would compel participants to leave: "It was ugly. It was very uncomfortable. I used to leave, I used to go to shopping centres, my family's houses" (Ellen). Renters in both social housing and private rentals experienced the exclusionary impacts of tenure, unable to make changes or plan ahead, often fear of landlord retribution stopping them from asking questions. Instead they tolerated inadequate conditions, including holes in the wall, blinds that didn't work and were permanently closed, and ineffective, expensive and unsafe heating and cooling.

Seeking affordable rents meant trading off preferred dwelling type, condition, availability, tenure and location in decision making. For example, participants left areas where they grew up to be able to afford to buy a place; smaller units were purchased rather than a house if the location was the primary consideration; and people stayed in inadequate rental properties for affordability, security and location.

In these accounts, the dwelling presents as both enabling comfort and safety, and a limitation to people being able to meet their needs. Emotional connections and expectations of home (Figure 12.1) are neither quantifiable nor tradeable, and the influence of time through memories and life changes

Figure 12.1: Changing life stages and emotional connection to 'home'

Source: Dr Sarah Robertson (reproduced with permission)

are not influenced by rational cost–benefit analysis and, instead, responsive to specific situations and contexts.

Social dimensions and experiences of retrofit

Experiences with retrofit are part of the ubiquitous phenomena of home improvements and of homemaking, within which knowledge, networks and capabilities are key determinants. Hence, whether (post-carbon) retrofit is achieved relative to other home improvements, that may increase overall environmental burdens, is a product of a range of affordances, imaginaries and access to practical knowledge. Functional services, such as those to heat and cool, point to evolving expectations and cultures of comfort, and appreciation of integration of both indoor and outdoor space. People require fit-for-purpose energy-related products and services and are reliant on sound services and advice. Capabilities relevant here include those associated with networks and relationships, knowing what one wants, access to information, ability to advocate for particular outcomes and availability of trusted suppliers.

People who have capabilities feel empowered and take on challenges and, in some cases, are able to achieve retrofits that meet their needs and goals. However, most often, participants report challenges of retrofit, including attaining multiple quotes; not knowing who to trust; having to sequence modifications; fear of other problems emerging as modifications are underway; escalating costs; and not having the time and money: "We just can't afford to do the whole thing. We just need more space. But it's very difficult when you come to trying to work out what to do with your own house. It is so hard, you don't know who to trust" (Alex).

One couple bought a house that they intended to renovate and found cascading hazards, including asbestos in the house and buried outside in the garden, and unstable foundations and building envelope. Housing presents opportunities and hazards (Figure 12.2). They were renovating quickly to prepare for their first child, who was due in six months:

> 'It was in such a state, you wouldn't have bought it, to be honest. It was too much work for us. ... But anyway, we just. ... You do what you do. But we should never have taken on just the sheer amount of work. We haven't even made it pretty, it's just habitable now. It's not warm, it's not pretty, it's just a roof over our head. And even that's, occasionally, when it rains, we still look at each other thinking, "Oh are we okay?"' (Sandra)

The market-based rationale occupies central ground within the retrofit imaginary, the idea that people can choose to retrofit their homes such that they have the information and resources they need to make decisions, and

Figure 12.2: Dwellings and their surrounds present as opportunities and constraints

Source: Dr Sarah Robertson (reproduced with permission)

the payback in energy savings over time will offset the initial cost, is a rational equation for utility. However, people's access to healthy, quality dwellings, and their abilities to initiate and advocate for change, rely on structural empowerment or disempowerment based on availability of resources, their tenure, access to suitable information, access to services and the conditions in the local area, their social support networks and differing abilities.

Inclusive, innovative, decommodified approaches

Across the diverse experiences of retrofit there were many examples of inclusive, innovative and decommodified approaches that are synonymous with informal, social arrangements; recycling, re-use, do-it-yourself (DIY) and other conservation behaviours; sharing and trading materials; and sharing knowledge and labour, including beyond immediate family and friends and within local communities. People draw on their neighbours, families and friends for advice specific to their needs, and people with practical skills are strongly relied upon and appreciated.

One participant (Clara) described living in a new development with a dirt driveway, and that "We got bogged [stuck in the mud] in the driveway. We got bogged in the front yard. We got bogged in the street." Support arose when working in a real estate agency, as a client (a concreter) had over-ordered concrete on a job and offered the excess to the staff. Clara accepted and the concreter put down two paths for the car to drive over: "If you haven't got the money to pay for it, you can wait." It took 40 years from buying their home before they were able to extend the work and concrete the garage floor. This story demonstrates the role of practices associated with financial management in a situation of limited resources, and the benefits of relationships, opportunism and sharing in achieving modifications.

Efforts to re-use and recycle were motivated by different values including environmental sustainability, identities of not being consumerist and being conservative, and saving money. Second-purchases, sharing items and seeking advice from locals via public forums were discussed in the interviews. There were stories of purchasing appliances second-hand, such as a stove through Gumtree (a website where people sell and give away items); sharing items via a roster managed through a community website; and seeking advice from the local community, including on energy providers. One participant was involved in a local 'food swap' (where people bring food that they grow, or have in excess, to swap with others) and during a food swap picked up an Energy Smart Thermometer from the local council to support temperature management as part of energy conservation. Conservation behaviours interact with home modification in the ways that people seek comfort, save money and express their values. This participant also conserved water:

> 'I save as much water as I can because I use some water for the gardens in summer. I like having a bucket in the shower and when it comes out, initially I save the cold water, before it gets hot, and I do that in the sink as well. And I re-use things like the pot of [water]. ... If I'm boiling an egg, I'll re-use that water a few times and then eventually put it on the garden. So, I try to save water as well.' (Katerina)

Such savings extended into contributing to immediate family and friends and the local community. One participant (Andrew) negotiated with neighbours to replace a 30-year-old hardwood fence. The fencer said that they could remove the old fence and take it to the local council to be mulched and used in council pathways. However, the participant chose to give half of the wood to a friend for their home firewood heater and to keep the rest of the wood to make sign boards about individual plants for the community garden. The community garden approved the design and the participant intended to make 50 sign boards (Figure 12.3).

Community values were grounded in cultural practices, past experiences of hardship and interviewees valuing opportunities that were afforded them, and that they could access while living in Australia. One participant who had recently travelled overseas reflected that, in Australia, "you're in your own

Figure 12.3: Sign boards for plants made from recycled wood

Source: Dr Sarah Robertson (reproduced with permission)

bubble", and that they try to "teach their kids not to abuse the privileges they have" (Miranda). Another couple reflected:

> 'You know what, people have got nothing, so ... still we've got a lot. ... You're always going to look at the worst [off] people, it's not like you've got to look at the highest. So at least we've got something. You remember when we used to live in Coburg, we had nothing.' (Jesse)

Conclusion

The rich diversity, resourcefulness and inventiveness across participants, and the challenges they face in accomplishing retrofit, prompted consideration of possible lines of action that might promote post-carbon inclusion in a more widespread retrofit practice. First, the idea of a 'silver bullet' solution is rejected, given that necessary social change will emerge in unpredictable ways from alignments of new discourses, new understandings or social 'rules', and/or new conventions and trusted knowledge. From such shifts, new bundles of retrofit practices might emerge, displacing existing practices. In any event, as participants showed, the social is invoked. Retrofit is a deeply social, rather than an individual or commoditized, activity. This observation is important as it informs the process of 'scaling-up' retrofit and the prospects for post-carbon housing inclusion displacing existing forms.

In this context, ideas of socio-technical transitions could draw more widely on degrowth, affective dimensions of social life and/or place-based social structures, as ways to shift the viewfinder from focusing on decarbonizing, to thinking about inclusive post-carbon arrangements, where retrofit is a ubiquitous social practice rather than an imaginary one-off event driven by rational economic, utility-maximizing behaviour. In turn, implications flow for the design and implementation of government-sponsored schemes and ways of shifting industry practices, towards local self-organized, inclusive and decommoditized approaches. 'Business as usual' low carbon retrofit is dangerous. However much resource is marshalled to help homeowners green up their homes, this will only drive further inequalities in the housing system and, in turn, jeopardize not only the lives of the dispossessed, but also place in peril the whole decarbonization project, by alienating sections of society from the changes needed.

The potential to realize inclusive approaches to retrofit at scale across the housing stock means rethinking what to do and how to do it, from a householder and retrofit stakeholder perspective, rather than from an assumed notion of the market–technology–behaviour paradigm. It follows that the latter can be implicated in structural resistance to such change – both directly in terms of protecting incumbent interests, and indirectly through a lack of awareness of the importance of social and affective dimensions of retrofit. In particular, engaging with the latter, combinations of two distinct approaches are worthy of attention. First, initiatives to shift industry practices such as through reskilling, building and support networks, and institutions and discourses that emphasize and make 'normal' the practices of inclusive post-carbon retrofit. This would include, for example, building connections between care providers and retrofit providers; building retrofit into home help; fostering intermediaries in the retrofit industry who have training and awareness of social and affective dimensions of retrofit, and so on. Second, an emphasis on local self-organized approaches (open experiments) to test how to scale-up retrofit in heterogeneous socio-material conditions. Retrofit mainstreaming in this context is about normalizing the local, the contingent and the contextual. Where agency combines with goodwill, the considerable voluntary time required is invested. Combined with well-designed programmes, new knowledge and standards of post-carbon retrofit inclusion, the potential conditions are created for requisite practices to emerge and spread.

Degrowth provides a means to think about how social and affective dimensions of retrofit might encourage new ways of understanding and institution building that could integrate and situate retrofit inclusion. In turn, this requires alternative approaches to support. Degrowth is highlighted here because, on the one hand, it serves to illustrate a tension between calls to deregulate housing – to provide more latitude for bottom-up, self-help, mutual aid and innovation – and calls, on the other hand, to add more formal regulation to, say, mandate upgrades and ensure quality workmanship to meet decarbonization targets. Elements of both need to be on the table. By elevating the necessary awareness of the consequences of each (intended or not), dissemination of the findings of this large, detailed study of households provides a contribution to the new discourses, the emerging practices and the ingenuity and innovation of households who are beginning to normalize post-carbon retrofit inclusion.

Note

[1] See https://cur.org.au/project/housing-energy-efficiency-transitions/

References

ABS (2022) 'Housing: census. Information on housing type and housing costs', *Australian Bureau of Statistics*. Available from: https://www.abs.gov.au/statistics/people/housing/housing-census/2021 [Accessed 22 December 2022].

Allon, F. (2008) *Renovation Nation: Our Obsession with Home*, Sydney: University of New South Wales Press.

Australian Government (2021) 'Australia reaches the 3 million solar milestone', *Clean Energy Regulator*, 10 November. Available from: https://www.cleanenergyregulator.gov.au/ [Accessed 4 April 2023].

Azpitarte, F., Johnson, V. and Sullivan, D. (2015) *Fuel Poverty, Household Income and Energy Spending: An Empirical Analysis for Australia Using HILDA Data*, Fitzroy: Brotherhood of St Laurence.

Baker, E. and Lester, L. (2017) 'Multiple housing problems: a view through the housing niche lens', *Cities*, 62: 146–51.

Baker, E., Mason, K. and Bentley, R. (2015) 'Measuring housing affordability: a longitudinal approach', *Urban Policy and Research*, 33(3): 275–90.

Blunt, A. and Dowling, R. (2006) *Home*, London: Routledge.

Bobrova, Y., Papachristos, G. and Chiu, L.F. (2021) 'Homeowner low carbon retrofits: implications for future UK policy', *Energy Policy*, 155: 112344.

Bouzarovski, S. and Tirado Herrero, S. (2017) 'Geographies of injustice: the socio-spatial determinants of energy poverty in Poland, the Czech Republic and Hungary', *Post-Communist Economies*, 29(1): 27–50.

Cauvain, J., Karvonen, A. and Petrova, S. (2018) 'Market-based low-carbon retrofit in social housing: insights from greater Manchester', *Journal of Urban Affairs*, 40(7): 937–51.

Coenen, L., Benneworth, P. and Truffer, B. (2012) 'Toward a spatial perspective on sustainability transitions', *Research Policy*, 41(6): 968–79.

Cuchi, A. and Sweatman, P. (2011) *A National Perspective on Spain's Buildings Sector: A Roadmap for a New Housing Sector*, Working Group for Rehabilitation, November. Available from: https://gbce.es/archivos/ckfinderfiles/Investigacion/libro_GTR_engl_postimprenta.pdf [Accessed 22 December 2022].

Daly, D., Halldorsson, J., Kempton, L. and Cooper, P. (2018) *Mainstreaming Low Carbon Retrofits in Social Housing*, Cooperative Research Centre for Low Carbon Living, May. Available from: https://apo.org.au/node/188491 [Accessed 31 May 2023].

Daniel, L., Moore, T., Baker, E., Beer, A., Willand, N., Horne, R. and Hamilton, C. (2020) *Warm, Cool and Energy-Affordable Housing Policy Solutions for Low-Income Renters*, AHURI Final Report No. 338, Melbourne: Australian Housing and Urban Research Institute.

Day, R., Walker, G. and Simcock, N. (2016) 'Conceptualising energy use and energy poverty using a capabilities framework', *Energy Policy*, 93: 255–64.

Desvallées, L. (2022) 'Low-carbon retrofits in social housing: energy efficiency, multidimensional energy poverty, and domestic comfort strategies in Southern Europe', *Energy Research & Social Science*, 85: 02413.

de Wilde, M. (2019) 'The sustainable housing question: on the role of interpersonal, impersonal and professional trust in low-carbon retrofit decisions by homeowners', *Energy Research & Social Science*, 51: 138–47.

Gabriel, M. and Watson, P. (2013) 'From modern housing to sustainable suburbia: how occupants and their dwellings are adapting to reduce home energy consumption', *Housing, Theory and Society*, 30(3): 219–36.

Gibson, C., Head, L., Gill, N. and Waitt, G. (2011) 'Climate change and household dynamics: beyond consumption, unbounding sustainability', *Transactions of the Institute of British Geographers*, 36(1): 3–8.

Graham, S. and Barnett, J. (2017) 'Accounting for justice in local government responses to sea-level rise: evidence from two local councils in Victoria, Australia', in Lukasiewicz, A., Dovers, S., Robin, L., Mckay, J., Schilizzi, S. and S. Graham (eds) *Natural Resources and Environmental Justice: Australian Perspectives*, Clayton South: CSIRO Publishing, pp 91–104.

Hand, M., Shove, E. and Southerton, D. (2007) 'Home extensions in the United Kingdom: space, time, and practice', *Environment and Planning D: Society and Space*, 25(4): 668–81.

Haughton, G. (1999) 'Environmental justice and the sustainable city', *Journal of Planning Education and Research*, 18(3): 233–43.

Hodson, M. and Marvin, S. (2017) 'The mutual construction of urban retrofit and scale: governing ON, IN and WITH in Greater Manchester', *Environment and Planning C: Government and Policy*, 35(7): 1198–217.

Horne, R. (2017) 'Urban low carbon transitions: housing and urban change', in Moore, T., Fjalar de Haan, F., Horne, R. and Gleeson, B.J. (eds) *Urban Sustainability Transitions: Australian Cases – International Perspectives*, Singapore: Springer, pp 3–18.

Horne, R. and Dalton, T. (2014) 'Transition to low carbon? An analysis of socio-technical change in housing renovation', *Urban Studies*, 51(16): 3445–58.

Horne, R., Willand, N., Dorignon, L. and Middha, B. (2021) 'Housing inequalities and resilience: the lived experience of COVID-19', *International Journal of Housing Policy*, November. DOI: 10.1080/19491247.2021.2002659

Jarvis, H. (2017) 'Sharing, togetherness and intentional degrowth', *Progress in Human Geography*, 43(2): 256–75.

Maller, C. and Horne, R. (2011) 'Living lightly: how does climate change feature in residential home improvements and what are the implications for policy?', *Urban Policy and Research*, 29(1): 59–72.

Melin, A., Day, R. and Jenkins, K.E.H. (2021) 'Energy justice and the capability approach: introduction to the special issue', *Journal of Human Development and Capabilities*, 22(2): 185–96.

Miller, D. (2012) *Consumption and Its Consequences*, Cambridge: Polity Press.

Moore, T., de Haan, F., Horne, R. and B. Gleeson (eds) (2017) *Urban Sustainability Transitions: Australian Cases – International Perspectives*, Singapore: Springer.

Nelson, A. and Schneider, F. (2018) *Housing for Degrowth: Principles, Models, Challenges, and Opportunities*, Abingdon: Routledge.

Oswald, D., Moore, T. and Baker, E. (2023) 'Exploring the wellbeing of renters during the COVID-19 pandemic', *International Journal of Housing Policy*, 23(2): 292–312. DOI: 10.1080/19491247.2022.2037177

Putnam, T. and Brown, D. (2021) 'Grassroots retrofit: community governance and residential energy transitions in the United Kingdom', *Energy Research & Social Science*, 78: 102102.

Sen, A. (2005) 'Human rights and capabilities', *Journal of Human Development*, 6(2): 151–66.

Shove, E. (2003) *Comfort, Cleanliness and Convenience: The Social Organization of Normality*, Oxford: Berg.

Sovacool, B.K. and Dworkin, M.H. (2015) 'Energy justice: conceptual insights and practical applications', *Applied Energy*, 142: 435–44.

Tingey, M., Webb, J. and Van der Horst, D. (2021) 'Housing retrofit: six types of local authority energy service models', *Buildings & Cities*, 2(1): 518–32.

Walker, G. and Day, R. (2012) 'Fuel poverty as injustice: integrating distribution, recognition and procedure in the struggle for affordable warmth', *Energy Policy*, 49: 69–75.

Walker, G., Karvonen, A. and Guy, S. (2015) 'Reflections on a policy denouement: the politics of mainstreaming zero-carbon housing', *Transactions of the Institute of British Geographers*, 41(1): 104–6.

Willand, N. and Horne, R. (2018) '"They are grinding us into the ground": the lived experience of energy (in)justice amongst low-income older households', *Applied Energy*, 226: 61–70.

Willand, W., Middha, B. and Walker, G. (2021) 'Using the capability approach to evaluate energy vulnerability policies and initiatives in Victoria, Australia', *Local Environment*, 26(9): 1109–27.

13

From an 'Imperial Mode of Living' to a 'Caring Commons'

Anitra Nelson

'Post-carbon inclusion' promises to address, in multidimensional ways, the two great challenges for humanity today – socio-economic inequities and ecological unsustainability. When they are applied, inclusionary policies are mainly limited to nation-state institutions that create, support and enact such policies. Yet, in the 21st century, nations are porous; global trade and mobility complicate assessing and creating targets for ecological sustainability and concerted cuts in carbon emissions. It is difficult to account for, let alone control or regulate, cradle-to-grave carbon emissions in the commodity chains and waste associated with the numerous and various goods and services consumed within city, state or national borders. Still, ecological indictors, such as carbon footprints incorporating all such emissions wherever they take place, are key to establishing zero- and negative-carbon living.

This chapter sketches a degrowth paradigm (introduced in Chapters 1 and 10) to reveal the challenge of inequities within global production for trade and flows of trade, then offers a Minority World analysis-cum-response of those implicated in an 'imperial mode of living'. Data derives from interviews conducted specifically for this chapter as well as from print and other media sources. An Australian activist is tracked as she tries to transform the imperial mode of living she was born into for a solidarity mode of living, with a focus on her engagement in eco-collaborative housing (a key housing-for-degrowth strategy). Accordingly, Zürich's 'radical young housing cooperatives' model is explored to argue that accessible, affordable and ecologically sustainable best practice models of eco-collaborative housing (incorporating aspects of an holistic, feminist, caring economy) have transformative potential to overturn the imperial mode of living and point towards a solidarity mode of living and caring commons. This discussion benefits from insights gained from interviews with degrowth-aligned Majority World activists. In short, this chapter engages with degrowth discourses taking account of global dimensions of post-carbon inclusion.

Global production for trade

Among others, Garmendia et al (2013: 1) call on those in the Minority World to cut down their resource dependency, to reduce production and consumption 'not only within their territory, but also abroad, where the commodity frontiers are expanding inexorably to access new resources'. By way of an illustration, Theine et al (2022: 1) find that, towards the end of the 2010s, households in Austria's highest income decile accounted for more than four times the emissions of the lowest decile, with the bottom half of the income distribution only responsible for around half the emissions of the top half. Significantly, '[t]wo thirds of the CO_2e emissions of final demand occur elsewhere', with Austria one of 10 countries characterized by net imports accounting for 'the most significant fraction of consumption emissions' (Theine et al, 2022: 2). In short, a national sense of inclusion has a high risk of being invisibly exclusive and inequitable compared with a global one.

Indeed, fair trade movements and international media remind Minority World residents that conditions in the Majority World are generally worse, more precarious and unjust. However, any sense of responsibility towards those in the Majority World whose basic needs remain unmet is undercut by mainstream Minority World economic rationalizations promoting production for trade and the purely monetary efficiencies of competitive capitalist markets as the best of all possible worlds. In the process, ethical discourses on inequities are marginalized, minimized and undermined.

In contrast, the degrowth movement takes a whole-of-Earth, socio-ecological perspective on inclusion. Degrowth advocates are troubled by ecologically unequal trade, unfair trade and the carbon costs of international trade. In particular, the movement recognizes 'the dark side of renewable energy' mitigation efforts by the Minority World relying on 'green' technologies, which assumes dispossession, degradation and dependent development in the Majority World where such appliances and equipment are produced (Kramarz et al, 2021), and costs associated with detrimental terms of trade for the Majority World.

Consequently, along with Callaghan and Mankin (2022), Hickel et al (2022) frame climate action in terms of responsibility, history and compensation. Significantly, Hickel et al (2022: e342) estimate that the one-sixth of the planet's population in high income nations accounted for three-quarters of global excess resource extraction during 1970–2017. The United States (US) and European Union countries contributed around one-quarter each, to account for just over one-half of the total, while 58 low-income countries, representing almost one-half of the world's population, lived within their global aliquot share (Hickel et al, 2022: e342). Hickel in ICTA-UAB (2022) concludes that 'wealthy nations bear the overwhelming responsibility for global ecological breakdown, and therefore owe an ecological debt to the rest of the world'. Consequently, 'these [wealthy] nations need to take the lead in making radical reductions in their resource use to avoid further degradation, which will likely require transformative post-growth and degrowth approaches' (Hickel in ICTA-UAB, 2022). A more nuanced approach is taken towards countries such as China, which sat on the sustainable side of the ledger in the 20th century but, since 2001, has registered increasingly unsustainable economic growth (Hickel et al, 2022: e345).

In short, Hickel and Slamersak (2022) argue that a *genuinely just transition* implies energy equity and convergence via solid and swift reductions in carbon emissions in the Minority World to meet the basic needs of all in the Majority World. They point out that climate mitigation scenarios on the Intergovernmental Panel on Climate Change agenda imply continuous disadvantages within the Majority World. For instance, negative emissions technology relying on bioenergy assumes that land in the Majority World is used to regenerate the status quo of far greater consumption in the Minority World, and is certain to deepen, not relieve, current dependence of the Minority World on the Majority World. Indeed, Wilting et al (2017: 3301) find that for almost one-third of their national and regional case studies 'environmental pressures outside their territory caused more than half of the[ir] biodiversity footprint'. Trade in foodstuffs derived from crops and pastures was a major contributor to biodiversity loss, just as biofuel and solar industries are future threats (Wilting et al, 2017: 3304).

From the 'imperial' to the 'solidarity' mode of living

In analysing and responding to injustices generated at a global scale, Ulrich Brand and Marcus Wissen (2017; 2021b) coin the concept 'imperial mode of living' to refer to standards of living in the Minority World that arise from and regenerate poor social and ecological conditions in the Majority World. 'Production and consumption patterns depend upon the import of under-priced commodities as well as on human and natural resources, not exclusively but particularly from the dependent countries of the world economy', write Brand and Wissen (2021a), with the waged in the Minority World 'forced into these patterns because of their subaltern status in capitalist societies'. These standards of living and terms of trade result from complex institutional and structural factors not from individual decision making.

National and international scale carbon mitigation strategies and policies are examples. They involve market mechanisms that frame carbon emissions as commodities to be traded, including as so-called 'offsets'. The United Nations (UN) Framework Convention on Climate Change REDD+ programme is one such initiative, designed to reduce emissions from deforestation and forest degradation so that forests are sustainably managed and land conserved in so-called developing countries. Within this programme, 'human pressure on forests that result in greenhouse gas emissions at the national level' is regarded as negative (UNFCCC, nd). For example, in San Martin (Peru), a Kichwa territory REDD+ project stands within 'a system of Natural Protected Areas based on a colonial and exclusionary conservation model that operates without consent' of Indigenous peoples and operates to 'undermine traditional territorial governance and reveal a disastrous distribution of benefits' (Ojeda del Arco, 2022).

Neither simplistic nor classless, the imperial mode of living concept was developed to heighten consciousness of, and facilitate agency to address, various forms of international inequity, exclusion and unsustainability expressed in complicated contemporary crises – from climate heating to absolute poverty and failed democracies. In a nutshell, 'the "ever more and ever faster" creed of constant production increasingly blocks an ecologically compatible mode of production and living' (Brand, 2020). Brand and Missen encapsulate within the term 'solidarity mode of living' many of the alternative futures pursued by degrowth activists and scholars, including holistic feminist visions of a care economy. They embrace various activities and strategies as the content of a 'movement of global solidarity that copes with multiple crises of *overcoming* the imperial mode of living' (Brand and Wissen, 2021b: xvi; emphasis in original).

This chapter takes an holistic caring commons approach, where caring exists as a generic approach to *all* work (Tronto, 1993; 2013; Habermann, 2016). This perspective enables an exploration of the hurdles and tensions encountered by activist scholar and policy-making change agents as they search for new hypotheses and drive novel experiments to transform away from imperial modes of living. Degrowth approaches to post-carbon inclusion require radical and holistic transformation demonstrated on the ground in cases of collective action (Chapter 10). Such cases openly acknowledge and attempt to redress the injustice of various types of exclusion between and within nations, for example, by embracing migrants and refugees. Similarly, degrowth activists prefer and develop localized production where the terms and conditions of workers and Earth are visibly fair and sustainable. Such cases of collective action can be treated as hybrid prefigurative exemplars of caring commons.

In contrast, mainstream households within capitalism mainly buy goods and services made in unknown places by invisible workers. Characteristically secretive capitalist production, in private firms, has only increased as intellectual and similar property rights are tailored to embrace novel technologies and techniques of production. At the retail end, many services are now delivered by gig economy 'workers' who actually have exploitative contracts with the firms they serve. Many mainstream 'eco' goods and services are suspect (De Freitas Netto et al, 2020) and capitalist co-option of products such as 'tiny houses', initially developed for ecologically sustainable living, proliferate (Anson, 2018; Arcilla, 2021).

Similarly, within the expansive and intensive growth of capitalism, affordable and sustainable initiatives are prone to the 'rebound effect'. Embodied material and energy efficiencies are reversed by subsequent overproduction and waste (Banihashemi et al, 2018), with more goods purchased for either excessive use or under-used (Freeman, 2018). In short, in urban cities, householders have few options to break out of this capitalist context of work and trade, unless they are prepared to self-provision or procure basic needs such as food in 'alternative' ways, say by joining in some type of degrowth activity and network ('formation'), as analysed in Chapter 10.

The production and use of alternative housing is an example of the complicated entangling of sustainability efforts within a dominant capitalist economy driven by growth. Contemporary planning, building, and financial regulations and mechanisms cater to building sectors dominated by large construction companies rolling out housing estates and high vertical apartment blocks; create exclusive zones for business, industry and government agencies; and cater to providers of services, such as water, communications and energy. Regulations are oriented around housing produced and sold as commodities and viewed by owners as assets. In Minority World regions such as North America and Australia, houses have grown in size over the past half-century, adding considerably to their population's disproportionately high carbon footprints (Nelson, 2018a).

As such, to varying degrees throughout the world, state and local building and planning regulations present difficult hurdles for individuals and collectives to co-create and inhabit 'alternative housing'. Due to concerns to live within Earth's limits, minimize carbon emissions and improve communities' resilience to the impacts of climate change, those aligned with a solidarity mode of living are often keen to repair, retrofit or self-build modest dwellings with appropriate off-grid energy and water services, or to collectively develop eco-collaborative housing with multiple dwellings sharing neighbourhood-oriented services (Tran, 2022). Here the limited agency of those in the Minority World does not stop various individuals from taking such alternative courses, which hint at the complexity and conditions for a potentially broader transition to post-carbon inclusion (Pickerill et al, 2024).

From individualism to collaboration and cooperation

When I interviewed Brenna Quinlan online on 3 December 2021 (from which all data here not otherwise referenced derives), she explained how she has attempted to live a one-planet footprint in Australia, a society in which the average footprint assumes four or five Earths.

After university, Brenna pursued interests and passions expressing a progressive agenda of reducing socio-economic inequities and improving ecological sustainability. She worked a bit and travelled within Canada via a network of hosts offering homestays on organic farms. Then, she rode her bike across the US down through Central America: "It took a year and it really shifted my understanding of how the world worked and my role in the world." Ironically, given that the co-originators of permaculture are Australian, Brenna learned about "activism through doing, which is my take on what permaculture is", as she journeyed overseas around for six years – taking up limited paid work and a range of offers to work alongside people in return for accommodation and food.

A significant amount of her time was spent in a range of intentional communities offering experiences of eco-collaborative living and collective permaculture provisioning to deliver sustainable and equitable practices. Beyond individual voluntary simplicity, such collective and cooperative responses enable money-free solidarity and the sharing of land, housing, facilities, appliances and equipment (Nelson, 2018a). Finally, Brenna made a difficult decision to leave a fulfilling community and partner, and return to her family in Australia. With all the carbon implications, "I didn't want to be flying across the world my whole life."

Back in Australia, Brenna sought similar milieux, initially gaining a practical internship in the Central Victorian household and permaculture demonstration site of the co-originator of permaculture, David Holmgren, and his partner, Su Dennett. After a few years at Melliodora, Brenna joined their team as a resident artist-illustrator, moving into their tiny T-house, a tenancy paid in-kind by working for them for around ten hours per week. Brenna's next move was with her partner Charlie in Big Red BEV, a firetruck converted into a waste vegetable oil-powered tiny house (Osmond, 2020). They travelled around 3,300 km west of Melliodora in Hepburn Springs (Victoria) to Denmark in Noongar Boodja country on the Western Australian coast to live in an eco-collaborative housing community.

The Living Waters property is composed of 18 quarter-acre sites for households, and several shared half-acre lots, with passive solar dwellings and solar power, dams, roads and paths, greywater and drainage systems. Ecovillage members in their 30s through to their 80s follow diverse practices, such as permaculture, regenerative farming and ecoforestry. They co-govern using principles and processes of 'sociocracy', an approach based on consent around shared goals and work, requiring co-learning and mutual caring, which develop and maintain trust between members. The community shares two communally owned wind turbines, a spring-fed dam and 90,000L water tank for fires and irrigation. Broader community activities include 'Soupie', a weekly meal open to all-comers, and sharing leftover freshly baked bread. The town sits on Denmark River with around 6,000 residents within a 1,843 km² municipality. Other intentional communities include the medium density urban DecoHousing Denmark, a co-housing project with a dozen hempcrete 9-star duplex dwellings, a common house, and other common spaces and facilities.

Brenna finds being a member of any inclusive community has numerous economic, social and sustainability benefits. While there are mandatory personal expenses, such as carrying a A$30,000 university fee debt and annual taxes, her approach relies on pursuing money-free relations, production and exchange within the neighbourhood. She economizes on food costs by growing her own; participating in, and accessing produce from, communal gardens; and networking with others who effectively collectively provision for one another. She estimated monetary payments for food at around A$50 monthly during the 2010s. Brenna has often worked for her board, camped, resided in tiny houses, and housesat. Since 2009 she hasn't paid any rent except for the five months when she worked and was a tenant in Canada. She estimates that half of her current earnings are spent on sustenance, such as food, and half on dwelling, such as now building her home. As a freelancer her income is precarious. But Brenna doesn't require an office space. She adapts to working more or less anywhere. Although she relies on digital tools and equipment for her income, she always buys electronics second-hand and economizes on internet use.

Collective living enables people like Brenna to live in caring relationships, and to develop skills in co-governing and practical collective sustainability. They live according to substantially more social and ecological values and relations than the average individual and household in Australia. Of course, to dismantle imperial modes of living at scale, socio-political and socio-economic change is necessary. But living 'alternatively' shows others its social benefits and ecological efficiencies, in direct contrast to mainstream imperial modes of living under state regulation and reliance on the market for everyday provisioning. Access to markets requires money, more often than not necessitating paid work and, if purchasing a house with a mortgage (the 'great Australian dream'), extraordinary debts held for decades.

Brenna is fortunate to live in a country where publicly funded basic healthcare, minimum schooling and welfare supports exist. She advocates for free tertiary education; neighbourhood-based infrastructure for services, such as renewable energy, water, and treated grey and black water; and minimizing waste. But lack of innovation and/or flexibility in Australian planning, building and financial sectors frustrates development of ecologically and socially rational eco-collaborative housing, such as cohousing and ecovillages, with their broader neighbourhood benefits. Brenna's experience shows an imperial mode of living dominating on every front.

Dwellings: in transition?

In many countries planning and building regulations target family, couple and single households, with no special category for co-governing collective residential settlements (Nelson, 2018a: 161–89). State and local government regulations are oriented around conventional market-based, carbon-emitting construction industries with expansive goals for bigger and more dwellings sold as commodities. Regulating for ecological sustainability and affordability are add-ons, demanding minimal standards from mainstream builders, allied professionals and trades. Such regulations rarely impinge on the size or number of dwellings constructed. Inappropriate developments continue apace, regenerating the carbon emitting imperial mode of living.

Significantly, the promotion of shared and co-governed housing, such as cohousing and ecovillages, is within the top ten most visible goals of degrowth policies (Fitzpatrick et al, 2022: 5, 8). In an overview of degrowth policies in select literature from 2005 to 2020 (1,166 articles, books, book chapters and student theses drawn from four bibliographic databases; including 446 with policy proposals) Fitzpatrick et al (2022: 5) discern 50 goals, 100 objectives and 340 instruments. Urban planning policies for housing include applying property taxes on excess floor space per dwelling; rental limits; expropriation and occupation of vacant buildings; expansion of social housing; and support for eco-collaborative housing with shared land and facilities; and eco-retrofits (Fitzpatrick et al, 2022: 8).

The collection *Housing for Degrowth* (Nelson and Schneider, 2018) emphasizes housing self-provisioning from self-to-collective builds to retrofits, with the editors urging governments to facilitate residents' engagement in project managing and directly contributing to building their housing. As Benson and Hamiduddin (2017: 6) point out, this inexpensive approach for prospective residents 'has been systematically undermined by land reform, the introduction of land use and planning regulation, bureaucracy and legislation', and obstacles to borrowing for self and collective builds in preference to 'speculative builders'. Yet in Western European countries such as Germany, 'over 60 per cent of homes are commissioned by individual households and built by local companies' (Benson and Hamiduddin, 2017: 6).

The radical 21st-century 'young housing cooperatives' movement in Zürich is realizing visions for greater equity and sustainability, through city-facilitated self-provisioning. Nelson and Chatterton (2022) detail how Zürich city support for housing cooperatives began in the early 20th century, emerging as a remarkable characteristic of the city's housing typology (see Chapter 6, this volume). Today, around seven in 20 dwellings in Zürich belong to housing cooperatives. A 2011 referendum committed the municipality to a housing cooperative target of one in three apartments. Each cooperative houses from hundreds through to thousands of residents in quality housing supported by council building, planning and financial provisions. Cooperatives expand and spawn new cooperatives. Member-tenants co-manage repaying decades-long loans with affordable rents typically around 20 per cent lower than private rents (COOP, 2020). Such safe, secure, affordable and quality housing tends to set a standard for privately owned housing and a ceiling for private rental rates in Zürich.

A special subset, Zürich's 'young [recent] housing cooperatives' are semi-autonomous, self-managing, and concerned with 'more than housing' matters, namely ecological sustainability and social justice (Hugentobler et al, 2016). Cooperatives, such as Kalkbreite in the city centre, offer solidarity and mutual support. Indeed, certain founders of Zürich's radical cooperatives recognized cooperative structures as vehicles for such transformation to degrowth futures. Well-oiled collaborations between architects, construction firms, bankers, lawyers, planners, councillors and city building bureaucrats support co-governed housing cooperatives to function and deliver in socially and environmentally sustainable ways (Boudet, 2017). Cooperative members participate in the design and realization of urban housing and planning while maintaining their neighbourhood in physical, material, social and political ways.

Compared with the Zürich average of 45 m^2 residential space per capita, each Kalkbreite resident takes up just 32 m^2 housing space (Müller Sigrist Architekten AG, 2017). All housing cooperatives abide by the city's policy of social mix, aiming for a housing demographic mirroring Zürich's demographic profile, which amplifies cultural diversity. Solidarity is displayed in democratic self-management and inclusive processes. The cooperative maintains open, responsible and outward-looking relations with Zürich citizens, municipal authorities and the housing industry more generally. Moreover, enforcing principles of environmental sustainability protects and ensures solidarity with and for future generations.

Radical global transformation

Minority World discussions of degrowth often include questions on Majority World discomfort with degrowth practices. Yet, Olivier De Schutter (2023), the UN special rapporteur on extreme poverty and human rights, argues that 'our focus should be on reducing inequality not increasing GDP'. Moreover, degrowth practices in the Minority World derive inspiration from Majority World philosophies. For instance, the South American concept '*buen vivir*' is compared with degrowth thinking. Eduardo Gudynas (in Balch, 2013) points out that: 'With buen vivir, the subject of wellbeing is not [about the] individual, but the individual in the social context of their community and in a unique environmental situation.'

By way of an example, a Majority World case study by Christie and Salong (2018: 80) shows that 'standard living practices in Vanuatu', especially in the outer islands, demonstrate degrowth practices implicitly. Ni-Vanuatu approaches to housing offer a model for the Minority World degrowth movement. Christie and Salong (2018: 80, 85) describe how self-reliant, convivial and resilient autonomous communities were primarily responsible for rebuilding ecologically sustainable dwellings after Tropical Cyclone Pam hit, with 280+ km per hour winds in mid-March 2015, destroying or damaging more than 20,000 dwellings.

Some 65 of Vanuatu's 83 islands support over 100 Indigenous cultures and languages, and customary governance practices with vernacular architecture unique to their environs. The maintenance of traditional building practices is significant, chiefs' meeting houses offering shelter in withstanding cyclones. Formal rebuilding responses were delayed and weak, characterized by 'an influx of international companies promoting and testing prefabricated housing modules' (Christie and Salong, 2018: 87). In contrast, grassroots recovery took an organic form of solidarity and mutual aid, acting creatively with materials at hand and through collective effort. Similar principles and synergies are likely to drive efforts in Majority and Minority Worlds with respect to decarbonizing futures challenged by impacts of global heating in the form of 'natural' disasters.

A related misconception in the Minority World is that Majority World countries want development and aspire to growth economies. Works of Majority World icons such as Ashish Kothari (2020; 2022), Gustavo Esteva (2017), Eduardo Galeano (in Nelson, 2018b) and Arturo Escobar (2022) point to the contrary. With respect to UN Sustainable Development Goals (SDGs), Larsen et al (2022: 21) contend that SDGs 'introduce or provide a new vocabulary of legitimacy that may easily further deepen development dispossession and inequalities'. Specifically, this agenda does not call for, nor can it drive, system change because SDGs fail to address 'root causes' or develop on 'a clear and explicitly stated bedrock of progressive values and ethics' (Larsen et al, 2022: 20).

Consequently, Larsen et al (2022: 24) call, instead, for an acknowledgement of 'local stewardship in building ecological integrity and resilience, where Indigenous Peoples and local communities are able to care for the diversity and maintenance of their cultural landscape ecosystems, whether in traditional or new ways'. Referring to Kurdish and Zapatista autonomous regions, city and locale-based assemblies and municipalism, they advocate direct democratic decision making on the basis of subsidiarity. They recognize that 'economic democracy would involve bringing communal rights and custodianship back to land and land-related common-pool resources, consumer-producer-prosumer collectives and alliances, and open localization with self-reliance for basic needs' – following calls and actions of La Via Campesina and similar peasant movements (Larsen et al, 2022: 24).

Simultaneously, they call for intersectional and locally customized responses, drawing on local knowledge, in order to overcome various inequities through direct participation, self-expression and decision making (Larsen et al, 2022: 24). Similarly, Kothari (2020: 259) emphasizes that Majority World peoples need to 'find their own home-grown visions and pathways of change'; in India's case '*ecoswaraj*' (*swaraj* is 'self-rule', as promoted by Gandhi) and 'radical ecological democracy' are examples. '*Ecoswaraj*' brings to the fore its holistic meaning as 'a combination of individual and collective autonomy, mutual responsibility, rights, and responsibilities' (Kothari, 2020: 261). Such 'post-development' frameworks offer Minority World degrowth activists and scholars a common language for their discourse (Kothari et al, 2019).

Various lineages of commoning in the practices and perspectives of First Nations peoples of all continents are envisioned anew in futures creatively drawing on 21st-century knowledge and skills. Arturo Escobar (2022: np), for instance, creates five 'design guidelines' to transition via collective perspectives and relocalized economies embracing all of life, drawing on the Oaxacan '*condicion nosótrica de ser*' ('we-condition of being') built on 'principles of love, care and compassion as ethics of living, starting with home, place and community … to prepare for greater sharing rooted in autonomy'. Vandana Shiva (2022: np) writes in her manifesto of 'economies of care', of 'reclaiming our minds, autonomy and creative potential, to preserve our freedoms and our rights to work in service to the Earth, our communities and future generations' and to 'stimulate creative freedom, justice and cohesion'.

Kalpavriksh

In late 2021, I interviewed two members of Kalpavriksh – a not-for-profit located in Pune, Maharashtra (India) – both active globally in supporting and advocating for communities and environments. I first met Ashish at the Fifth International Degrowth Conference in Budapest (Hungary) in 2016 and Shrishtee at the 2018 Sixth International Degrowth Conference: Dialogues in Turbulent Times held in Malmö (Sweden). Even if the contexts within which degrowth activists and advocates of the Majority and Minority Worlds act determine differences in perspectives and priorities, inequity and injustice are common concerns along with a keen interest in self-reliant communities, collectives and movements, including autonomous regions advancing substantive and direct democratic institutions. There are common interests in co-creating knowledge to enrich joint perspectives and actions.

Kalpavriksh co-founder Ashish Kothari is a prolific writer, teacher, researcher and activist whom I interviewed online on 22 November 2021. Ashish has worked in universities and many movements, including the ICCA

Consortium – the formal body of a global movement based in territories and areas conserved by Indigenous peoples and local communities ('territories of life'), promoting equity in conservation. Several years ago, after completing her Master's in Development Studies, Shrishtee Bajpai joined Kalpavriksh due to its holistic post-development approach, the priority given to nature rather than capital, and to communities 'struggling and creating things'. I interviewed Shrishtee online on 10 December 2021. A core team member of Global Tapestry of Alternatives (exploring and extending connections between movements and actions all over the world), Shrishtee researches, documents and networks around radical alternatives, particularly those associated with Indigenous, traditional and customary perspectives, ways of living and decision making. All data from hereon in not otherwise referenced derives from these two interviews.

Kalpavriksh has been convening a Vikalp Sangam ('Alternatives Confluence') process for Indian groups and people working on alternative transformations to analyse the appropriateness and strategic value of specific alternatives. In this process an holistic perspective has evolved, confirming the elemental principles of ecological integrity and resilience, social wellbeing and justice, direct and delegated democracy, economic democracy, cultural diversity, and knowledge democracy. A Kalpavriksh (2017) report shows an evolving set of values:

- Self-governance / autonomy (*swashasan / swaraj*)
- Cooperation, collectivity, solidarity and 'commons'
- Rights with responsibilities
- Dignity of labour (*shram*)
- Work as livelihood (integrating pleasure, creativity, purpose, meaning)
- Livelihoods as ways of life (*jeevanshali*)
- Respect for subsistence and self-reliance (*swavalamban*)
- Qualitative pursuit of happiness
- Equity / justice / inclusion (gender, caste, class, ethnic … *sarvodaya*)
- Simplicity / sufficiency / enoughness / living well with less (*aparigraha*)
- Respect for all life forms (*vasudhaiv kutumbakam*)
- Non-violence, peace, harmony (*ahimsa*)
- Reciprocity and inter-connectedness
- Pluralism and diversity. (Kalpavriksh, 2017: np; italics added)

This list is quoted to illustrate the many consistencies between concerns of movements for degrowth and ecological justice in the Minority World and like-movements in the Majority World. This is not to suggest unity but rather an independent evolution of similar perspectives, in this case of '*eco-swaraj*' meeting, engaging and collaborating with degrowth activist-scholars to greatly enrich the latter in the course of such working relationships.

Care commoning approach

Contemporary works by queer feminist Friederike Habermann and certain members of the Feminisms and Degrowth Alliance (FaDA) strongly resonate with the care commoning approach (Habermann, 2016; Saave-Harnack et al, 2019; Dengler and Lang, 2022). FaDA (2020) argues for 'a caring economy that democratizes all dimensions of life, delinks livelihood security from wage-work, equitably revalues both paid and unpaid care work and promotes its gender-just redistribution'. Mariam Abazeri (2022: 5), for instance, presents 'a decolonial feminist approach that ... sustains degrowth principles, situating community action within localized knowledge traditions while contesting and reimagining the practices and expectations of socialization that further embed participative governance, ecological sustainability, community building, local wealth circulation, and creative expression into the fabric of intersubjective relations'.

The type of transition required by our current political, economic and ecological conjuncture – expressed in demands from Majority World and ecofeminist forces – requires radical transformation. Brand (2020: np) argues for trade unions to become concerned with 'international entanglements' of globalized production and trade rather than matters of economic self-interest, ecological modernization and support for sustainable growth. Not only must 'socio-ecological tasks ... become core issues for trade unions', but also 'nothing less than fundamentally questioning the capitalist growth imperative is needed' (Brand, 2020: np).

Radical agents of transformation challenge states and markets, within which we now live and operate. Existing capitalist and socialist states are market and growth-oriented. Radical movements such as degrowth point, instead, in the direction of community autonomy; with ecological, social, and infrastructural networks within and between such communities; and all living within the natural limits of Earth. The decentralized horizontal politics of such movements, and the experimental forms of organization they spawn, demonstrate such new formations (see Chapter 10, this volume). In contrast to states and markets failing to meet the challenge of growing socio-economic inequity and ecological unsustainability, the achievements of socio-ecological movements emerge starkly – within distinctive perspectives, offering institutional futures of solidarity and care within which individuals are perceived and treated respectfully.

Towards a conclusion

Particular socio-material challenges of exclusion, inequity and carbonization play out within global trade and mobility. The imperial mode of living identifies incumbents who drive and benefit from global capitalism and mainstream societal and economic obduracies. A solidarity mode of living suggests pathways for transformation. Best practice eco-collaborative living is a way forward, facilitating solidarity and a caring economy-cum-commoning. Degrowth, and allied discourses and grassroots activities, offer promising lines of agency to promote post-carbon inclusion. Such agency is centred on relatively novel practices requiring political engagement and policy changes for amplification – scaling out via adapting models for replication, and spreading inclusive decarbonizing principles through networks and relationships of sharing, support and solidarity. As such, Majority World movements and actions for just transitions and decolonization can be integrated within Minority World activism and campaigns.

This chapter has focused on degrowth analyses and approaches that aim to achieve post-carbon living and *international* inclusion. This demands wholescale transformation, such as top-down reforms facilitating a transition of power to grassroots agents enabling low carbon practices, caring economy approaches and, ultimately, even universal (glocal) commoning. Do sufficient and increasing numbers of people have the collective will necessary to politically and practically challenge economic orthodoxies and mainstream prejudices in order to change their everyday habits? Resistance to change is likely to endure in claims to unjust privileges, substantially in the Minority World but also among the rich and powerful in the Majority World. Yet most of the underprivileged in both the Minority and Majority Worlds have much to gain from degrowth visions of satisfying every single person's basic needs within Earth's regenerative limits.

For those in the Minority World, a George Orwell quote in Solnit (2021: 183, 288n) is apposite – Orwell provocatively challenged the British last century, 'You have got to choose between liberating India and having extra sugar. Which do you prefer?' Significantly, this century, is the point that resistance to transformational change greatly reduces the chances of secure and sustainable living for *all of humanity* in the not so distant future.

References

Abazeri, M. (2022) 'Decolonial feminisms and degrowth', *Futures*, 136: 102902.

Anson, A. (2018) 'Framing degrowth: the radical potential of tiny house mobility', in Nelson, A. and Schneider, F. (eds), *Housing for Degrowth: Principles, Models, Challenges and Opportunities*, Abingdon and New York: Routledge, pp 68–79.

Arcilla, P. (2021) 'Tiny homes, big capitalism', *Kill Your Darlings*, 12 July. Available from: https://www.killyourdarlings.com.au/article/tiny-homes-big-capitalism/ [Accessed 8 June 2023].

Balch, O. (2013) 'Buen vivir: the social philosophy inspiring movements in South America', *The Guardian*, 4 February. Available from: https://www.theguardian.com/sustainable-business/blog/buen-vivir-philosophy-south-america-eduardo-gudynas [Accessed 8 June 2023].

Banihashemi, S., Tabadkanib, A. and Reza Hosseinic, M. (2018) 'Integration of parametric design into modular coordination: a construction waste reduction workflow', *Automation in Construction*, 88(April): 1–12.

Benson, M. and Hamiduddin, I. (2017) *Self-Build Homes*, London: UCL Press.

Boudet, D. (2017) *New Housing in Zürich: Typologies for a Changing Society*, Zürich: Park Books.

Brand, U. (2020) 'Ways out of the growth trap', *The Bullet*, 1 January. Available from: https://socialistproject.ca/2020/01/ways-out-of-the-growth-trap/#more [Accessed 8 June 2023].

Brand, U. and Wissen, M. (2017) *Imperiale Lebensweise: Zur Ausbeutung von Mensch und Natur in Zeiten des Globalen Kapitalismus*, München: Oekom Verlag GmbH.

Brand, U. and Wissen, M. (2021a) 'Imperial mode of living: how capitalism affirms Its hegemony even in times of crisis', *Progress in Political Economy*, 6 July. Available from: https://www.ppesydney.net/imperial-mode-of-living-how-capitalism-affirms-its-hegemony-even-in-times-of-crisis/ [Accessed 8 June 2023].

Brand, U. and Wissen, M. (2021b) *The Imperial Mode of Living: Everyday Life and the Ecological Crisis of Capitalism*, London and Brooklyn: Verso.

Callaghan, C.W. and Mankin, J.S. (2022) 'National attribution of historic climate damages', *Climatic Change*, 172: 40.

Christie, W. and Salong, J. (2018) 'Housing and climate change resilience: Vanuatu' in Nelson, A. and Schneider, F. (eds), *Housing for Degrowth: Principles Models Challenges and Opportunities*, Abingdon and New York: Routledge, pp 80–95.

COOP (2020) 'About Switzerland', *Cooperative Housing International*. Available from: https://www.housinginternational.coop/co-ops/switzerland/ [Accessed 8 June 2023].

De Freitas Netto, S.V., Sobral, M.F.F., Ribeiro, A.R.B and Da Luz Soares, G.R. (2020) 'Concepts and forms of greenwashing: a systematic review', *Environmental Sciences Europe*, 32: 19.

Dengler, C. and Lang, M. (2022) 'Commoning care: feminist degrowth visions for a socio-ecological transformation', *Feminist Economics*, 28(1): 1–28.

De Schutter, O. (2023) 'Economic growth is not a magic wand for ending poverty', *The Guardian*, 20 March. Available from: https://www.theguardian.com/global-development/2023/mar/20/economic-growth-is-not-a-magic-wand-for-ending-poverty [Accessed 16 October 2023].

Escobar, A. (2022) 'Five axes of transition: imagining "alternatives" for the post-pandemic future', *Radical Ecological Democracy*, 30 July. Available from: https://radicalecologicaldemocracy.org/five-axes-of-transition-imagining-alternatives-for-the-post-pandemic-future/ [Accessed 8 June 2023].

Esteva, G. (2017) 'A path to freedom', *Radical Ecological Democracy*, 27 September. Available from: https://radicalecologicaldemocracy.org/a-path-to-freedom/ [Accessed 8 June 2023].

FaDA (2020) 'Feminist degrowth', [one-page statement], tweet by Feminisms and Degrowth Alliance, [@fem_degrowth], 24 April. Available from: https://twitter.com/fem_degrowth/status/1253403063987159041 [Accessed 8 June 2023].

Fitzpatrick N., Parrique T. and Cosme, I. (2022) 'Exploring degrowth policy proposals: a systematic mapping with thematic synthesis', *Journal of Cleaner Production*, 365: 132764.

Freeman, R. (2018) 'A theory on the future of the rebound effect in a resource-constrained world', *Frontiers in Energy Research*, 6: 81.

Garmendia, E., Urkidi, L. and Arto, I. (2013) 'The Basque ecological debt: global socio-ecological impacts of a small open economy', *BC3 Policy Briefing Series* July 04-2013, Bilbao: Basque Centre for Climate Change (BC3).

Habermann, F. (2016) *Ecommony: UmCare zum Miteinander*, Sulzbach: Ulrike Helmer.

Hickel, J. and Slamersak, A. (2022) 'Existing climate mitigation scenarios perpetuate colonial inequalities', *The Lancet Planetary Health*, 6(7): E628–31.

Hickel, J., O'Neill, D.W., Fanning, A.L. and Zoomkawala, H. (2022) 'National responsibility for ecological breakdown: a fair-shares assessment of resource use, 1970–2017', *The Lancet Planetary Health*, 6(4): E342–9.

Hugentobler, M., Hofer, A. and Simmendinger, P. (eds) (2016) *More than Housing: Cooperative Planning – A Case Study in Zürich*, Basel: Birkhäuser.

ICTA-UAB (2022) 'The United States and the European Union are responsible for the majority of ecological damage caused by excess use of raw materials', Institut de Ciència i Tecnologia Ambientals, University Autonomous Barcelona (Press Room), 8 April. Available from: https://www.uab.cat/web/newsroom/news-detail/the-united-states-and-the-european-union-are-responsible-for-the-majority-of-ecological-damage-caused-by-excess-use-of-raw-materials-1345830290613.html [Accessed 8 June 2023].

Kalpavriksh (2017) *Transformation Format: A Process for Self-Assessment and Facilitation Towards Radical Change*, 20 February, prepared for ACKnowl-EJ project, Pune: Kalpavriksh.

Kothari, A. (2020) 'Radical ecological democracy: reflections from the South on the degrowth', in Burkhardt, C. Schmelzer, M. and Treu, N. (eds), *Degrowth in Movement(s): Exploring Pathways for Transformation*, Winchester and Washington: Zer0 Books, pp 258–71.

Kothari, A. (2022) 'The flower of transformation: alternatives for justice, sustainability and equity', *Meer Magazine*, 13 March. Available from: https://www.meer.com/en/68872-the-flower-of-transformation [Accessed 8 June 2023].

Kothari, A., Salleh, A., Escobar, A., Demaria, F. and Acosta, A. (eds) (2019) *Pluriverse: A Post-Development Dictionary*, New Delhi: Tulika Books.

Kramarz, T., Park, S. and Johnson, C. (2021) 'Governing the dark side of renewable energy: a typology of global displacements', *Energy Research & Social Science*, 74: 101902.

Larsen, P.B., Haller, T. and Kothari, A. (2022) 'Sanctioning disciplined grabs (SDGs): from SDGs as green anti-politics machine to radical alternatives?', *Geoforum*, 131: 20–6.

Müller Sigrist Architekten (2017) '04_Live-work complex Kalkbreite', *Premio Europeo di Architettura Matilda Baffa Ugo Rivolta*. Available from: http://premiobaffarivolta.ordinearchitetti.mi.it/portfolio_page/04_live-work-complex-kalkbreite-muller-sigrist-architekten-ag/ [Accessed 8 June 2023].

Nelson, A. (2018a) *Small is Necessary: Shared Living on a Shared Planet*, London: Pluto Press.

Nelson, A. (2018b) 'The political economy of space and time in Eduardo Galeano', *Progress in Political Economy*, 20 February. Available from: https://www.ppesydney.net/political-economy-space-time-eduardo-galeano/ [Accessed 8 June 2023].

Nelson, A. and Schneider, F. (2018) *Housing for Degrowth: Principles Models Challenges and Opportunities*, Abingdon and New York: Routledge.

Nelson, A. and Chatterton, P. (2022) 'Dwelling beyond growth: negotiating the state, mutualism and commons', in Savini, F., Ferreira, A. and von Schönfeld, K. (eds), *Post-Growth Planning: Cities Beyond the Market Economy*, New York and Abingdon: Routledge, pp 49–62.

Ojeda del Arco, M.P. (2022) 'Carbon commodification in the Peruvian Amazon: the Kichwa people's struggle against territorial and climate destruction', *Radical Ecological Democracy*, 26 July. Available from: https://radicalecologicaldemocracy.org/carbon-commodification-in-the-peruvian-amazon-the-kichwa-peoples-struggle-against-territorial-and-climate-destruction/ [Accessed 8 June 2023].

Osmond, J. (2020) *Epic Fire Truck Tiny House: The Tiny House Fire Truck That Runs on Waste Vegetable Oil!*, video. Available from: https://www.youtube.com/watch?v=LbU27pZp2W0 [Accessed 8 June 2023].

Pickerill, J., Chitewere, T., Cornea, N., Lockyer, J., Macrorie, R., Maly Blažek, J. and Nelson, A (2024) 'Urban ecological futures: five eco-community strategies for more sustainable and equitable cities', *International Journal of Urban and Regional Research*, 48(1): 161–76.

Saave-Harnack, A., Dengler, C. and Muraca, B. (2019) 'Feminisms and degrowth: alliance or foundational relation?', *Global Dialogue*, 9(1): 29–30. Available from: http://globaldialogue.isa-sociology.org/feminisms-and-degrowth-alliance-or-foundational-relation/ [Accessed 8 June 2023].

Shiva, V. (2022) 'Manifesto on economies of care and Earth democracy', *Navdanya International*. Available from: https://navdanyainternational.org/publications/manifesto-on-economies-of-care-and-earth-democracy/ [Accessed 6 June 2023].

Solnit, R. (2021) *Orwell's Roses*, London: Granta.

Theine, H., Humer S., Moser M. and Schnetzer, M. (2022) 'Emissions inequality: disparities in income, expenditure, and the carbon footprint in Austria', *Ecological Economics*, 197: 107435.

Tran, N. (dir) (2022) *Never Too Small: Paris Architect's Small Family Loft Extension*, New Mac Video Agency, 5 May. Available from: https://www.youtube.com/watch?v=MERY9V4AzrY [Accessed 6 June 2023].

Tronto, J. (1993) *Moral Boundaries: A Political Argument for an Ethic of Care*, New York: Routledge.

Tronto, J. (2013) *Caring Democracy: Markets, Equality, and Justice*, New York: New York University Press.

UNFCCC (nd) 'What is REDD+?', *United Nations Framework Convention on Climate Change*. Available from: https://unfccc.int/topics/land-use/workstreams/redd/what-is-redd [Accessed 8 June 2023].

Wilting, H.C., Schipper, A.M., Bakkenes, M., Meijer, J.R. and Huijbregts, M.A.J. (2017) 'Quantifying biodiversity losses due to human consumption: a global-scale footprint analysis', *Environmental Science and Technology*, 51(6): 3298–306.

Further reading: relevant websites

Degrowth.info (online international webportal): https://www.degrowth.info/

FaDA, Feminisms and Degrowth Alliance: https://www.degrowth.info/en/feminisms-and-degrowth-alliance-fada/collective-research-notebook/

Global Tapestry of Alternatives (a global, South and North, network of alternatives): https://www.globaltapestryofalternatives.org/

14

Future Directions for Post-Carbon Inclusion

Ralph Horne, Anitra Nelson, Gordon Walker and Aimee Ambrose

Ecological modernization and business-as-usual approaches to decarbonization are dangerous. They mainly exacerbate inequalities and fail to address challenging social questions related to contemporary governance, technologies and economies. Helping homeowners to decarbonize their homes along current market-oriented lines, such as subsidies for purchasing new 'green' goods and services, only drives further inequity in housing and transport systems. Increasing inequity not only jeopardizes the lives of the dispossessed but also means that those on lower incomes have more pressured and precarious lives. Alienating these major sections of society from the universal change required places in peril the whole decarbonization project (Chapter 12). As such, the importance of incorporating inclusion within the post-carbon imperative cannot be overestimated, as this whole collection has sought to illustrate.

A normative focus on economic growth and technology over wellbeing and socially determined limits marginalizes 'alternatives' to the status quo to fringe experiments. In fact, such alternatives attempt to challenge precisely those mainstream practices which hamper effective decarbonization. Current settings allow overconsumption by those most able to purchase green goods and services (Chapter 11). Moreover, they background degrowth, which is potentially a transformative pathway towards post-carbon inclusion (Chapters 10 and 13). Illustrating the possibilities when inclusion is centre-stage, Chapter 5 offers an alternative framework for 'just transitions' to promote the virtues of generosity and care as foundations for achieving justice. In concert, these virtues have the potential to bridge communities (Castro, 2021). Furthermore, the alternative values that they uphold can shape transitions and justice from the starting point of genuine concern for the wellbeing of others.

This chapter presents a forward-oriented agenda drawing upon the insights of contributors to this volume, as they explain the dangers of business-as-usual decarbonization policies and programmes, analyse their implications for research and practice, and present potential routes to post-carbon futures.

Dangers of business-as-usual decarbonization

This book engages with questions of justice, inclusion and transformation to explore possible changes to currently sedimented societal, economic and infrastructural histories and trajectories. In doing so, we enter deeply politicized territory (Newell and Mulvaney, 2013; Armstrong and McLaren, 2022). To call for post-carbon inclusion in the terms we establish is not a neutral act that can be neatly bundled into techno-managerialist terms, seeking change without disruption to ongoing accumulation strategies and societal order. *Politics is central.*

Yet, contradictions and alignments of political positions and arguments flowing through current transition and net zero debates are often complex. They can take quite unexpected forms, presenting distinct challenges as well as opportunities. Recent interest in degrowth by the Intergovernmental Panel on Climate Change (Chapter 1) and the European Commission (Deconinck, 2023) is a case in point. Degrowth challenges the central growth ideal of contemporary economies and states. Chapters 10 and 13 are devoted to exploring degrowth interventions, veritable disruptions to commonplace socio-material boundaries, incumbencies and power relations. However, as policy makers and politicians are attracted to this new movement calling for limits, so the risks of contortion and co-option of degrowth principles accumulate, as apparent in capitalist-inclined 'postgrowth'.

We might normally expect climate activists' concerns for inequality, justice and inclusion to align with progressive perspectives on the political left or centre ground, positions seeking simultaneous attention to climate and social objectives, from local through to global scales. However, in recent years, populist and radical right proponents have opportunistically supported the cause of those disadvantaged by the impact of decarbonization policies. Typically, they assert that households and communities on low incomes cannot afford the service costs of rapid and substantial carbon action, as in requiring a turn from non-renewable energy sources (gas and coal) to renewable ones (wind and solar) and cannot purchase expensive (as such 'middle-class') goods, such as heat pumps and electric vehicles.

At first sight, such popular and radical right arguments mimic progressive political ones and related legitimate concerns raised in various chapters in this collection. However, more often than not, mobilizing inequality objections is a political right tactic seeking to delay and disrupt climate action, rather than a call for policy synergies and ways forward towards post-carbon that promote justice and inclusion. Various commentators note a shift in the discourses of climate sceptics and denial towards narrating a strategy of delay and obstruction (Lamb et al, 2020; Low and Boettcher, 2020). In their analysis, 'concern' for the distribution of costs and benefits, and burden on those already disadvantaged, is just one of a series of moves to slow down climate action, muddy the political waters and promote political fragmentation. Such developments lead to disarray and friction, just when strong and concerted political action to decarbonize is most needed.

In particular, the chrono-urbanist concept of the '15-minute city', engaged with in a United Kingdom (UK) context within Chapter 4, shows further ways in which climate action and inclusion can become ensnared in some of the worst excesses of right-wing populist politics. The idea of enabling easy accessibility via walking and cycling to services through planning for mixed, liveable and green neighbourhoods offers co-benefits of various forms to urban communities and draws on long, largely uncontroversial, traditions of land use and transport planning. Risks of gentrification and exclusion identified in Chapter 4 do not undermine the 15-minute city proposal or intent but, rather, call for attention to managing in socially responsible ways who benefits and exactly how '15-minute' and related policies are applied.

However, once refracted through populist politics and inflected with variants of post-COVID-19 conspiracy theory, the 15-minute city concept has been attacked in social media as a means of exerting social control, a move to monitor what people do and where they go, as if *requiring* them to stay within 15 minutes of their homes rather than making it *possible* for them to satisfy many of their everyday basic needs quickly and easily (Calafati et al, 2023; Loader, 2023). Such wild claims have now infected mainstream politics within the UK, with the Conservative government seeking political advantage by positioning themselves against 15-minute city initiatives and related local transport planning schemes to support active travel and reduce traffic emissions (Wainwright, 2023).

In short, in seeking shifts towards post-carbon inclusion, there is copious political territory to navigate. In this febrile political atmosphere, concerns raised about potentially deepening various forms of exclusion, inequalities and vulnerabilities risk being appropriated to the ends of those not so much seeking better climate action and decarbonization as much less of it. Not radical and just transformation, but incremental advancement of the status quo, protecting the interests of incumbents and seeking to keep structures of elite accumulation and mass-disadvantage firmly in place. This philosophy is illustrated in Chapter 11, which highlights a glaring, but seemingly inconspicuous, research and policy lacuna around high consuming groups, a striking omission given that half of all greenhouse gas emissions emanate from the wealthiest 10 per cent in society (Hubacek et al, 2017). Focusing research attention and policy interventions on such highly influential groups remains a radical prospect suggesting how delicately a degrowth aligned research agenda is likely to be approached.

Implications for post-carbon inclusion research and practice

Beyond arguing that we must only contemplate decarbonization projects where inclusion is embedded as a procedural intention and outcome, discourses in this collection present a set of related political and economic implications. Here they are grouped into three entangled and overlapping agendas, of mapping the terrain, of rights and justice, and of empowerment and agency. These agendas are envisaged as core directions for future research and policy communities working in partnership in this growing field of post-carbon inclusion studies.

Mapping the terrain

Currently, deep understandings of the actual nature of social life and of how capabilities and lived practices entangle with decarbonization agendas, ideas and projects is essential yet in short supply. In advancing without such understandings, the neoliberal ecomodernist approach to decarbonization puts in peril the whole project to save both people and planet. Working on flatter ontological and epistemological terrain, and plugging the gaps in normative framings of decarbonization, is urgently needed. This is why contributors to this collection present opportunities to draw on practice theory and justice as 'capabilities'.

Walker (2013: 187) highlights that 'successful performances of practice are distributed across populations' and that it is crucial to recognize 'this as a reflection of differences in the capability to perform'. Inequality is about recruitment to, and the performance of, particular practices that differ according to exclusionary societal factors, such as wealth creation and resultant poverty, minorities produced by majorities, and so on. These differences reflect differences in capability (Halkier and Holm, 2021). Linking capabilities and social structures, agency and practices in this way usefully draws attention away from individual performance and behaviour towards societal changes that support broad spread capabilities and embeds social justice as central to social practice analyses (Willand et al, 2021).

Rights and justice

As the terrain of uneven capabilities is revealed in more ways and in more situations, it opens up scope to reframe justice rights and rules – social and otherwise. For example, as deep qualitative research reveals how energy poverty shortens lives and contravenes human rights, so ideas of universal rights to basic energy services take hold. An example is identified by Olsen et al (2018) in the Italian housing movement where campaigns have advanced from the 'right to the city' to the 'right to metabolism'. The search for fairness in energy service access and distribution entails ethical, moral and value-based work (Sovacool and Dworkin, 2014; Jenkins et al, 2016; Sovacool et al, 2016) and leads to questions about defining 'essential' energy (Chapters 7 and 12). Some successfully hide their energy poverty by only turning on winter heating when a care worker or other visitor is expected. As such their mortal danger, a pernicious form of energy injustice, is hidden from friendly observation or formal support systems (Willand et al, 2023).

Access to clean air is widely regarded as a basic human right, yet brutal contraventions of this right continue to expand (Chapter 7). Deliberate greenhouse gas emissions are a violent act, given that we know the science of climate change and that human and ecological harm is underway and accelerating, indeed out of regulatory control. Protection of those most exposed to such human-induced violence is essential in an unequal world. The contradictions of systems based on greed juxtaposed to a climate emergency inevitably lead researchers and policy makers into the domains of rights and justice. It makes little sense to expect people to voluntarily limit high energy consumption while allowing the prolific existence of consumption advertising (Chapter 11). If consumption is a problem (and it is) then it needs to be policed at the points of production and distribution.

Empowerment

The editors of this volume are not unique in concluding that precursors to post-carbon inclusion require systematically structured, locally responsive and relevant mechanisms for building coalitions. Intermediary functions are needed to share knowledge, connect and mediate across experiments, regions, neighbourhoods and initiatives. Engagement and co-design are not only contemporary methods based on principles of reciprocity and respect but also are essential underpinnings of post-carbon inclusion. The United Nations Sustainable Development Goals call for leaving no one behind, which is laudable but woefully insufficient. Identifying who is vulnerable and excluded, whose needs should be prioritized (Chapter 5) and integrating everyone into decision making are more meaningful goals. The opposite extremes of poverty and profligacy and the absence of inclusion in the post-carbon agenda places the planet in great peril.

Knowledge, insight and learning are all essential, but they only matter if we add agency. This points to the dual importance, first, of practising post-carbon inclusion research with both near and far neighbours, activists, and those who already feel disempowered and, second, of working across the boundaries of the immediately practical horizon (what can actually be done now to progress post-carbon inclusion) and essential future horizons (imaginaries of post-carbon inclusion and models of future planetary governance).

Agency calls attention to both capabilities and governance, to lines of representation and accountability that genuinely empower those who have been left out from a share in the spoils of capital accumulation. Agency relies on different supports in various contexts, from socio-technical and socio-material bundles to new constellations and institutions, from fresh discourses and practices to revisions in common understandings and accepted social truths. How might such promising lines of agency spread outwards, upwards or otherwise to become more pervasive and, in so doing, supersede existing obduracies and incumbencies?

Discussions and analyses of agency highlight the significance of experiments in living arrangements that demonstrate and test post-carbon futures. Chapters 2 and 10 offer different, arguably complementary, perspectives. The alternative concept of the solidarity mode of living is counterposed to the contemporary imperial mode of living in Chapter 13. Altogether, Chapters 5, 7, 10 and 13 argue the needs for, and show ways to, amplify, legitimize and celebrate multiple and diverse degrowth variants, with associated virtues of empathy, care, generosity, solidarity, cooperation, dialogue and sharing.

Routes to post-carbon futures

Highlighted by Naomi Klein (Winship, 2016) in 'there are no non-radical futures', an ongoing search for post-capitalist, post-carbon futures evolves in the face of increasingly inadequate mainstream responses. Aside from tensions between needs to sustain and improve human wellbeing and needs to decarbonize (Chapter 9), protecting planetary health is a task beyond the narrowly circumscribed interests and motivations of markets and national states. While markets create the poverty and the social boundaries that imperil decarbonization, national governments protect national interests against planetary interests, inter-generational interests and inter-species interests. This is especially the case given that these interests often diverge, so requiring subtle and sensitive analyses to form optimum outcomes.

The exemplary and evidentiary fact that, for example, significant land-use changes in the Amazon influence water resources and climate conditions globally, highlights the significance of 'planetary boundaries' defining safe operating parameters for humanity and a regenerative living planet (Rockström et al, 2009). Sterner et al (2019) point out that complex earth systems must be analysed across boundaries and synthetically as well as taking into account politics in order to govern for global carrying capacity.

Can neoclassical economics, tied as it is to a modernization project that is alienated from the planet (du Plessis, 2012), be fundamentally rethought (Grubb et al, 2016)? Degrowth, as explicated and illustrated in various chapters in this volume, proposes one paradigm. As Gibbons (2020) details, ideas of regenerative science propose a co-creative partnership with nature, positioned beyond simply human sustainability, with additional layers of restoration, reconciliation and regeneration. Moreover, regenerative futures explore how futures thinking can promote regenerative development (Camrass, 2020).

But, who will action these grand ideas at the broad scale necessary? How will such narratives be realized? Normatively, as the corporate world engages with commodified concepts of 'energy-positive' buildings and 'the green rebranding of cattle' (Cusworth et al, 2022), the boundaries seem drawn around what is amenable to globalized mechanisms of accumulation. Can the corporate world contribute to post-carbon inclusion? Hope lies in debunking corporate myths about reinventing itself to behave better in a newly fashioned suit made from recycled fibres.

As pointed out by movements of environmental justice, degrowth and social justice, hope lies in new forms of engagement, in new agents and actors operating in new ways. Chapter 2 finds urban experiments increasingly collaborating with arts communities to bring the necessary ingenuity to interpret and engage human imagination in addressing the climate crisis and its roots in a system that exacerbates exclusion of people and planet. Collective solidarity, respecting Earth, and political awareness, are central to this project (Chapter 13).

The planetary scale interactions of climate change and inequality open up the field of post-carbon inclusion research to interact with related social and environmental movements in creative and constructive ways. While much normative debate about decarbonization is around learning new technologies, the post-carbon inclusion project points towards mass mobilizations and engagement with the great unlearning of the 'truths' of late neoliberalism around wealth creation.

Contributors to this volume dipped their toes into post-carbon inclusion futures. Immediately, we found hurdles and road blocks, so much so, our chapters focus on describing the knotted nets in front of researchers, activists and policy makers addressing the challenges of global heating, climate change and ways of approaching a very necessary transition to modes of relational living. We as a species confront politico-economic and ecological circumstances largely of our own making and seem unable, yet, to undo and move past our predicament. However, we can change our practices, and this book has sought to identify some starting points. This makes a forward-oriented agenda a beacon of hope for researchers, policy makers, practitioners and, indeed, all of us.

References

Armstrong, C. and McLaren, D. (2022) 'Which net zero? Climate justice and net zero emissions', *Ethics and International Affairs*, 36(4): 505–26.

Calafati, L., Froud, J., Haslam, C., Johal, S. and Williams, K. (2023) *Habitation and the Ideal of the 15-Minute City in Wales*, Working Paper 12 (September), Foundational Economy Collective. Available from: https://foundationaleconomycom.files.wordpress.com/2023/09/habitation-and-the-ideal-of-the-15-minute-city-in-wales-wp12.pdf [Accessed 1 November 2023).

Camrass, K. (2020) 'Regenerative futures', *Foresight*, 22(4): 401–15.

Castro, E. (2021) 'Hacia una ética de la generosidad' [Towards an ethics of generosity], IV Encuentro de Filosofía Intercultura, 28 May, Instituto Hamalgama Métrica, Las Palmas de Gran Canaria, Canary Islands. Available from: https://www.youtube.com/watch?v=FjNwR1n1eSY [Accessed 28 May 2023].

Cusworth, G., Lorimer, J., Brice, J. and Garnett, T. (2022) 'Green rebranding: regenerative agriculture, future-pasts, and the naturalisation of livestock', *Transactions of the Institute of British Geographers*, 47(4): 1009–27.

Deconinck, C. (2023) 'European Commission gave €10 million to "degrowth" research', *Brussels Signal*. Available from: https://brusselssignal.eu/2023/08/european-commission-gave-e10-million-to-degrowth-research [Accessed 1 November 2023].

Dubuisson-Quellier, S. (2022) 'How does affluent consumption come to consumers? A research agenda for exploring the foundations and lock-ins of affluent consumption', *Consumption and Society*, 1(1): 31–50.

du Plessis, C. (2012) 'Towards a regenerative paradigm for the built environment', *Building Research & Information*, 40(1): 7–22.

Gibbons, L.V. (2020) 'Regenerative – the new sustainable?' *Sustainability*, 12(13): Article 5483.

Grubb, M., Hourcade, J. and Neuhoff, K. (2016) *Planetary Economics: Energy, Climate Change and the Three Domains of Sustainable Development*, Abingdon and New York: Routledge.

Halkier, B. and Holm, L. (2021) 'Linking socioeconomic disadvantage to healthiness of food practices: can a practice-theoretical perspective sharpen everyday life analysis?', *Sociology of Health & Illness*, 43(3): 750–63.

Hubacek, K., Baiocchi, G., Feng, K., Muñoz Castillo, R., Sun, L. and Xue, J. (2017) 'Global carbon inequality', *Energy, Ecology and Environment*, 2(6): 361–9.

Jenkins, K., McCauley, D., Heffron, R., Stephan, H. and Rehner, R. (2016) 'Energy justice: a conceptual review', *Energy Research & Social Science*, 11: 174–82.

Lamb, W., Mattioli, G., Levi, S., Roberts, J., Capstick, S., Creutzig, F. et al (2020) 'Discourses of climate delay', *Global Sustainability*, 3: E17.

Loader, I. (2023) '15-minute cities and the denial(s) of auto-freedom', *IPPR Progressive Review*, 30(1): 56–60.

Low, S. and Boettcher, M. (2020) 'Delaying decarbonization: climate governmentalities and sociotechnical strategies from Copenhagen to Paris', *Earth System Governance*, 5: Article 100073.

Newell, P. and Mulvaney, D. (2013) 'The political economy of the "just transition"', *The Geographical Journal*, 179(2): 132–40.

Olsen, E., Orefice, M. and Pietrangeli, G. (2018) 'From the "right to the city" to the "right to metabolism"', in Nelson, A. and Schneider, F. (eds) *Housing for Degrowth: Principles, Models, Challenges and Opportunities*, Abingdon and New York: Routledge, pp 33–43.

Rockström, J., Steffen, W., Noone, K., Persson, Å., Chapin III, F.S., Lambin, E. et al (2009) 'Planetary boundaries: exploring the safe operating space for humanity', *Ecology and Society*, 14(2): Article 32.

Sovacool, B.K. and Dworkin, M.H. (2014) *Global Energy Justice: Principles, Problems, and Practices*, Cambridge: Cambridge University Press.

Sovacool, B.K., Heffron, R., McCauley, D. and Goldthau, A. (2016) 'Energy decisions reframed as justice and ethical concerns', *Nature Energy*, 1: Article 16024.

Sterner, T., Barbier, E.B., Bateman, I., van den Bijgaart, I., Crépin, A., Edenhofer, O. et al (2019) 'Policy design for the Anthropocene', *Nature Sustainability*, 2: 14–21.

Wainwright, O. (2023) 'In praise of the "15-minute city": the mundane planning theory terrifying conspiracists', *The Guardian*, 16 February. Available from: https://www.theguardian.com/commentisfree/2023/feb/16/15-minute-city-planning-theory-conspiracists [Accessed 2 November 2023].

Walker, G. (2013) 'Inequality, sustainability and capability: locating justice in social practice', in Shove, E. and Spurling, N. (eds), *Sustainable Practices: Social Theory and Climate Change*, London: Routledge, pp 181–96.

Willand, N., Middha, B. and Walker, G. (2021) 'Using the capability approach to evaluate energy vulnerability policies and initiatives in Victoria, Australia', *Local Environment*, 26(9): 1109–27. DOI: 10.1080/13549839.2021.1962830

Willand, N., Torabi, N. and Horne, R. (2023) 'Recognition justice in Australia: hidden energy vulnerability through the experiences of intermediaries', *Energy Research & Social Science*, 98: Article 103013.

Winship, M. (2016) 'Naomi Klein: "There are no non-radical options left before us"', *Salon*, 4 February. Available from: https://www.salon.com/2016/02/04/naomi_klein_there_are_no_non_radical_options_left_before_us_partner/ [Accessed 1 November 2023].

Index

Page numbers in *italic* type refer to figures; those in **bold** type refer to tables.

15-minute city concept 26, 54, 60, *61*, 62–5, **63**, 66, 227

A

Abazeri, M. 219
Abidoye, R. 91
Adam, B. 56, 57
adaptive thermal comfort model 141
ADEME 28
Adloff, F. 165
Africa 75, 107, 139
agency 229–30
Aguayo-Krauthausen, R. 165–6
air conditioning 138, 139, 141, 144, 151, 152
air pollution 11, 104–5, 113–14, 229
 and active mobility 105, 109
 co-benefits of transition for 11, 104, 105, 108–10, *110*
 deaths from 106–7, 108
 inequality and injustice 11, 104–5, 105–8
 during transition 110–13
 and urban vegetation 109–10, *110*
air source heat pumps 36, 175
Aldred, R. 113
Alteralia 27
'Alternatives Confluence' (Vikalp Sangam) 218
Altman, R. 122
altruistic transition 74–5, 77
Amazon 109, 230
Anastasiu, I. 130
anti-capitalism 8
Apple 124
Arab Spring 157
Architecture et Précarités **24**, 26, 29–30, 31, 32
Aristotle 74
art 165
Askins, K. 128
aspirational consumers 175, 176
 see also high consumers

Australia
 housing 86, 87, 90, 190
  DecoHousing Denmark 213
  domestic photovoltaic (PV) transition 191
  homeownership 191–2, 213
  Housing Energy Efficiency Transitions Project research findings 190, 195–202, *197, 199, 201*
  housing financialization 85–6
  Living Waters eco-collaborative housing 212
  Nightingale (Baugruppen) 94–5
  rental housing 190, 191, 196–7
  social housing 183, 192
 waste policies 126–7
Austria 122–3, 208
Avelino, F. 20

B

Bajpai, S. 217, 218
Ball, M. 86
Barcelona, Spain 63
Baugruppen model 94
Bebbington, J. 129
BedZED (Beddington Zero Energy Development) 26, 93–4
behavioural psychology 138
Benson, M. 214
Berlin Conference Beyond Growth 169
Berry, M. 97–8
biodegradable substitutes, and waste 126
BioRegional Development Group 93, 94
Bitterballen 130
Bobrova, Y. 193
Bobulescu, R. 165
bodily rhythms of mobility 62–3, 65
Bouzarovski, S. 91
Brand, U. 9, 13, 209, 210, 219
Brill, F. 85
Brown, D. 193
Brynskov, M. 130

'*buen vivir*' concept 215
Bulkeley, H. 32, 128
business-as-usual approach to decarbonization 225, 226–8
Butler, C. 38

C

C4 cities network 104
Caisse des Dépôts et Consignations 29
Callaghan, C.W. 208
Cameroon 150–1
Campania, Italy 127
Campbell, S. 149
Canada, Government of
 'Task Force: just transition for Canadian coal power workers and communities' (2019) 4, 19, 72
capability approach 6, 128, 228, 229–30
 cooling 139, 146–7, *148*, 149, 150, 151–2
 energy justice 190–1, 194
 secondary capabilities 147
capitalism 8, 156, 210–11
carbon (CO_2) emissions 2, 3, 75, 171
 Austria 208
 carbon capture technologies 112
 carbon mitigation strategies 209–10
 high consumers 175–6, 177
 impact of urban decarbonization on 18
 and urban air pollution 104–5, 108–14, *110*
 see also GHG (greenhouse gases)
care commoning approach 210, 219, 220
Cargonomia, Budapest, Hungary 160–1, 162–4
caring economies 13, 165, 167, 220
caring transition 70–1, 77–80, 81
carrying capacity 194, 230
cars
 and the 15-minute city 64
 freedom from motorized traffic 26–7
 impact of EVs (electric vehicles) on air pollution 111–12
 LTNs (low-traffic neighbourhoods) 113
Castro, E. 76
Catapult Connected Places 26
Central Europe 145
central heating 39, 41, 43, 47, 48
 see also gas
Chatterton, P. 96, 214
Chatterton, T. 176, 178
children
 cooling issues 139, 141
 domestic heating 48
 urban air pollution 106
 vulnerability of 79–80
China 209
 air pollution 108
 banning of waste imports 120
 carbon emissions 75

Christie, W. 215–16
chrono-urbanism, and de-energization 10, 53–4, 65–6, 227
 15-minute city 54, 60, *61*, 62–5, **63**, 66
 de-energization principles 65–6
 deceleration 10, 53, 57, 60, 63, **63**, 66
 localization 10, 53, 58–9, 60, 63, **63**, 66
 reconnection 10, 53, 57–8, 59, 60, 63, **63**, 66
 sharing 10, 53, 59–60, 63, **63**, 66
 urban rhythms and energies 54–5
circular economies 1, 5
 circular economy approach to waste 11–12, 120–4, 129, 130, 131
 'responsibilization' 120, 121–2
cities
 energy consumption in 55
 greening of, and air pollution 109–10, *110*
 multi-level governance 17
 see also chrono-urbanism, and de-energization; urban ...
city governments 17, 21
Civil Rights Movement, US 71
Clapham, D. 88
Clean Air Act (1956), UK 43–4
climate adaptation 138, 139
climate change, inclusion in post-carbon urban experiments 22–3, *23*, **24–5**, 26–8, 230
climate justice 71, 104
 see also just transitions; justice
climate mitigation 3, 79
 and cooling 138, 139
climate scepticism/denial 227
coal
 coal-powered power generation, India 112
 for domestic heating 36, 37, 42, 45–6, 105
 transitional support for coal-based communities 11, 19–20
co-housing 93
 see also eco-collaborative housing
commerce, 15-minute city component 60, *61*, 63
communities
 role in socio-technical transitions 21
 role of in urban experiments 18, 19
compact city concept 62
 see also 15-minute city concept
compensatory consumption 184
compostable substitutes, and waste 126
Conservative government, UK 227
consumerism
 negative consequences of 179
 see also high consumers
consumption 210–11, 229
 compensatory 184
 lowering of 9

and waste 125, 128
see also high consumers
'convivial technologies' principle 165
cooling 12, 138–40, 151–2
　air conditioning 138, 139, 141, 144–5, 151, 152
　CA (capability approach) 139, 146–7, *148*, 149, 150, 151–2
　cool inclusion 140, 146, 151–2
　cooling behaviours 141–2
　cooling exclusion, Global South 12, 149–51
　cooling 'services' 147, *148*
　inequality in ability to keep cool 138–9, 144–5
　thermal autonomy 139–40, 145
　thermal comfort 140–1
　thermal inequalities and thermal violence 144–6
　thermal management 142, *143*, 144
　thermal violence 139–40, 144–6
Corvellec, H. 122–3
cost-benefit analysis, housing retrofitting 189, 192, 193
'counter economies' 165
covenant systems, housing 95
COVID-19 pandemic 21–2, 26, 64, 90, 162, 164
creative precincts 22
creativity 165
cross-sectoral cooperation 19
cultural change, and high consumption 181
cycling 65, 227
　bodily rhythms of mobility 62–3, 65
Cyclonomia 160, 162

D

Daly, D. 192–3
Damgaard, C.S. 78
Darby, S.J. 38, 48, 176
Davis, L. 152
Davoudi, S. 85
Day, R. 147, 149, 194
De Schutter, O. 215
De Wilde, M. 193
decarbonization 1, 2, 3, 4, 19, 231
　business-as-usual approach to 225, 226–8
　see also post-carbon inclusion
deceleration (urban de-energization principle) 10, 53, 57, 60, 63, **63**, 66
DecoHousing Denmark, Australia 213
de-energization 2, 3
　and chrono-urbanism 10, 53–4, 65–6
　15-minute city 54, 60, *61*, 62–5, **63**, 66
　de-energization principles 10, 53, 57–60, 63, **63**, 65–6
　urban rhythms and energies 54–5
deep ecology 56
deforestation 2, 105, 109, 210

degrowth 1, 4, 7–8, 56, 156, 207–8, 210, 220, 225, 226, 231
　'degrowth formations' 12, 157, 211
　and high consumers 176
　and housing
　　alternative housing 212–13, 214–15
　　retrofitting 13, 193–4, 202, 203
　　prefigurative degrowth hybrids 12, 156–60
　　Cargonomia, Budapest, Hungary 160–1, 162–4
　　Haus des Wandels (House of Change/House for Transformation), Heinersdorf, Germany 160, 161, 164–8
　　Konzeptwerk Neue Ökonomiec (A Laboratory for New Economic Ideas), Leipzig, Germany 160, 161–2, 168–70
　　and transformation 170–2
　radical global transformation 215–19
　and waste 131
deindustrialization 10–11, 72
Denmark, 'loss and damage' payments 75, 76
Dennett, S. 212
digital cities 21
digitalization of employment, and the 15-minute city 64
DiMuzio, T. 177
disabled people, waste and exclusionary practices 125
disadvantaged groups, and urban air pollution 106–8
discard studies 124, 126
distributive governance 19
distributive justice 20
district heating systems 37, 39, 43
domestic heating *see* heating, of domestic homes
domestic waste *see* waste
Douala, Cameroon 150–1
drinking straw substitutes 125
Dubuisson-Quellier, S. 178
Dunster, B. 93
Durrant, D. 85

E

Eastern Europe 145
eco-ableism 124
eco-collaborative housing 12, 93, 207, 211, 220
　Australia 212–13
eco-districts 21, 22
ecofeminism 219
economic growth 8, 156, 225
　see also degrowth
'economies of care' 217
education, 15-minute city component 60, *61*, 63
electricity
　cooling 'services' 147, *148*, 149
　for domestic heating 37

INDEX

elite consumption 180
  see also high consumers
Eltahir, E.A.B. 150
'empire of things' 73
employment
  part-time working 170
  working, as a 15-minute city component 60, *61*, 64
empowerment 229–30
energy
  domestic PV (photovoltaic) systems 92
  'energy biographies' 38
  energy efficiency 3, 8, 92
  energy justice 3, 71, 85, 110
  energy poverty 36, 46, 110, 113, 144, 179, 229
  Australia 190, 192–3
  UK 191
energy studies, and high consumers 176, 183
energy transitions, domestic heating 37, 38–9, 48, 49–50
ENSA Paris-Belleville 29
entertainment, 15-minute city component 60, *61*, 63
environmental justice 71, 128, 231
  and urban air pollution 11, 104–5, 105–8, 111, 112, 114
'environmentality' 130
Erös, L. 162
Escobar, A. 159, 216, 217
Esteva, G. 216
ETH Zürich (Swiss Federal Institute of Technology) 158
ethics 9
  and power 6–7
ethics of care *see* caring transition
European Commission 156, 226
  The Just Transition Mechanism: Making Sure No-one is Left Behind (2020) 4, 7, 19, 71, 81
European Union 75, 208
  Green Deal programme 4, 7, 71
European Waste Framework Directive 123
Evans, J. 17, 18, 32
EVs (electric vehicles), impact on air pollution 111–12
extravagance 74

F

FaDA (Feminisms and Degrowth Alliance) 219
Fawcett, T. 176
Fernández Arrigiotia, M. 159, 167
Fieldwork 28
Fifth International Degrowth Conference, Budapest, Hungary (2016) 217
financialization of housing 11, 84, 85–6, 87, 88, 90–1, 92, 97, 98, 189
First Nations people 217

Fitzpatrick, N. 157, 214
flying, by high consumers 176
food sharing 167
food waste 126, 128
foodstuffs, international trade on 209
forest burning 105, 109, 210
fossil fuels 1–2, 3, 4
  for domestic heating 36, 37, 42, 45–6, 105, 110
  industrial use of 105
  and urban air pollution 104, 110–11
Foth, M. 130
Fouquet, R. 47
Foye, C. 88
Fritscheova, A. 165
Fundamental Human Needs theory 181

G

Gabriel, I. 73, 74
Galeano, E. 216
garden waste 126
Garmendia, E. 208
gas
  for domestic heating 36, 37, 39, 44, 175
  as a 'transition' energy 2
Geels, F. 21
gender-just redistribution 219
generous transitions 4, 70–1, 73–7, 78, 81
Geneva, Switzerland 109
gentrification 18, 30, 90–1, 95, 227
  and the 15-minute city 64–5
  green 59, 64, 98, 113
Germany
  self-build housing 214
Geyer, R. 121
GHG (greenhouse gases) 2, 27, 90, 128, 175, 210, 227–8, 229
  see also carbon (CO_2) emissions
Gibbons, L.V. 231
Giddens, A. 178, 182
gift economies 165
Glaeser, E. 64
global elites, carbon emissions 3
global financial crisis, 2008 87
Global North 3, 5, 21, 74, 180
  air pollution mitigation 111, 112
Global South 3, 5, 74
  air pollution 107, 112, 114
  and cool inclusion/exclusion 12, 140, 149–51, 152
Global Tapestry of Alternatives 218
González-Pijuan, I. 79–80
good life, definitions of 180–1
Goodchild, B. 38, 47
grand narratives, of domestic heating 37, 46, 48, 49
Great Britain
  air pollution 111
  see also UK

green public space 22
greenhouse gases (GHG) 2, 27, 90, 128, 175, 210, 227–8, 229
  see also carbon (CO_2) emissions
Greenpeace 124
greenwashing 73
greenways 110
Grenfell Tower fire, London, 2017 88
gross domestic product 7
ground source heat pumps 36
Gudynas, E. 215

H

Habermann, F. 219
Hamiduddin, I. 214
happiness, and high consumers 177, 178, 182
Haughton, G. 191
Haus des Wandels (House of Change/House for Transformation), Heinersdorf, Germany 160, 161, 164–8
Havas, A. 162
Hawkins, G. 124, 126
healthcare, 15-minute city component 60, 61, 63
heat 140–2, *143*
  air conditioning 138, 139, 141, 144–5, 151, 152
  heat exposure 142, 144
  impact on health 138, 144
  physiological acclimatization 149–50
  thermal comfort 140–1
  thermal management 142, *143*, 144
heat island effects 27, 32, 138
heating, domestic 10, 36–9, 49–50
  cold homes 40–1
  cold water 41–2
  gendered division of labour 47–8
  gendered roles 43
  grand narratives of 37, 46, 48, 49
  lost practices of 44–5
  research approach 39–40
  research findings 40–6
  transitions in 36–7, 175
Held, M. 66
Henckel, D. 55
Hendrickson, C. 159, 167
"hero stories' of energy efficiency 8
Heslop, J. 88
Hickel, J. 208–9
high consumers 12–13, 174–5, 183–5, 225, 227–8
  academic and stakeholder perspectives on 179–81
  compensatory consumption 184
  defining high consumption 179–81
  drivers of high consumption 177–8, 184
  elite consumption 180
  and happiness 177, 178, 182
  IE (institutional ethnography) research 183
  impact on carbon emissions 175–6, 177
  improving understanding of 182–3
  lack of academic and policy focus on 176–7
  negative consequences of high consumption for 178–9, 182
  problem of 175–6
  research difficulties 181–2
  and status 177, 178, 182
Hildago, Anne 60
Hirsch, D. 180
Hirsch, R.F. 39
Hobson, K. 122, 130, 131
Holmgren, D. 212
home working, and the 15-minute city 64
housing 3, 5, 11, 84–6, 211
  and the 15-minute city 64
  affordability issues 84, 85
  alternative 211, 214–15
  as commodity-cum-asset 11, 85, 87
  'deliberative developments' 94
  DIY/DIO (do-it-ourselves) projects 93
  eco-housing niche 93, 97
  financialization of 11, 84, 85–6, 87, 88, 90–1, 92, 97, 98, 189
  green-tech systems 92–3
  as 'home' 11, 85, 88, 92, 99, 195–8, *197*
  homeownership (owner occupation) 11, 84, 85, 86, 99, 190
  housing shortages 88–9
  inclusion and low carbon housing narratives 88–93, **89**, 97–9
  inclusive low carbon housing experiments
    BedZED (Beddington Zero Energy Development) 26, 93–4
    degrowth housing models 95–7, 98
    Nightingale (Baugruppen) 94–5
  mid-rise housing, Getafe, Madrid, Spain 32
  origins of Westernized housing 86
  post-carbon inclusive housing 11, 85
  post-millennium high-rise apartment blocks 84, 87
  rental housing 87, 88
    Australia 190, 191, 196–7
  retrofitting and renovation 13, 84, 90, 91, 189–90, 201–3
    epistemologies of 192–4
    homeowner-dominated policy context 190–2
    Housing Energy Efficiency Transitions Project research findings 195–201, *197*, *199*, *201*
    inclusive, innovative, decommodified approaches 199–201, *201*
  right-to-buy schemes 90
  self-build 214
  shared equity 90, 94, 98
  social housing 89, 90, 91, 94, 98
    Australia 183, 192
    UK 193

INDEX

urban renewal 90–1
as utility 11, 85
see also eco-collaborative housing
Housing Energy Efficiency Transitions Project research findings 190, 195–202, *197*, *199*, *201*
Hugentobler, M. 215
human rights 71, 229
Hyderabad, India 150–1

I

ICCA Consortium 217–18
IE (institutional ethnography), and high consumers research 183
Illich, I. 57
ILO (International Labour Organization) 4, 71
'imperial mode of living' 9, 13, 207, 209–10, 213, 230
inclusion 4
15-minute city 60, 63–5
chrono-urbanism, and de-energization 54, 57, 58, 59, 60, 66
inclusive governance in post-carbon urban experiments 22–3, *23*, **24–5**, 26
participatory inclusion 114
and post-carbon urban experiments 18
incubators 22
India 112, 150–1, 217–18
Indonesia 109, 150–1
industrial ecology 121
inequality 3, 4, 6–7
inclusion in post-carbon urban experiments 22–3, *23*, **24–5**, 26
infrastructure projects 22
innovation precincts 22
innovative precincts 21
integrated precincts 21
International Labour Organization (ILO) 4, 71
IPCC (Intergovernmental Panel on Climate Change) 209, 226
Climate Change 2021: The Physical Science Basis (2022) 138
Climate Change 2022: Impacts, Adaptation, and Vulnerability (2022) 175
Climate Change 2022: Mitigation of Climate Change (2022) 7–8
and degrowth 156
Global Warming of 1.5% (2019) 2
Ipraus 29

J

Jakarta, Indonesia 150–1
Jalas, M. 55, 58
Janda, K.B. 8
Jarvis, H. 170
Johansson, N. 122–3
Jones, C.F. 39

just transitions 1, 4–5, 7, 18, 19–20, 71–3, 80–1, 209, 225–6
justice 4, 19–20, 71–3, 228–9, 231
accomplishment-based 6
alternatives to 10–11, 70–1, 73, 80–1
altruistic transition 74–5, 77
caring transition 70–1, 77–80, 81
generous transition 4, 70–1, 73–7, 78, 81
and cool inclusion 140
housing retrofitting 194
loss and damage, responsibility/recompense for 75–7, 78

K

Kalbreite 'young housing cooperative,' Zürich, Switzerland 96, 215
Kallaugher, L. 158
Kalpavriksh, Pune, Maharashtra, India 217–18
Kanner, A.D. 179
Karachi, Pakistan 150–1
Kasser, T. 179
Kębłowski, W. 130
Kemeny, J. 88
Klein, Naomi 230
knowledge cities 21
knowledge networks 22
Konzeptwerk Neue Ökonomie (A Laboratory for New Economic Ideas), Leipzig, Germany 160, 161–2, 168–70
Kothari, A. 216, 217–18
Kotsila, P. 159
Kraftwerk 1 'young housing cooperative,' Zürich, Switzerland 96
Kruger, R.M. 127

L

La Via Campesina 216–17
Lamb, W.F. 3
landscapes, poly-energetic 59
Landsmark, T. 7
Lane, H.M. 107
language, and justice in transitions 81
Larsen, P.M. 216–17
Lazányi, O. 160, 163–4
Lazendorf, M. 89
leadership, diversification of 7
Leahy, T. 158
learning stories 8
Lefebvre, H. 54–5
Lepawsky, J. 124, 131
Liboiron, M. 124, 131
Liegey, V. 160, 162
Lilac (low impact living affordable community), Leeds, UK 96
Lindsay, J. 125
Lisiére d'une Tierce Forêt (Edge of a Third Forest), France **24**, 26, 27–8, 31, 32
living, 15-minute city component 60, *61*

living labs 21
Living Waters eco-collaborative housing, Australia 212
local futures movements 18
local governments
  energy service models 193
  relationship with national governments 17
  and urban experiments 17
localization (urban de-energization principle) 10, 53, 58–9, 60, 63, **63**, 66
low carbon communities 56
low carbon inclusion, present practices of 7–9
low-income households 175, 179
LTNs (low-traffic neighbourhoods) 113
Lund, Sweden
  domestic heating 10, 37, 39, 41, 42–3, 44–5, 46–7
  cold water 41–2, 47
Luscher, D. 64

M

Maher, J. 125
Majority World, degrowth practices 215–16
Makerspace at the Docklands Library, Melbourne, Australia 26
makerspaces 26
Mallet, S. 66
Mankin, J.S. 208
market-based solutions to climate crisis, failure of 5
Marsden, G. 64
Martin, C.J. 60
Mata, E. 85
material anthropology 194
materialism. negative consequences of 179
Max-Neef, M. 181
Meadowcroft, J. 20
Meitschäuser Syndikat 96–7
Melbourne, Australia 123
Melin, A. 190
mental health, and heat exposure 144
methane 2
  see also GHG (greenhouse gases)
Mexico 110
Meyerricks, S. 165
Minority World
  carbon (CO_2) emissions reduction 209
  housing size 211
  'imperial mode of living' 207
  need to reduce consumption 208
Mitchell, G. 111
mobility
  active mobility, and urban air pollution 105, 109, 113
  rhythms of 62–3, 65
  waste and exclusionary practices 125
moderation, practices of 9
Monticelli, L. 158, 159
Moreno, C. 60, 62

motorized traffic
  freedom from 26–7
  see also cars
Mullen, C. 64

N

Nagle, R. 124
Naidoo, S. 104
national governments, relationship with local/city governments 17
natural rhythms, reconnection with 10, 53, 57–8, 59
negative gearing 87
Nelson, A. 96, 214
net zero 3, 22
New Public Management 11–12, 121
'niche level' 21
Nieuwe Meent housing project, Amsterdam, the Netherlands 98
Nightingale (Baugruppen) 94–5
nitrogen dioxide (NO_2) pollution 111
  see also GHG (greenhouse gases)
nitrous oxide 2
  see also GHG (greenhouse gases)
North America, housing financialization 85–6
Nussbaum, M. 6, 146, 147

O

Occupy movement 157
oil, for domestic heating 36
Ojedo del Arco, M.P. 210
older people
  cooling issues 139, 141
  urban air pollution 106
  waste and exclusionary practices 125
Olsen, E. 229
One Planet Framework 94
'one planet living' 158, 212
Oppermann, E. 150
oral histories see heating, of domestic homes
organic vegetable box schemes 160, 163
Ormerod, E. 88
Orwell, G. 220
ozone 106

P

Pakistan 150–1
Pal, J.S. 150
Palgan, Y.V. 20
paper recycling 122
Paris Agreement 108
Paris, France, 15-minute city 60, *61*, 62
Paris&Co. 28
Parkinson, S. 158
participatory inclusion 114
particulate pollution
  and deforestation 109
  and EVs (electric vehicles) 112–13

INDEX

part-time working 170
Peabody Trust 93
Pearson, P. 47
peasant movements 216–17
Pel, B. 7
permaculture initiatives 18, 212
personal responsibility, and high consumers 178
personality traits, and high consumers 178, 182
'planetary boundaries' 230
planetary repair 2
planned obsolescence 124
planning policies, and alternative housing 214
plastic bag bans 123, 125
plastic water bottles 126
political change, and high consumption 181
populist politics 226–8
'post localism' 167
post-carbon inclusion 1–2, 3, 4, 5
   as an heuristic concept 9–10
   assessment of 21–2
   future directions for 14, 225–31
   purposive and just urban transitions 19–20
   research and practice 228–30
post-carbon urban experiments 10.230, 17–19, 30–3
   Architecture et Précarités **24**, 26, 29–30, 31, 32
   empirical framework 22–3, *23*, **24–5**, 26
   Lisiére d'une Tierce Forêt (Edge of a Third Forest) **24**, 26, 27–8, 31, 32
   Superblock Barcelona **24**, 26–7, 30, 32
   see also urban experiments
postgrowth 226
   see also degrowth
power, and ethics 6–7
prefigurative degrowth hybrids 12, 156–60
prefigurative politics 156, 157–8
psychology, and high consumers 178, 182, 184
Putnam, T. 193

Q

'quiet activism' 31
Quinlan, B. 211–13

R

Race, K. 126
racism, and residential segregation 107
Raven, R. 21
'rebound effect' 211
reconnection (urban de-energization principle) 10, 53, 57–8, 59, 60, 63, **63**, 66
recycling
   waste 121–2, 128
      kerbside recycling 120–1, 122–3
      'wishcycling' 121–2
recycling, and housing retrofitting 199–201, *201*
regenerative science 231

Regulier, C. 54
renewable energy 3, 21
rental housing 87, 88
   Australia 190, 191, 196–7
rhythmanalysis 53, 54–5
   see also chrono-urbanism, and de-energization
rights 228–9
   'right to metabolism' 229
   'right to the city' 19, 229
right-wing politics 226–8
road traffic
   and the 15-minute city 62–3
   see also cars
Rohse, M. 48
Rosa, H. 57, 58
Rucker, D.D. 178
rural areas, air pollution 106
Russia, invasion of Ukraine 167

S

safeguarding, and ethics of care 78–80
Salong, J. 215–16
San Martin, Peru 210
Savini, F. 98
Schneider, F. 214
Schwanen, T. 65
Scientists for Global Responsibility 1.5°C Living Targets 158
Scottish Government
   Just Transition - A Fairer, Greener Scotland (2021) 72
   Just Transition Commission (2020) 4, 19
   Zero Waste Scotland policy 129
SDGs (Sustainable Development Goals), UN 216, 229
secondary capabilities 147
Selzer, S. 89
Sen, A. 6, 128, 139, 146, 190–1, 194
Sengers, F. 20
sequential sharing 59–60
Seward, C. 147
sharing (urban de-energization principle) 10, 53, 59–60, 63, **63**, 66
Sheffield, UK, domestic heating 10, 37, 39–40, 40–1, 42, 43–4, 45–6, 46–7
shelter, cooling 'services' 147, *148*
Shiva, V. 217
Shove, E. 121, 122
Singer, P. 74
single-use plastics bans 127
Sixth International Degrowth Conference: Dialogues in Turbulent Times, Malmö, Sweden (2018) 217
Slamersak, A. 209
'slow streets' 26
Smith, M.L. 147
social housing 89, 90, 91, 94, 98
   Australia 183, 192
   UK 193

social practice theory 194
'society is culture' principle 165
socio-technical transitions 1, 4, 18, 19
  housing retrofitting 13, 194, 202
solid fuels *see* coal; wood
solidarity 8, 231
solidarity economies 165
solidarity mode of living 207, 210, 211, 220, 230
Solnit, R. 220
South Africa, residential segregation 107
South Asia 139
Southwest Asia 150
Sovacool, B.K. 3, 79
speed 57
  see also deceleration
Stapeln Open Makerspace, Malmö, Sweden 26
Starosielski, N. 145
status, and high consumers 177, 178, 182
Stephens, J.C. 7
Sterner, T. 230
street trees 110
Strenchock, L. 160, 163
'sufficiency' 8, 156, 175, 176, 178, 183
Superblock Barcelona **24**, 26–7, 30, 32
SuperHomes network, UK 193
sustainability, and temporality 56
sustainability transitions literature, and waste 124
Sustainable Development Goals (SDGs), UN 216, 229
sustainable precincts 21
Sutton, London Borough of 93
Sweden 47
  domestic waste policy 122–3
Swiss Federal Institute of Technology (ETH Zürich) 158
synchronized sharing 59

T

tactical urbanism 26, 31
tax, and high consumption 181
temporal justice 66
  see also chrono-urbanism, and de-energization
temporality
  and sustainability 56
  see chrono-urbanism, and de-energization
temporary experimentation sites 22
Teng, F. 108
'territorial resilience' 28
Theine, H. 208
thermal autonomy 139–40, 145
thermal comfort 140–1
thermal inequalities 144–6
thermal management 142, *143*, 144
  see also cooling; heating, domestic
thermal violence 139–40, 144–6
third spaces 21, 26
Thomson, H. 145
thrift, practices of 9
Tingey, M. 193
Topouzi, M. 8
Törnberg, A. 157, 158
trade, global production for 208–9
trade unions 219
transition towns 18, 56
transitions
  altruistic 74–5, 77
  caring 70–1, 77–80, 81
  energy transitions, domestic heating 37, 38–9, 48, 49–50
  generous 4, 70–1, 73–7, 78, 81
  governing of 6–7
  just transitions 1, 4–5, 7, 18, 19–20, 71–3, 80–1, 209, 225–6
  socio-technical transitions 1, 4, 13, 18, 19, 194, 202
transnational corporations, carbon emissions 3
transport studies, and high consumers 176, 183
Trentmann, F. 72–3
Treu, N. 162
Tunstall, R. 98

U

UK
  air pollution, deaths from 107
  energy transitions 175
  housing 86, 88
    retrofitting 193
    social housing 193
  LTNs (low-traffic neighbourhoods) 113
Ukraine, Russian invasion of 167
ULLs (urban living labs) 7, 12, 18, 19, 20–1, 22, 32
UN (United Nations) 71
  'Cooling for All' 139
  Sustainable Development Goals (SDGs) 216, 229
UNFCCC (United Nations Framework Convention on Climate Change) 4
  COP 27 71, 76
  REDD+ programme 210
unwell people, cooling issues 139, 141
urban decarbonization *see* decarbonization
urban elites, role in socio-technical transitions 21
urban energies 54–5
  see also chrono-urbanism, and de-energization
urban experiments 7, 10, 17–19, 21
  role of community in 18, 19
  see also post-carbon urban experiments
urban forest 110
urban innovation 21

INDEX

urban living labs (ULLs) 7, 12, 18, 19, 20–1, 22, 32
urban net zero 22
urban planning, and alternative housing 214
urban rhythms 54–5
  see also chrono-urbanism, and de-energization
urban think tanks 21
urban vegetation, and air pollution 109–10, *110*
US
  air conditioning 144–5
  carbon emissions 75
  environmental justice 71, 105–6, 112
  global excess resource extraction 208
  housing 86
  just transition movement 72
  residential segregation 107
  waste policies 127
'utopian hospitality' 167

V

Vandyck, T. 108
Vanuatu 215–16
vegetation
  cooling 'services' 147, *148*
  urban vegetation, and air pollution 109–10, *110*
Verlinghieri, E. 65
Vetter, A. 161, 162, 165
Vikalp Sangam ('Alternatives Confluence') 218
violence, and heat exposure 144, 151
Volcovico, V. 75

W

Walker, G. 6, 107–8, 129, 228
walking 65, 227
  bodily rhythms of mobility 62–3, 65
waste 131
  banning of products 123
  banning of waste imports 120
  biodegradable and compostable substitutes 126
  CE (circular economy) approach 11–12, 120–4, 129, 130, 131
  and degrowth 131
  designing out of 123–4
  discard studies 124, 126
  and exclusion 122, 124–5
  future domestic discard regime 121, 127–9
  and inclusion 121, 122, 124–7
  recycling 121–2, 128
    kerbside recycling 120–1, 122–3
    'wishcycling' 121–2
  relational-informed local waste governance 121, 128, 129–31
    everyday waste routines 130
    governance bundles 129
    infrastructure and affective bundles 130–1
  social practices and the capabilities approach 121
  social practices capability framework 128–9
  waste governance 126
  waste-to-energy incineration systems 123
wastefulness 74
water
  cooling 'services' 147, *148*, 149
  domestic, cold water 41–2, 47
  domestic conservation measures 200
  plastic water bottles 126
water retention 27
Weber, R. 85, 97
Western Australia 125
Willand, W. 191
Williams, J. 94
Wilting, H.C. 209
Wishart, L.J. 129
'wishcycling' 121–2
Wissen, M. 9, 13, 209, 210
Wittmayer, J.M. 20
women, 'double burden' on 48
wood, for domestic heating 37, 42–3, 44–5, 45–6, 47
working
  15-minute city component 60, *61*, 64
  see also employment

Y

Yang, X. 108
Yates, L. 60
'young housing cooperatives,' Zürich, Switzerland 96, 158, 207, 214–15

Z

'zero waste' 120, 124, 129
Zink, T, 121
Zografos, C. 27
Zsamboki Biokert 160, 163
Zürich, Switzerland
  'young housing cooperatives' 96, 158, 207, 214–15

www.ingramcontent.com/pod-product-compliance
Lightning Source LLC
Chambersburg PA
CBHW070042040426
42333CB00041B/1950